HomePlaygrounds

For Karl and Erik
The days that make us happy make us wise.

HomePlaygrounds

The Harrowsmith Guide to Building Backyard Play Structures

Merilyn Mohr

Camden House

© Copyright 1987 by Camden House Publishing Ltd.

Canadian Cataloguing in Publication Data

Mohr, Merilyn
    Home playgrounds

Includes index.

ISBN 0-920656-62-5

1. Playgrounds - Equipment and supplies -Design and construction. 2. Playgrounds -Design and construction. I. Title.

GV425.M63   1987   796'.06'8   C87-093550-X

Trade distribution by
Firefly Books
3520 Pharmacy Avenue, Unit 1-C
Scarborough, Ontario
Canada M1W 2T8

Printed in Canada for
Camden House Publishing Ltd.
7 Queen Victoria Road
Camden East, Ontario
K0K 1J0

Front Cover: Left: Frank B. Edwards
             Top Right: Frank B. Edwards
             Bottom Right: Linda J. Menyes
Back Cover: Linda J. Menyes

Colour separations by
Herzig Somerville Limited
Toronto, Ontario

Printed and bound in Canada by
D.W. Friesen & Sons
Altona, Manitoba

Printed on 60 lb. Friesen #1 Offset

Acknowledgments

The author gratefully acknowledges the generous assistance of play consultant Polly Hill and the Children's Environments Advisory Service of Canada Mortgage and Housing Corporation; Shirley Post of the Canadian Institute of Child Health, whose task force on play spaces and equipment chaired by Dr. Satya Brink provided much valuable information; and Canadian play-equipment manufacturers, particularly Al Potvin of Hilan Creative Playstructures and Rick Henke of Children's Playgrounds Inc., for their advice on the design and construction of specific play equipment. Sincere thanks to Ross Rogers for his practical suggestions and to Michael Webster, Linda Menyes, Tracy C. Read, Patricia Denard-Hinch and Charlotte DuChene for guiding the manuscript through publication.

Contents

Preface

Play's the thing

If we get started in the right direction, we can play our way into paradise.

Malcolm Wells, architect

The little boy's eyes stretched wide with excitement as his father knelt on the back lawn to bend open the heavy copper staples fastening one side of a long cardboard box. As soon as one corner was freed, the youngster squeezed his pudgy fingers under the flap and lifted it up to peek at the jumble of red- and blue-swirled pipes. "Is this gonna be fun, Dad? Just like the park?" he asked, pulling at the chains that slithered across the bottom of the box.

Three hours later, swing set assembled, the boy climbed first on one seat, then on the other, pumping back and forth with all his 5-year-old might. "Look at me! Look at me!" he called, letting go of the swing chains and stretching his arms out wide. He stood on the seat, then lay across it on his stomach, trailing his fingers and toes in the grass. He rode it sideways as if it were a stallion, clutching one chain with both hands and yelling "giddy-up" as he alternately rammed the frame and the other swing. Dismounting his steed, he left the chuckwagon for the circus, swinging by his hands from the side bars of the frame. Then he grabbed the swing seat and hurled it high into the air, catching it as it fell and pitching it back toward the frame, again and again. The rhythmic clang of metal on metal finally roused his father from the house. "I'm bored, Dad. Can we go to the park?"

In two hours—less time than it took his father to put the swing set together—this preschooler discovered just about everything that piece of play equipment had to offer. Over the next few weeks, he enjoyed an occasional mid-afternoon swing and one short burst of renewed enthusiasm while he mastered the art of shinnying up the frame to hang by his knees from the cross bar, but by the end of summer, the swing set stood untouched in its corner of the yard, abandoned to rust and roosting starlings.

Although the play equipment in schoolyards and parks has changed dramatically in the past two decades, parents shopping for something to entertain children outdoors at home find only the same swing sets that littered their own childhoods. Libraries have little to offer those willing to build their own outdoor playthings: shelves of books are available on public playgrounds, but home-based play is virtually ignored. Yet kids like to play at home and parents are eager to have them there—if only they knew how to create a good playground in the family backyard. This book is the result of my own quest for the quintessential home-built swing-set substitute. What I discovered in my search is that there is more to children's play than stretching muscles and letting off steam and more to creating a home playspace than bolting 4 by 4s together to build swings, slides and climbers.

Play is not just something kids do in their spare time; it is the way they learn about themselves and the world. The 4-year-olds darting from behind the lilac bushes, towel capes flapping and garbage-can-lid shields brandished high, are exercising their imaginations as vigorously as they are their muscles, and the toddler repeatedly dumping sand down the slide is not being defiant—he is defining for himself the law of gravity. The first play structures, built 100 years ago, ignored the creative and intellectual aspects of play, meeting only kids' rough-and-tumble physical needs. It took designers 50 years to supplement those original swings, slides and teeter-totters with more sophisticated structures that encourage dramatic and social play as well as solitary exercise. This second-wave play equipment, bedecked with wooden platforms, rope nets, tube slides

Public playgrounds have changed dramatically since their inception a century ago. Rows of iron swings, slides and climbers have been replaced by wooden play structures with platforms and several ways of getting up and down to encourage dramatic and social play as well as solitary exercise.

Play is part of growing up— and always has been, **previous page**—but only recently have parents begun to realize that a creative home playspace is as important to a child's development as are the structures in the city park or the school playground.

and clatter bridges, is an improvement over its plumbing-pipe predecessors, but children need more than structures to play on: they need a play *space*, an environment designed to stimulate probing young minds, a personal domain honeycombed with child-sized nooks and crannies where a young body can curl up to contemplate the world in all its wonder.

Creative playspaces are beyond the scope of municipal parks departments and schools. Charged with the safety and supervision of large numbers of kids, they must provide playgrounds that are durable, low-maintenance and low-risk. But a more creative playspace is ideally suited to the backyard. With a little ingenuity and good planning, even a stamp-sized city lot can be converted into a stimulating and challenging play area. On home turf, where a little mess and risk can be tolerated, let kids make their own playthings with blocks and boards, water and sand—raw materials that enlighten as much as they entertain. Well-designed swings and climbers are still important for developing young bodies, but instead of installing them on a flat expanse of Kentucky bluegrass, plant a potpourri of colour, shape and texture to pique the senses. Ultimately, parents cannot force children to play creatively in the same way they coerce them into making their beds or brushing their teeth, but they can develop an outdoor setting that encourages kids to stretch their minds, their muscles and their hearts through play.

Until now, the essential design and construction information necessary to create playspaces that nurture the whole child has not been available to the people best equipped to do the job: the members of the family themselves. This book attempts to correct that. It includes more than 40 pages of plans for tire

A creative playspace piques children's natural curiosity about the world around them. Since a backyard can accommodate more risk and mess than a schoolyard, a home playground can better challenge young bodies and minds.

swings, mound slides, jungle-gym climbers, playhouses, hollow blocks, sand gardens, play streams and dozens of other pieces of constructed play equipment, as well as detailed suggestions for improving the play value of the backyard landscape. Chapter 4 takes the family step-by-step through the design process, helping it to assess the property, choose the play components and lay them out effectively in the yard—useful information whether one is building the equipment at home or installing custom-built playthings purchased from the manufacturers listed in the Sources section at the end of this book. Sample playspaces at the end of Chapter 4 illustrate how a yard can evolve as children grow, continuing to challenge and stimulate them through their developing years. But before a family decides whether to build a playhouse or a jungle gym, it has to understand the nature and importance of play. The opening chapter explains the role of play in a child's development and shows why the standard metal swing set is so inadequate. It may seem that the

faithful old swing set is unfairly maligned, but it is criticized not so much for what it is as for what it is not. Plunking a play set in a corner of the yard is a token gesture that meets only a fraction of children's play needs. It does not absolve parents of their responsibility to provide a well-rounded play environment. This book aims to overcome that benign neglect by providing workable, inexpensive ways of converting a conventional backyard into a creative playspace.

Readers may have noticed that although youngsters are occasionally referred to as children, preschoolers and adolescents, most often they are just "kids." Let me assure those who are eager to remind me that kids are baby goats: the choice is a conscious one. A quick poll of my neighbourhood confirmed my sense that kids prefer to be called kids, associating the label "child" with reprimands and visiting relatives. I apologize in advance to those who may be offended by this decision, but I suspect there won't be a kid among them.

1 Child's Play

Putting play into perspective

Mankind owes to the child the best it has to give.

United Nations Declaration

A hundred years ago, when most Canadians were still reading by gaslight and a railway to the Pacific was only a national dream, Marie Zakrzewska disembarked from a steamship in Boston harbour with an idea that would change the face of North America. Fresh in her mind were the public parks she had visited in the German capital of Berlin, delightful green spaces dotted with "sand gardens" – heaps of sand supplied by the local government for kids to dig in and clamber through under the watchful eyes of trained supervisors. Inspired by the revolutionary notion of a space reserved solely for children's outdoor play, Zakrzewska returned to Boston to transplant the seeds of the German play movement to the New World. By the late 1880s, the Massachusetts Emergency and Hygiene Association had established three sand gardens for Boston's children, but Zakrzewska and her philanthropic cohorts soon realized that their pseudo-beaches attracted only the very young; something else was needed to lure older children off the crowded city streets.

At their request, Harvard physical education professor Dudley Sargent adapted gymnasium exercise equipment to outdoor use, designing iron frames with ladders, swings, teeter-totters, climbing ropes and poles. In 1889, a boys' exercise frame and a less rigorous, modesty-preserving girls' frame were installed on a strip of wasteland along the banks of the Charles River named Charlesbank Park, discreetly separated by sandboxes, benches and a running track. And so the first North American playground was born, the offspring of philanthropy and physical education.

Today, it is hard to imagine a school without a playground or a city without public parks studded with swings and slides, but a century ago, most people scoffed at the idea of devoting public space and money to something as frivolous as children's play. Nevertheless, Zakrzewska's movement persisted and spread, led by social reformers appalled by the overcrowded conditions in the nation's industrialized cities. Fearing that the devil would make work for the idle hands of children recently released from their gruelling factory jobs, philanthropists pressed for open public spaces where kids could play. Before long, play was hailed as a panacea for the worst evils wrought by society's newly forged technology. At the first annual convention of the Playground Association of America, held in 1907, founding president Luther Halsey Gulick described the playground as "our great ethical laboratory. The sandpile for the small child, the playground for the middle-sized child, these are the fundamental conditions without which democracy cannot continue." Not only were playgrounds the route to political utopia, they were the antidote to crime. According to play advocate Jane Addams, "amusement is stronger than vice, and it alone can stifle the lust for it." Playgrounds were even promoted as a preventive medicine for tuberculosis, the most dreaded disease of the first part of this century. One writer maintained that "almost every one of these [tuberculosis] deaths would have been prevented if these children from infancy had had a proper amount of open-air play." There was nothing, it seemed, that a little play could not cure. A 1909 textbook on playground design and construction extravagantly claimed that "through the play of children, the unfavourable conditions of both city and country life may be remedied."

The equipment in those first playgrounds was a clear reflection of 19th-century theories on why children

Strongly influenced by Darwin, the first theories of play characterized it as a primitive impulse that helped children ''evolve'' into adults. So in addition to being sexually segregated, the first adult-designed playground equipment concentrated on swinging, balancing and other monkeylike activities.

The first playgrounds were built by philanthropists concerned that the devil would make work for the idle hands of youngsters recently released from factory jobs by child labour laws. Today, however, play is considered essential for the creative, intellectual and physical development of modern children, **previous page**.

play, most of them strongly influenced by Darwin's writings on evolution. The **surplus energy theory** maintained that since civilized people do not need all their energy to meet life's basic needs of food and shelter, kids play to ''let off steam,'' releasing the pent-up energy left over from a stage in human development when life was not so soft. The **instinct theory** proposed that play is an inherited impulse by which humans prepare for life, much as kittens practise mouse-stalking techniques on a ball of yarn. According to this view, children do not play because they are young; rather, youth exists so that children can play and hone their inherent skills. The **recapitulation theory** took this genetic view of play one step further, suggesting that through play, children repeat the stages of human evolution: the toddler digging in

the sand is reenacting the exploits of early land animals, the 10-year-old shinnying up a tree has advanced to the primate phase, and teenagers scrimmaging over a football are playing out early tribal rituals. Because all these original theories saw play as a visceral, primitive impulse, it is not surprising that the first play equipment relied heavily on swings, ''monkey'' bars and ''jungle'' gyms.

Play in Theory

Such theories prevailed until the 1930s when Freud and Piaget revolutionized the way society viewed childhood and play. Both men concentrated on how kids benefit from play: according to Freud's **psychoanalytic theory**, children incorporate elements of real-life events into their play, thus gaining control over the emotions those events provoke; Piaget's **cognitive theory** describes play as a child's way of learning new behaviour. Unlike early theorists who only emphasized its physical basis, psychologists now view play as the way kids learn, express themselves and become comfortable with their emotional and physical surroundings. Even at home, attitudes have changed: turn-of-the-century parents tolerated play, assuming that children would later settle down to the serious business of studies and chores, but modern families actively encourage it as the source of creative, intellectual and physical development.

This new outlook on play and childhood spawned a startlingly new type of playground in postwar Europe. Conceived by Danish landscape architect C. Th. Sorenson, the **adventure playground** was totally child-centred. Under trained but unintrusive supervision, kids built, destroyed and reconstructed their own

play equipment from a stockpile of scrap materials. Established on the rubble of bomb sites throughout Europe, the ''junk play yard'' movement had little impact in North America, possibly because neither public attitudes nor the terrain had been as dishevelled by war.

Nevertheless, Americans were also searching for an alternative to the original exercise-yard playgrounds, and in the early 1950s, the first **creative playground** was built in California. Designed to develop young minds and imaginations as well as muscles, the creative playground has at its core a multilevel play frame with a series of platforms connected by ramps, ladders, slides and bridges. Often made of wood and custom-designed for a particular site, the creative playground offers vigorous physical play opportunities with varied levels of challenge as well as room for social and dramatic play. Kids use the platforms for private rendezvous or as jail cells in rousing games of cops and robbers. They soon get bored with an ordinary playground slide, but when it is incorporated into a play frame as one more way of escaping capture or disposing of prisoners, kids play happily for hours. Creative playgrounds gradually spread across the continent, and soft sand and complex platform climbers have now replaced metal jungle gyms and asphalt as the standard play equipment in parks and schoolyards.

In the continent's backyards, though, this evolution has yet to occur. Creative playgrounds have been part of the public landscape for 20 years, but at home, parents continue to make do with a scaled-down version of Professor Sargent's outdoor gym, which, despite bright paint, plastic seats and space motifs, is as out of place in today's backyard as a penny-farthing bicycle. However, to replace the tired old swing set with a miniature replica of the creative play frame in the city park would be to repeat the mistakes of a century ago. As much as this second generation of public play equipment is an improvement over its purely physical predecessors, it still centres on a piece of "furniture." What kids really need is a play environment – a creative playspace – that titillates the senses and invites exploration and experimentation, both physical and mental. Instead of adapting the limitations of public equipment to private use, the backyards of North America can become the leading edge of the third wave of children's playground design.

Why bother, though, when there are public playgrounds around virtually every corner? Because it seems that society has reached a plateau at least as critical as the one in 1889 that spawned

Although they are an improvement over their metal predecessors, wooden structures do not meet all of children's play needs. A well-rounded playground also includes a rich natural environment that stimulates the senses and encourages kids to explore.

Boston's Charlesbank Park. On one hand, children are increasingly passive, absorbing long hours of television and video, living vicariously through miniature characters and learning about their world from a two-dimensional screen that offers sight and sound but never touch, smell or taste. Children – and adults – desperately need the first-hand physical, intellectual and emotional stimulation of play. On the other hand, as family size dwindles, parental expectations are focused on one or two offspring, putting children under pressure to achieve both at school and in organized "play" activities. These hurried and harried children are pushed to learn, grow and excel during every waking moment. The modern emphasis on "meaningful" activity is uncomfortably close to the 19th-century dictum that "the devil makes work for idle hands," though dawdling is now despised not as an evil but as a squandered opportunity.

15

A creative backyard playspace is a healthy antidote to today's pressures, a place where kids set their own rules, grow at their own pace and explore, dream and have fun in their own way.

Caterpillars & Castles

Before they can transform their golf-course lawns into stimulating and amusing creative playspaces, parents need to understand what "play" is, in all the subtle forms it takes as kids grow from toddlers to teenagers. Psychologists do not agree on a precise definition of play, but there are certain identifying characteristics that all play activities share. If a mother tells her daughter to go splash in a puddle and the child obediently complies, she is not playing; yet kids love to play in puddles, pressing the thin skin of spring ice with the toe of a running shoe until squeak turns to crack and water gushes through to soak the foot. The difference is that true play is self-motivated, initiated by the child and not by some outside force. Too often, well-meaning parents meddle in a child's world, imposing their own goals and standards on the child either directly ("Build a castle like this") or indirectly ("Don't get those clothes dirty"). This restricts the freedom and spontaneity that are implicit in real play. Although no one would bar parents from playing with their kids, purely child-initiated play is important in developing self-confidence and a feeling of control over one's surroundings. To encourage self-motivated play, a playspace should include child-sized hiding spots and unobtrusive adult seating so parents can supervise their children without hovering.

Watch a youngster on hands and knees push a block of wood through a sandbox, lips pursed and sputtering; there is no doubt that bulldozer is as real to the child as any Caterpillar. When immersed in their make-believe world, kids shrug aside the physical laws, expectations and consequences of real life and enter a domain where they make the rules, bending physical reality as easily as time and space. If she so decrees and her younger brother agrees, Sara really can be Morgan, faerie enchantress; the rock she carries becomes a bottle of magic potion that turns uncooperative princes and siblings into frogs; and the hole in the hedge is undoubtedly the dragon's lair. Kids do not need anything remotely resembling a castle or a spaceship to create their own worlds. In fact, too much detail gets in the way of a good fantasy: a toy bulldozer could never be a Roman chariot, though a child's imagination easily transforms the tail end of a 2 by 4 into either. To stimulate strong

imaginations, bypass the quaintly detailed Hansel-and-Gretel table and chairs in favour of nondescript props such as big hollow blocks that kids can shape into a dining room suite or a spaceship console as the make-believe world of the moment dictates.

To be stimulating and fun, play must be uncertain, with no one—least of all the child playing—sure how it will turn out. The real downfall of traditional play equipment is that it is predictable. The designer of the old-fashioned assembly-line slide expected children to repeatedly climb single file up the steps, sit on the ramp and slip to the bottom, all for the sake of a momentary thrill. In reality, a child goes through the exercise a few times until, bored with the anticipated outcome, he creates new uncertainties: walking up the slide, first on the ramp, then on the rails; diving down headfirst, then sideways and straddling a friend's back; even skateboarding down the slope. Such antics often earn sharp rebukes and accusations of misbehaviour or even vandalism, but in fact, the fault lies with the designer, not the kids: only a monkey would mindlessly climb stairs to slide down a ramp, time and time and time again. Instead, give kids play equipment with varying degrees of risk and challenge and choices at every turn to ensure that the outcome is never predetermined—platforms with multiple entrances and exits so a child can climb up the rope ladder or clatter bridge and leave via the sliding pole, the tube slide or the cargo net. Furthermore, supply playthings that kids can manipulate and change—movable ramps and platforms for a jungle gym—and they can then create a playspace that is continually fresh, exciting and uncertain.

"Play, like virtue, is its own reward," wrote American playground designer

As well as static play structures like climbers and slides, where the outcome of play is predetermined, kids need playthings they can manipulate and change, learning how the world works and exercising some control over it.

Richard Dattner. Kids play because the process itself is enjoyable, not because the activity produces some tangible result. The apparent purposelessness of play may explain why historically it has been held in such derision: with no defined goals and no measurable end products, play runs counter to the principles of the Protestant work ethic that powers North American society. Play is traditionally characterized as the opposite of work, with "what needs to be done" facing off against "what is fun to do." Yet studies show that playfulness is an important part of useful work, that play and creativity are a hairbreadth apart. A child toying with patterns of stones in the sand is applying the same processes as a chemist fiddling with formulae for a new solar-collector fluid. By encouraging the exploratory, superficially unproductive nature of play, thus allowing children to dally with ideas instead of always working toward a set goal, parents can help heal the rift between work and play, and they will rear a generation of adults more able to devise creative solutions to the problems they face.

Play activity may be seen as self-motivated, uncertain and purposeless make-believe, but such a definition misses the heart and spirit of play. Ask kids what play is, and they will say, quite simply, "Fun." Kids play to have a good time, just for the joy of it. If in designing a play environment, parents combine the right elements of challenge, privacy, diversity, flexibility and control but leave out the fun, they might as well buy a swing set. The chemistry that draws kids to a play area is highly individual—the 10-foot tower that thrills Meredith and fires her imagination may intimidate Candyce, who really wanted a sandbox and her own ant farm —so include the kids in the planning

process. Watch how they play, and listen to their ideas to be sure the playspace is delightful and not merely developmentally correct.

Types of Play

Visiting a friend's backyard playspace recently, I observed four preschoolers deeply immersed in play: Corina, the rambunctious leader, was concentrating hard on mastering a tire net that drooped from the play platform; underneath, her younger sister Jessica and best friend Naomi were hanging blankets on the cross braces to create a tent for their Cabbage Patch Kids; and nearby, the baby of the family, Joshua, lifted a shovelful of sand into the air, tipped it slowly and stared at the grains as they fell back to earth, then scooped up another shovelful and intently repeated the exercise. Purposeless, otherworldly,

self-motivated, uncertain fun—all the adjectives fit all the kids' activities, yet they were all playing in at least one of four distinctly different ways. Joshua was absorbed in learning how this mysterious world works, Naomi and Jessica were deep in imaginative play, which they also shared as social play, and Corina was conditioning her body with physical play. Although it is an oversimplification to pigeonhole play in this way—each type of play always includes elements of the others— understanding them separately allows parents to design a playspace that includes them all.

"Children are not playing: they are finding out how the universe works," noted Buckminster Fuller, one of the 20th century's most innovative architects. A 4-year-old may not be able to explain in scientific terms why wet

No one can dispute that play is important to a child's development, but the psychologists' analyses of play often miss a fundamental ingredient— fun. Kids play to have a good time, and equipment that is developmentally correct will not be used unless it is also a delight to play on.

Kids need few props for play. A couple of upturned flowerpots have sparked this child's imagination, sending him down the garden path on an absorbing space walk that stretches muscles and tests his low-gravity balance.

sand is heavier than dry sand, but after a day in the sandbox, she knows it is true. Unlike the cerebral kind of book learning typical of schools and even many homes, learning through play involves the whole person – body, mind and senses – and as a result, the child absorbs new information freely, painlessly and fully.

A playspace designed for learning is complex, with open-ended activities and equipment that kids can move and change, producing effects that are under their control. As they test new facts and redefine old ones, children extend their intellectual horizons and develop the basis for good personal judgment. Although a playspace must be intellectually challenging, do not push kids beyond their levels: match the design to their abilities, letting them live each stage fully, providing new challenges when they are ready to tackle them. And don't forget that much of the intellectual play value of a backyard comes not from a piece of equipment but from a landscape rich in colours, textures, shapes, smells and spaces which all help to stimulate a child's natural sense of wonder.

A child gazing at a hummingbird hovering above the crimson azalea might wonder how the tiny bird manages to hang suspended in midair, but when he closes his eyes and climbs astride that iridescent back and swoops from flower to flower aboard the Nectar Express, arms clasped around its ruby neck, imagination, not intellect, is at play. Eric McMillan, one of the world's best designers of large-scale creative play environments, including those at Ontario Place and Vancouver's Expo 86, believes that "play is the path to an open mind," and much of that openness comes from an active, well-developed imagination which lets kids put

themselves in other people's shoes without moving a muscle. Starting at about age 3, kids try on other personae – perhaps BBC's Dr. Who or the surgeon who took out their tonsils last week – and thus are able to handle their emotional reactions to real or fictional events, experiment with different points of view and rehearse the roles of the adult world they will eventually join.

"We know very well how to kill creativity," observes Polly Hill, one of Canada's preeminent play consultants, "but little about how to nurture it." In her opinion, creative, imaginative play is encouraged in much the same way as an enquiring mind – by designing a play environment with variety, flexibility, sensual stimulation and, above all, lots of child-initiated activity. Children don't need a stage to be dramatic, but they do

need a private enclave to foster the illusion that they are outside real time and space. A finely detailed landscape also sparks kids' imaginations by providing the props for flights of fancy: a bayberry hedge that is a hideout for crooks and ogres, a brick path that is a superhighway one minute and a treacherous no-man's-land between good- and bad-guy territory the next. In the end, though, children's creativity probably has more to do with parental attitudes than with either playspace design or equipment. If parents encourage an active imagination, taking the time to help tie on a towel cape or carve a wood-block ray gun, the kids will do the rest.

Children often act out solitary fantasies, signing on a dog and a teddy bear as extras, but imaginative play is sometimes shared. When a child solicits a friend to play Darth Vader to his Luke Skywalker, though, he relinquishes some control over the make-believe world: Lord Vader may suddenly decide to kidnap R2D2, sending the plot off in a direction Luke did not intend. Learning to cope with another – often conflicting – point of view teaches kids ways of dealing with each other that form the basis of adult relationships. Some psychologists believe that play, frivolous and carefree though it may seem, is actually one of the most important avenues of social development.

At about age 2½, kids begin to enjoy social play, and, according to noted child-development psychologist Arnold Gesell, by the time children start school, the neighbour's yard begins to look more attractive than their own. From this point on, play becomes largely social and the backyard playspace will likely entertain as many friends as it does family members. Design it to encourage both solitary and social play, including traditional play equipment such as swings, slides and monkey bars, which are fun for one child, and components designed for group play, such as horizontal tire swings and platforms. Playhouses are a social mecca for kids from 3 to 13, but remember to include private retreats where they can indulge in solitary reverie.

A playspace that stimulates kids' minds and imaginations but ignores their bodies is no better than the swing set, which does just the opposite. To develop physically, children need a playspace that promotes both whole body movement and specific muscle development: open areas for running, equipment such as horizontal ladders to develop upper body strength and coordination, ramps for eye-foot coordination and soft, flexible climbers such as nets and tires that teach kids to adjust to dynamic surfaces and the movements of others. Once they have learned to stand fairly steadily on their feet, toddlers like to push and pull, to climb on low structures and to dig and swing. Children from ages 2 to 6 experiment more vigorously with their bodies, climbing higher, turning somersaults and lugging big objects around like indefatigable house movers. School-age children need larger and more complex equipment to challenge their rapidly growing bodies: taller, more intricate climbers, horizontal bars and trapeze rings. At this stage, interest in formal and group games begins to emerge, increasing in importance as the child grows into adolescence, but the need for physical play does not diminish as the toddler becomes a teenager. In my own backyard, the Tarzan rope swing that dangles over the gully is still a major attraction for local 15-year-olds bent on proving their prowess.

A good home playground includes something for the body as well as the imagination. Design physical play equipment to match the kids' abilities and preferences. As these happy 10-year-olds will attest, monkey bars are a favourite of school-age children.

19

Surrounded by dense forest on three sides and a busy country road on the fourth, the Waltons built a backyard playspace for their three sons, using a rusted swing set frame to anchor the two-part swinging bridge that angles from the playhouse to the sandbox below.

In other times and cultures, these physical challenges unfolded naturally as kids clambered up rocks, slid down sand hills, jumped from stone to stone across a rushing stream and dangled by their arms from the branches of a spreading oak tree. But most urban backyards are barren by comparison, and though rural areas offer more opportunities for physical play, safety concerns often keep children, especially the very young, close to home.

"In some ways, a backyard playspace is even more important in the country than in the city," says Wendy Walton, whose house is surrounded by the deep forests of northeastern Ontario. "When the children are little, they can't go into the woods. It would be so easy to get lost, and once they got in there, you'd never find them. There are also bears and wolves and other animals that country kids have to be made aware of before they can be allowed to play beyond the yard. And there are no sidewalks, so the road is out of bounds until they are a responsible age. Living where we do, we felt it was essential to have something fun and interesting for the kids right here in the yard."

Whether in the country or the city, parents can construct play equipment that is as rich in physical challenge as forest and field, but structures that are physically challenging inevitably involve danger. "There is always a certain risk in being alive," observed the playwright Henrik Ibsen, "and if you are more alive, there is more risk." When they play, kids constantly stretch beyond the limits of what they know they can do in order to learn something new. The first time a 6-year-old girl leans forward to clutch the starting rung of the monkey bars, she doesn't know for sure if she can hold her own weight, let alone whether she will be able to "walk" hand-over-hand to the other side. She'll never know if she doesn't try, but if she fails, will she hurt herself? Risk has become an important issue in public playground design, particularly since injury-related lawsuits have sharply increased playground insurance costs. Safety is no less a concern for the homeowner considering a backyard playspace, but there is a real danger that, in their eagerness to make play equipment safe, designers and manufacturers will eliminate challenge and, with it, the fun and learning which are the *raison d'être* of play.

It is very difficult to assess exactly how hazardous play equipment is. Statistics from the United States show that in 1982, 194,041 children were injured and 45 were killed in playground-related accidents. No overall playground injury statistics are kept in Canada, but three children's hospitals and two general hospitals contribute their records to Canadian Accident

Injury Reporting and Evaluation (CAIRE). According to their April to September 1984 figures, monkey bars and swings ranked second and third behind bicycles as the products most frequently involved in the injuries of 5-to-9-year-olds, but such data probably says more about how kids spend their time than about the safety of those particular items. A British study concluded that three times more children are hospitalized for dog bites than for playground accidents and that a child is five times safer using play equipment than playing an organized sport. Nevertheless, there have been a few gruesome playground-related deaths: an Ontario youngster was recently strangled when her scarf became caught on the top of a park slide.

Sad as such incidents are, it is wrong to conclude that playgrounds are implicitly dangerous. Instead of excluding a piece of play equipment that might cause an accident, design and construct it to reduce the potential for serious injury in the event of a mishap. Eliminate obvious hazards – protruding bolts, widely spaced railings that can trap small heads, or slides that end abruptly 2 feet above the ground – at the drawing-board stage, and lay a resilient ground cover under physical play equipment to cushion falls, the greatest cause of playground injuries. Good layout and close attention to clearances prevent such accidents as kids running into a cable ride or swings colliding with each other or a nearby fence. Playspace safety requires careful planning, but it does not have to dull the challenge or the fun. (See Safety Checklist on page 140.)

Although safety is a persistent theme in the following chapters, parents must recognize from the outset that there is no such thing as risk-free play. "If that is the goal, we'll end up with a foam-rubber world," says Al Potvin of Hilan Creative Playstructures. What is important is relative safety. Kids develop a healthy respect for danger if they are exposed to graduated, manageable risks where there is minimal potential for serious injury. Recently, a group of 10-year-olds roughhousing on a play frame in a public park were pushing each other with taunts and dares to slide "no hands" down the fire-station pole. But when one boy started physically pushing another over the platform guardrail, the others gave him a tongue-lashing. "My brother got pushed and broke his leg, so back off!" commanded one youngster. The kids knew when risk had degenerated into danger.

Parents must learn to trust their children's ability to estimate risk. Back-yard play is not always well supervised, and with several kids in the family, a size-5 child inevitably ends up experimenting with a size-10 challenge. Fortunately, most children are better at this than their parents give them credit for. They may even be better at it than the parents themselves. Spend an afternoon observing children on a climber, and it soon becomes apparent that they push their limits by very small degrees, unlike those adults who, after a decade of inactivity, force their bodies through a rousing game of tennis that sends them to the doctor with pulled muscles or inflamed joints.

The best plan is to make the surroundings as safe as possible, then give kids some latitude and accept the scraped elbows, bumped noses and skinned knees that are the inevitable consequences of body-stretching play. If adult discretion builds in too great a safety factor, the play equipment will be uninteresting and unused, driving kids

to seek thrills where there is real danger and not simply challenge. "Life demands courage, endurance and strength," writes Lady Allen of Hurtwood, who brought adventure playgrounds to Britain, "but we continue to underestimate the capacity of children for taking risks, enjoying the stimulation of danger and finding things out for themselves. It is often difficult to permit children to take risks, but over-concern prevents them from growing up."

Because kids of several ages will undoubtedly play on the backyard play frame, youngsters will inevitably experiment with challenges that are beyond their skills. Parents should design and build the equipment to minimize injuries, but in the end, they have to learn to trust their children's ability to assess risk.

2

Swings and Things

The constructed play environment

How do you like to go up in a
   swing,
Up in the air so blue?
Oh, I do think it the pleasantest
   thing
Ever a child can do!

Robert Louis Stevenson

Ten-year-old Ross Saunders paused a moment, waiting for the orange crate under his feet to stop wobbling, then he stretched his arms and gripped the trapeze bar swaying lightly overhead. He gave it a couple of tentative tugs. The two lengths of electrical wire filched from his father's toolbox seemed to hold just fine. Using his best Cub Scout knots, Ross had looped one end of each wire around a low branch of the big red maple and hitched the other ends to a split broom handle from the woodshed. Hands clutching the bar, he squeezed his eyes shut and began his first swing, the roar of the crowd thundering in his ears. For a moment, his daring young body soared through the air with the greatest of ease, then the applause collapsed with a crash, and he lay sprawled in a jumble of splintered wood, the bar still clenched in his fists, frayed copper wires trailing in the breeze.

Kids love to swing, tumble, climb and slide, but they do not have to learn the hard way – as Ross did – how to build play equipment that will not let them down in midair. This chapter is devoted to the constructed elements of a child's recreational environment: it discusses the kinds of activity that tire swings, cargo nets, hollow blocks and other playthings stimulate, their changing appeal as a youngster grows and develops and the design elements and safety features parents must consider when buying or building each piece of play equipment for the backyard.

Some of the familiar fixtures of public playgrounds – freestanding slides, roundabouts and teeter-totters – are notably absent. Of limited play value, these single-function pieces of equipment cost too much to build and take up too much space to be practical for the family yard. Since no mandatory safety standards exist, the technical recommendations in this chapter are based on discussions with play-equipment manufacturers and consultants. In cases of conflicting opinion, this book takes the most conservative stance, but in the final analysis, no set of rules is a substitute for well-honed common sense.

Swings

The 1919 Spalding sports-equipment catalogue proudly proclaimed its new metal swing a technological breakthrough, destined to push aside forever the traditional rope swing with its wooden seat smoothed and hollowed by generations of bottoms: "The modern playground needs something better adapted to its requirements – a perfect mechanical device designed to stand incessant wear under any and all conditions." Corporate advice notwithstanding, swings have survived and evolved in the family yard, offering new variations on the pendulum theme that allow adults as well as kids to satisfy their craving for the soothing and thrilling sway of a swing.

The responsive rhythms of a swing make it one of the all-time favourites among backyard playthings. Cradling the swinger in gently rocking arms, it can be a comforting retreat for kids of all ages, but it can also exhilarate the swinger who arches her back, toes straining to touch the sky, then swoops back in a breathtaking arc, only to fly forward again. The adrenaline rush is addictive – what else can explain the lemming-like dash that recurs every morning when the buses pull into my son's schoolyard and 90 youngsters race to claim one of nine playground swings?

From the time they can sit until they are actively walking (8 to 18 months), children need "baby swings" that

apart on a single frame – some horizontal, some vertical – creates a swaying obstacle-course swing climber guaranteed to keep 12-year-old Tarzans on their toes. A single rope with knotted or wooden footholds tempts kids well into their teens, especially if it dangles over a pond or ravine, but adolescents, like adults, revel most in the privacy and self-indulgence of a cozy, full-size hammock, pulling up the fringes to obliterate all but a gently swaying slice of sky.

Meeting all the needs of kids as they grow from toddlers to teens does not entail building a new swing every other year; instead, a parent can design and construct a single frame to accommodate a succession of swings. For example, at the University of Guelph preschool play yard, a simple wooden post-and-beam frame with permanent hooks to hang three swings stands near a storage cupboard containing an assortment of traditional swings, horizontal and vertical tire swings, trapeze bars and rings. Simply changing what is hung from the frame will ensure that the swing is always novel and appropriate to the child using it. This solution is especially suitable for family backyards, where 2-year-olds and 10-year-olds share the same space and where the equipment serves virtually all ages over its life span.

The swing frame can be as simple as a branch if the backyard is blessed with a good swing tree. But don't tie a rope tightly around the limb: that will ringbark the branch, strangling it to death. Instead, hang the swing from S-hooks and hitching rings attached to heavy eyebolts passed right through the centre of the branch. This will not harm the tree branch, which will eventually grow over the bolts. If good swing trees are in short supply, fasten the eyebolts to

support them at the waist and have a between-the-legs strap to keep them from slipping out. As the toddler grows and begins to climb, a low-slung swing suspended 14 inches or more off the ground provides the physical challenge of trying to mount a horse that won't stay still, followed by a rewarding swing every time the beast is tamed. By the age of 3 or 4, kids enjoy swinging together on a horizontally suspended tire, which they will also use as a social gathering place or a swaying stage for dramas set on the high seas. This "social swing" will inevitably be used as a climber, with several kids coordinating their collective muscle power to prod a few physical thrills from even this sluggish sideways pendulum. For older school-age children, traditional swings suspended on long ropes or chains are challenging and fun, though the single tire remains a welcome place to flop on lazy summer days. Hanging a series of tires a yard a sturdy frame anchored firmly enough that the uprights will not sway no matter how hard a child pumps. Ideally, the swing frame will be a separate unit, isolated from other play equipment and designed to discourage kids from climbing on the sides and top. If swings are combined with a play frame, suspend them away from the physical action. To prevent collisions, make sure there is at least a 30-inch clearance between the swing and its frame and between adjacent swings. Tire swings, which move in all directions, should never be mounted on the same frame as traditional swings, and because children can fall off them at any point of the compass, tire swings need more clearance—at least 6 feet between the maximum reach of the tire and any obstacle.

The swing hangers that connect the rope or chain to the frame are the most important part of swing design because if they fail, not only will the child crash to the ground, but heavy hardware could land on his head. For traditional swings, the simplest connections are eyebolts and hitching rings installed so the full circle of each eye is visible if one stands in front of the swing. An S-hook connects each hitching ring to a swing chain. If installed this way, the ring acts as a bearing, absorbing the friction of the to-and-fro motion. Otherwise, says Rick Henke of Children's Playgrounds Inc., the S-hook on a well-used backyard swing can wear out in three weeks. For the same reason, it is also advisable to use a ring at the seat connection. Henke suggests that stability can be improved by spacing the eyebolts on the frame an inch or two farther apart than the width of the seat so the chains are slightly V-shaped instead of hanging parallel. More durable—and more expensive—suspension systems are available from play-equipment manufacturers: hangers

with lubricated bearings for pendulum swings and swivels designed for multi-axis tire swings that let the seats pivot without twisting the chains. Whatever the suspension hardware, though, maintenance is the key to safety; inspect the suspension system and lubricate bearings several times a year. Replace worn parts before they fail.

Swing seats are suspended by either ropes or chains. Metal is cold to the touch in winter and large chainlinks can pinch small fingers, but both these problems can be avoided by sheathing the handgrip portion with flexible rubber or plastic hose. The S-hook joining the chain to the hitching ring or bearing hanger must be tightly clinched to ensure that the chain does not jump out when a child swings very high. Once the S-hook is clinched, chains cannot be readily adjusted to raise the seat as a

child grows. Rope, on the other hand, is more comfortable to grasp, especially in winter, and is also easily adjustable. Splice the rope ends back into the main cord to create an eye to hang on the S-hook. Clinch the hook tightly, then feed the other end of the rope through the hitching ring and back through the S-hook as illustrated on page 111. The loop then can be lengthened or shortened.

Because of safety concerns, seats have probably changed more than any other part of the traditional swing. A thwack on the head from a swing seat is one of the most common playground injuries, and whether empty or occupied, wood and metal seats are heavy and hard enough to harm a child seriously. A rigid seat is only acceptable if it is very light (under 3 pounds) or is designed to reduce impact. For instance, the perimeter of one British seat is Swiss-cheesed with holes that act as air cushions. It successfully passes the European "egg test": when released from a height of 3 feet, the seat does not hit an egg hard enough to break it. A safe alternative to wood, metal and rigid plastic is a belt or strap seat made of flexible material. Lightweight and nonslip, belt or strap seats may wear faster than wood or metal, but they conform nicely to any size bottom. Tires also make good swing seats, either factory-reject new tires or recycled used tires that still have some tread. Avoid worn steel-belted tires if there is any danger that the metal strands will poke through and injure the kids.

The hardware that connects the seat to the rope or chains can also be a hazard—I recently saw a youngster being dragged back and forth through the gravel under a playground swing because her shorts had caught in the open S-hook joining the seat to the chains. Be sure S-hooks are tightly

With lots of room for two or more, a swivelling tire is more than just a swing. It is a climber, a meeting place and a swaying stage for plays set on the high seas.

Suspend swings from a separate frame or from a beam extended to one side of the play frame, well away from the kids who are sliding and climbing. Provide enough clearance in all directions so the swing will not strike any obstacles.

clinched, and avoid seat connectors with 4-to-9-inch-wide openings that might trap small heads.

For older children, consider suspending trapeze bars or rings from the frame. The cross member of a trapeze bar does not present the same safety hazard as a seat since it swings above the heads of toddlers, who are most likely to unwittingly walk into the path of moving objects. For the budding acrobat, buy a metal bar with fused suspension rings, or make one by suspending a hardwood dowel horizontally from two ropes or chains. To avoid head entrapment, rings should be less than 4 inches or greater than 9 inches in diameter, a difficult standard to meet without making rings uncomfortably small or large. One solution is a triangular "ring" that has an inside diameter of less than 4 inches but a longer grasping surface. Hang trapeze bars and rings no more than 6 inches above a child's maximum reach, between 5 and 8 feet off the ground.

Swings are involved in a high percentage of playground accidents, partly because they are popular but also because not enough thought is given to their design and installation. Remember to locate swings out of the main flow of playground traffic where kids cannot easily walk behind them. Put them in a corner near a fence or building, nestled into shrubs so kids are encouraged to get on from the front. Be sure there is sufficient clearance for the swing to extend in full flight without hitting any obstacles.

Even with these precautions, parents should assume that kids will occasionally fall off their swings. The best defence against injury from those inevitable tumbles is a soft landing. Cushion the area under a swing's path – a swath approximately 20 inches wide and 5 feet long – with a resilient ground cover. Aside from its safety value, a good ground cover also eliminates the unsightly, muddy ruts worn in the lawn by the repeated braking of pint-sized feet.

Cable ride

Extravagantly labelled the "Slide for Life" in Arthur and Lorna Leland's 1909 textbook on play but more commonly called the cable ride or pulley glide, this thrilling variation on the swing will be a magnet for every school-age kid in the neighbourhood. At our house, the cable ride (we call it an aerial runway) is the first thing the boys show off to new visitors, and it never fails to elicit whoops of delight. Gripping the rope handle, the rider leaps bravely off a raised platform and swoops through the air, drawn by a pulley racing smoothly along a steel cable strung between two trees. Few pieces of play equipment are more fun or give the upper torso a better workout than the cable ride, but it can also be dangerous if not properly designed and built.

The ideal setting for a cable ride is a gentle slope – about 1:25 (vertical height:

Strung the length of the yard close to a bordering hedge, a cable ride takes up little space and is simple to build but gives kids a unique kind of fun and exercise.

27

Stout trees make the most secure endposts for cable rides. To create an artificial slope, fasten the steel cable to an eyebolt inserted high in the tree and build a take-off platform and ramp.

running height)—with a stout tree at the top and two trees 6 or 8 feet apart at the bottom. If the terrain is flat, create an artificial incline by fastening the cable higher at the take-off point than at the terminus and building a platform or ramp from which to start the ride—a ramp lets kids decide when to become airborne instead of forcing them to leap into midair. Periodically, our sons revive a long-standing scheme for a supercable strung from their bedroom window to their friends' house a quarter-mile downhill, but as they discovered, a cable ride does not have to be long to be fun. It does not even have to be very high: by tucking up their knees, kids can get that free-floating feeling even if their toes are just inches off the ground. Suspend the cable so its highest point is no more than 6 inches above the reach of the tallest user, but be sure it is high enough that people playing around the site will not run into it. The scar just above my Adam's apple is proof that anyone can be seriously hurt by low-slung wires that disappear in poor light.

Ideally, the ride should be installed along a fence or property edge where it is out of the traffic flow. Be sure the entire length of the ride is unobstructed and the surface underneath the cable is soft in case the rider lets go midway. If the runway is in the woods, clear away rocks and stumps: ferns and underbrush will provide a soft landing, but a chunk of granite underneath could cause a serious injury. A rubber mat is expensive but cushions falls effectively and protects the hillside from being worn away by sliding feet; sand is a good alternative, especially under the drop-off point.

The rider's speed is controlled by adjusting the slope and tautness of the cable. The pulley should reach its maximum speed near the middle of the

run, slowing down before it reaches the end. Instead of fastening the cable to a single end post, suspend it from a cross beam bridging two posts or trees so the child finishes the run in a clearing rather than heading straight for an obstacle. If there is only one end post, cushion it with a tire "bumper" spiked to the pole to absorb the shock of landing. Install a brake—a tire impaled on the cable—to stop the pulley at least 6 feet short of the end posts, and be sure to test the

mechanism before kids are allowed to ride—even a brake will not prevent injuries when the cable is too taut or the ride too fast. If they hit the brake with too much force, kids' lightweight bodies can be propelled forward much farther than 6 feet.

Trees make the best takeoff and end posts because their root systems anchor them firmly against the formidable lateral stress of kids and adults throwing their weight into the ride. The alternative is to suspend the cable between posts sunk deeply into the ground. The Playground of the Century at Century School in Ottawa, built for the 7th World Conference of the International Playground Association, included a cable ride with posts sunk 6 feet in well-tamped ground, but its designer, Paul Hogan, suggests that 8 or 10 feet is not extreme. With wooden knee braces to give the posts extra stability, 4 to 6 feet is adequate. Bolt the cross beam to the back of the posts or trees so the stress pulls the joints together rather than apart.

Heavy rope knotted with a bowline around one tree and an adjustable hitching knot around the other is acceptable only for a temporary (one day) cable ride. Anything more permanent requires a ⅜-inch galvanized steel cable fastened to heavy eyebolts set in the cross beam. The pulley can be a standard wooden pulley block or one of the specially designed metal glides sold by play-equipment manufacturers that feature two self-lubricating rollers enclosed in a rustproof aluminum casing. In either case, the moving parts must be fully enclosed and out of children's reach. In separate incidents in Germany recently, two girls were scalped when their long hair became caught in cable-ride pulleys. A mechanism designed specifically for the job is worth the price. Commercial pulleys for public playgrounds cost over $500, but both Children's Playgrounds Inc. and Hilan Creative Playstructures sell enclosed backyard models for less than $100. Play-equipment dealers sell pulleys with T-bar or trapeze-ring handgrips, but kids can make their own out of rope or dowelling. Because kids tend to "whip" the pulleys back to the starting point with some force, the handgrips should be higher than the tallest child, with a retrieval rope dangling low enough to be grasped without stretching.

Slides

Slides come in many shapes – spirals, waves, tubes, tunnels – and in about as many sizes as kids – tall and skinny, short and wide and truly gargantuan, like the concrete slide at Tokyo's Ota-ku Playground. At 15 feet high and 200 feet wide, it is big enough to handle a hundred squealing, tumbling kids at a time. But whatever form they take, slides are an indispensable part of every playground, because nothing can replace the thrill of standing high above the world, then whooshing, weightless, back to earth.

For a toddler, the slide is as frighteningly fun as a roller coaster, and although it continues to appeal to kids of all ages, a slide has to change in size and complexity to maintain that adrenaline rush as the child grows. A study by Texan play psychologist Joe Frost shows that for children under the age of 6, slides were second only to sandboxes as the most preferred piece of play equipment. For these youngsters, low, wide slides offer the physical exercise of climbing, early lessons in the physics of gravity and acceleration and good social-play opportunities when two or three tackle the slope together.

However, their preferences change by the time kids reach school. When Vancouver play researcher Marilyn Reid asked a sample of local children what they liked best about their schools' creative playgrounds, slides were near the bottom of the list. That does not necessarily mean that school kids do not like slides, just that the slides they had were not much fun. To hold the interest of children over the age of 6, slides have to be very fast or very long or have wily contours for a wild and bumpy ride. The challenge for slide designers is to let kids have their kicks safely.

There are four basic types of slides: freestanding slides with a ramp and steps combined as a single piece of equipment and installed on a level patch of lawn; combination slides where the bedway is part of a play frame that incorporates several ways of getting to the top of the slide; embankment or mound slides that are embedded into a hillside and follow the contour of the land; and spiral slides, which are generally beyond the space and budget limitations of a family and its backyard.

The traditional playground slide is freestanding, tall and narrow (up to 16 feet high and only 16 inches wide) with a small platform at the top where the child makes the transition from climbing up to

Count on kids to test play equipment to its limits, running up and leaping down a slide after the thrill of conventional use wears thin. Encourage children's natural quest for challenge by building equipment that can withstand such abuse: reduce its accident potential by designing safety features such as smooth slide beds, handrails and a soft ground cover.

29

A mound slide embedded in a gentle slope is both fun and safe since there is nowhere to fall if kids tumble over the side. There are many ways other than stairs to get back to the top: kids can pull themselves up a knotted rope, follow stepping-stones that zigzag up the hill or simply crawl up the grassy slope.

sitting and sliding down. As a single-function piece of play equipment, it is impractical for home play yards because it costs too much to build and takes up too much room for its limited play value. Combination and mound slides, on the other hand, make better use of limited space and enhance both the complexity and the flexibility of a play area. They offer almost limitless imaginative possibilities, serving as an escape route from pirate invasions or a speedy beam-down from Starship Enterprise to an alien planet. Attached to a play-frame platform, a slide provides only one of many exits and becomes an element in the overall flow of physical play instead of an isolated up-and-down exercise. As the child grows, the slide can be lengthened and attached higher on the frame to provide a bigger thrill. It can also be widened to 3, 4 or more feet, since kids seem to like squeezing together to slide down a slope even better than taking a solo plunge.

The bedway of a freestanding or combination slide slopes through midair, making railings essential both as handholds for the timid and as barriers to keep kids from sliding over the edge; however, kids have nowhere to fall if they tumble over the side of a mound slide. If the slide is built into an existing hillside or a created hillock (practical only with a major restructuring of the backyard landscape), the lie of the land can be shaped to give it some tummy-tickling swells. Landscape the other sides of the mound to give kids alternative routes to the top: log or stone steps embedded in the grass, hard rubber or metal hoops as handholds for climbing or a knotted rope tied to a stake for scaling the peak. Because it is an integral part of the natural landscape, a mound slide will probably get more year-round use than other types: in

winter, it is a ready-made flying-saucer run; a sheet of 10-mil plastic and a running garden hose will convert it to a water slide to counter a July heat wave.

The winter potential of slides has been sadly underappreciated. In their rural backyard near Nipissing Village in

northern Ontario, Raymond and Wendy Walton built a 3-foot-wide, 7-foot-tall freestanding slide. The bedway, fashioned from salvaged enamelled-metal roofing, extends 25 feet, long enough to give their school-age sons lots of summer sliding fun. But in winter, the slide becomes a major attraction for the parents and their friends as much as for the kids. Using a snowblower, Raymond builds a run-out more than 100 feet long at the end of the slide, extending it

into a swath cleared in the woods and banking the path like a bobsled run before icing it smooth with a hose. Perched on plastic Crazy Carpets, sliders whip down the slope and around the bend, swooping out of sight through the trees until they come to rest in a bed of soft snow.

In summer, there are no snowdrifts to cushion runaway sliders, but slope the bedway gently enough and kids will not reach uncontrollable speeds. The incline of a slide should average no more than 30 degrees from the horizontal, and if it is wavy, each change in angle should have a radius of at least 39 inches. As a rule of thumb, make the bedway twice as long as it is high – install an 8-foot slide 4 feet high for preschoolers and a 14-foot slide 7 feet high for school-age children. The sliding surface also affects speed. Because water slides are three times faster than steel or plastic, build them at only a 10-degree angle, or have a splash pool at the bottom to cushion the landing.

On traditional freestanding slides, the narrow platform at the peak is often the site of accidents. After climbing up the steps, children need to have enough room to tuck their legs under and sit down, a complicated manoeuvre for young children just learning to use their bodies. Combination and mound slides bypass the problem by providing large platforms and giving kids other ways of getting down if they "chicken out" at the last minute. Whatever the design, the platform at the top of the slide should be at least as wide as the sliding surface and, on a freestanding slide, a minimum of 20 inches long, with guardrails to prevent the child from falling off.

Whether a slide is freestanding or attached to a play frame, the means of getting to the top – rungs, steps or stairs – should be scaled to the size of the

Taking the plunge with a friend is often more fun than a solo slide, especially for young children. Instead of building a traditional 20-inch-wide slide, expand the bedway to 3 or 4 feet to create a "social slide."

sliders. Space steps and rungs evenly, with 4 to 14 inches between them to accommodate the arm and leg reaches of kids. If steps are 4 to 9 inches apart, close them in at the back to avoid head entrapment. Steps should be horizontal and at least 16 inches wide, with a tread depth of 5 to 10 inches. There should be continuous handrails at a height that allows kids to stand erect. Avoid unnatural climbing angles: ladders with rungs should be sloped 55 to 90 degrees from horizontal, ladders with steps should have a slope of 35 to 55 degrees, and stairways should tilt no more than 35 degrees.

Getting youngsters safely off the slide can be as much of a challenge as getting them on. Just as swings provide a steady clientele for orthodontists, slides make good business for orthopaedic surgeons. On a slide with a simple straight slope, children gather speed on their way down, then crash to the ground on their tailbones. Lowering the slope enough to make it safe would defeat the purpose of a slide. Instead, many public playground slides have a short horizontal extension on the bottom that slows sliders to normal walking speed so they can regain balance before getting off. Although ideal, this solution may not be practical for the backyard where relatively short slides rarely cause excessive speeds. It is important, however, for kids to land on a soft surface. Make sure the exit lip is low enough that when kids sit on it, their feet touch the ground—3 to 14 inches off the ground, depending on the size of the kids. If it is too high, kids can hit the back of their skulls on the exit lip when they land. For very young children, bury the exit lip in the sand or gravel to prevent a crash landing.

Many of these safety features are standard on ready-made slides. And most play-equipment manufacturers willingly sell slides to individuals, an option worth considering since slides are expensive and challenging to build. Purchased models are made of polyethylene, steel, aluminum or, occasionally, fibreglass, but homemade versions can be constructed with hardwood planks or metal sheeting (stainless steel or galvanized aluminum) over exterior-grade plywood. Homeowners can reasonably build short slides, but bedways over 6 to 8 feet long are difficult. If seams are not carefully joined, rough edges and narrow gaps can snag kids' clothes, causing problems that range from rips and tears to injury and even death.

Climbers

From a perch near the top of a broad-leaved tree, the landscape seems small enough to fit in the palm of the hand, the streetcars mere toys and the fierce dog next door just a china shop ornament. Climbing gives children an exhilarating sense of dominion over a world that is often overwhelming, but good places to climb are notably absent from most backyards. City kids may have few opportunities to exercise their natural affinity for scaling heights and scrambling over rugged terrain, making a constructed climber especially important to the home playspace.

As soon as babies learn to crawl, they take delight in trying to climb over the Cabbage Patch dolls and Duplo blocks that get in their way. From the age of 9 months, when they develop a sense of depth perception and begin to master the concept of height variation, kids need to climb. Physically, climbing strengthens important arm, leg and back muscles and develops postural control, but it also offers new perspectives that help kids come to terms with their world. One observational study concluded that small children prefer to play 3 to 6 feet above ground level, which elevates them to adult eye level or better, a height from which they can suddenly look down on a world they spend most of their time looking up to. Sitting on the grass, they see only daffodils around the birdbath base and the bottom step of the deck, but from the top of the play frame, their vista magically expands to encompass the whole yard, giving order and meaning to the single elements that loom so large when seen up close.

A child's preference for heights does not alter with advancing age, but how high children want to go is directly related to how they get there: the simpler the climber, the higher kids like to be, but if the route is a tricky cargo net or rigorous rope climb, they are content with a lower destination.

A climbing mountain gives kids the physical challenge of climbing without dominating the backyard landscape. Embed peeled cedar logs upright in the ground at irregular heights, or cluster small rocks around a large central boulder, filling the gaps between stumps or stones with sand to prevent small feet from getting trapped. As well as stretching the muscles, these custom-built mountains are perfect for ambushing desperadoes or for hiding from all the king's men.

Though not very high off the ground, balance beams provide a popular form of climbing for kids from 3 to 13, with young schoolchildren being especially adept at the kind of daredevil antics this climber inspires. Balance beams are easy to make: simply secure a 6-to-10-foot peeled log or rounded timber to two posts so that it rests 18 to 30 inches off the ground. Increase the challenge for older kids by suspending the beam with chains, by raising one end so kids have to balance up an incline or by changing the beam to a lumberjack's log roller, a narrow log suspended on bearings between two posts. A series of balance beams can be used as kids' benches and as low fencing to separate activity areas in the yard, or they can be integrated into the physical play area as a novel way of getting from one piece of equipment to another.

In the 1960s, tires were recycled into playground climbers largely because they were plentiful and free, but the practice persists because the big rubber O's add a unique textural and physical dimension to kids' play. Smooth and sculptured to the touch, tires are not firm underfoot like wood or metal: they lean and stretch with children's weight, forcing them to match their movements to the material. A tire crawler, a series of big tires spaced 18 inches apart and sunk vertically halfway into the ground, is a credible obstacle course for preschoolers to climb through and leap over. Bolt as few as two or as many as a dozen tires to a post to create a tire tree, or fasten them to each other with a "flex link" (see page 125) to make a tire net strung between two posts or from a play deck.

Though the tires themselves are cheap (use factory seconds or old tires that are undamaged and still have some tread), bolting them together is a laborious job, and hardware is expensive but unavoidable: if tires are not well supported, they sag and tear, becoming

Kids love to climb, rising above the backyard to get a new perspective on their world. Climbers also give kids a good physical workout, exercising leg and back muscles on the ascent and arms and shoulders on accessories such as knotted ropes, sliding poles and monkey bars.

what had been exclusively used as climbing frames. In the process, the physical element was almost completely designed out of some structures, reducing them to little more than heavily built play towers with good dramatic possibilities but little potential for either rigorous exercise or physical challenge. These multipurpose play frames take up a lot of space, and parents who buy or build them must carefully assess the kinds of activity they promote. If thoughtfully designed, however, a play frame can be wonderfully flexible, with interchangeable accessories that extend both physical and imaginative play and keep the backyard playspace challenging as the children grow and develop.

An amorphous piece of equipment, each play frame can be shaped to suit family needs and preferences as well as the topography of the yard. Whatever its final form, it should include vertical and sloped climbing to exercise the legs and lower back, horizontal climbing to strengthen the arms and upper torso, and platforms for social play and stopovers where kids can assess their accomplishments and decide what to do next. With a careful choice of accessories, a play frame can stimulate the full range of physical activities and provide graduated challenges so children can progress at their own pace, enjoying the thrill of success as fresh opportunities beckon. The Waltons' play frame has ladders, monkey bars, a swinging bridge and a sliding pole. According to Wendy Walton, "The more ways there are to climb up and hang off the frame, the better the kids like it."

Most of the accessories are simply muscle-stretching ways of getting to and from platforms, the simplest being vertical climbers. A ladder is the most obvious choice—certainly it is the most overused in commercial designs—and it

frustrating, dangerous and unsightly.

On traditional playgrounds, kids get their climbing kicks by scaling the jungle gym. According to play consultant Polly Hill, this original piece of physical play equipment did a pretty good job of exercising young bodies: "There is nothing new about a jungle gym, but it still has lots of play value and is one of the best pieces of equipment for physical development so far invented." The advantage of the jungle gym is that kids use their legs as they climb up the rungs, their whole bodies as they weave in and out of the spaces between, and develop arm coordination and strength (brachiation) when they hang by their hands and move hand-over-hand across the structure. Like the other equipment described above, it develops spatial judgment and individual muscles, but the jungle gym is unique in that it gives

kids a good overall workout.

Parents can make their own jungle gyms out of posts and hardwood dowels, building 2-foot-square modules to match the physical size and abilities of their children. For preschoolers, a 6-foot cube is sufficient: it takes up little space yet can be used imaginatively by very young children, especially if they have props such as cleated boards that fit between rungs to form temporary, movable platforms. As they become more physically competent, older school-age kids need climbers that are high and challenging: extend the gym up to 10 feet high for 6-to-14-year-olds and make it increasingly complex.

As creative playgrounds evolved, designers tried to combine the physical benefits of jungle gyms with opportunities for imaginative and social play by adding permanent platforms to

An amorphous piece of equipment, each play frame can be custom-designed for the particular yard and the children who will use it. Raised platforms form the core of a play frame, with accessories to create a variety of challenging ways to get up and down—cargo nets, sliding poles, monkey bars and slides.

can be incorporated permanently into the side of the play frame or constructed as a separate unit to hook onto the structure wherever they want. Spaced to match a child's arm and leg reach, rungs are usually made of ¾-to-1½-inch wooden dowels because they are easy to grip and comfortable to handle in summer or winter. If possible, vary the basic ladder concept by changing the rung material (ropes, wooden steps) and the incline to give the child as many different up-and-down climbing experiences as possible.

Though kids under 5 generally lack the muscle coordination and strength to hoist their small bodies up a knotted rope, it makes a challenging vertical climber for older children. Pulling themselves hand-over-hand up a hemp rope also has potent imaginative appeal, transforming a shy 10-year-old into a valiant Robin Hood scaling the walls of Nottingham to rescue Maid Marian. And should the Sheriff's men arrive on the scene, a sliding pole provides a good way to make a quick exit. A sliding pole is extremely popular with school-age kids and is easy to install. Position the pole 18 to 20 inches from the platform—close enough for a child to reach without leaning and far enough that he won't hit the play frame while sliding down. Barricade the play frame at ground level, and children won't be tempted to run out from under the deck into the path of the slider, and if the pole passes two platforms, add a guardrail to the lower one so kids can't mount the pole from below, colliding with someone already on his way down.

Sloped climbers—steps and ramps— appeal mostly to very young children, for whom the gradual change in elevation builds strong leg and back muscles and develops good eye-foot coordination. Ramps can be made a permanent part of the frame, but attaching them temporarily is better, since the incline can be increased as the child's skill improves. Make a portable ramp by fastening two or three boards with cleats that double as stops to hook over the ladder rungs on the play frame. Preschoolers will use ramps as a freeway for racing cars, a gangplank for crawling up to the pirates' den or, hitched to a high rung, as a lean-to cover for impromptu tea parties.

A kinesiologist once told Polly Hill that if all adults had hung by their arms for an hour a day as children, back problems would not be as epidemic as they are today. Whether or not they reduce potential medical problems, horizontal climbers such as monkey bars are good exercisers, and kids love them. Before age 4 or 5, children lack the upper-torso muscle development to climb hand-over-hand, but by age 8, they hang by their hands, their knees and any other part of their anatomy they can hook over the bars. The bars should be small enough in diameter—¾ to 1½ inches—for kids to grip easily and spaced comfortably for their average reach—12 to 20 inches. Children will inevitably try walking across the top of this horizontal ladder, so suspend it as low to the ground as possible (4 to 5 feet) while still allowing the tallest child to hang by her hands without touching the ground. A 4-foot-wide ladder accommodates more than one child at a time, though the dowelling for the rungs has to be thicker to safely bridge the gap. The greatest hazard with traditional monkey bars is the child's falling on the adjoining ladder rung as he starts or finishes his hand-over-hand climb. Avoid this by raising the top step or by setting the first monkey bar in far enough that the child has to reach for it, thus leaning clear of the steps.

Horizontal ladders are a test of endurance as well as strength. To challenge kids of many different ages, slope the monkey bars, adding 3 feet of height over a 10-foot length. Young children will climb down and try the lower reaches, while older children will tackle the entire uphill climb.

On a public playground, monkey bars are usually a separate piece of play equipment, but in a backyard where space is at a premium, it makes more sense to add them to the play frame as an outrigger. Likewise, use a frame post to support one side of a chinning bar, which appeals to the same age group and exercises many of the same muscles. By installing tall support posts, the chinning bar or monkey bars can be raised as the children grow, eventually becoming high enough to give parents a good workout.

Complex play-frame layouts often support two or more parallel platforms connected by bridges designed to provide a physical challenge as well as a visual and functional link between play-equipment components. A footbridge need not be suspended very high off the ground for its gentle sway to give kids a few good thrills and lots of practice developing balance and strong leg muscles. Make a clatter bridge out of wood slats held together with rope, chains or steel cable, or for more challenge, bridge the space between platforms with a tire or rope net. Whether it joins two high platforms, crosses a play stream or connects a ground-level playhouse with a tree house, calculate spans carefully and provide rope, chain or wood handrails.

Rope and tire bridges fall into the category of flexible climbers, relatively new additions to the playground that develop coordination, balance and judgment as well as strong muscles.

Once kids have mastered climbing on solid surfaces (usually by age 4 or 5), they are ready to tackle climbers made from soft materials such as rubber conveyor belts, tires and rope that respond to the climbers' every move. Not only must children adapt to the flexible, dynamic surface, they have to readjust their bodies each time another climber changes position. Rope or tire nets can be draped from a platform to the ground, slung between two platforms or suspended between posts as an entirely separate piece of equipment. Commercial play frames sometimes use chain instead of rope because it is more durable, but metal is unpleasantly cold in winter and hot in summer, and it lacks the resilient textures of fibre. Buy rope cargo-net climbers from play-equipment manufacturers, or make one at home using basic splicing or macramé techniques – a big job but one that realizes considerable savings.

Platforms – the raised flat surfaces on play frames – can be big enough for a space invasion by half a dozen toddlers or small enough to be way stations with just enough room for a timid child to decide whether to climb up the other side of the frame or cross the bridge and clamber down the cargo net. Small platforms tend to keep kids moving, turning the play frame into a kind of three-dimensional fitness trail, whereas large platforms encourage social and dramatic play interspersed with muscle-building exercise.

Platforms can be fixed or movable; a good play frame includes both. Permanently incorporate into the design platforms that differentiate levels of climbing difficulty, but also make cleated boards for the kids so they can create their own platforms, adjusting the play-frame design to suit each new make-believe world. The height of the

platform should match the size and development level of the children using it. In general, experts recommend that for 2- and 3-year-olds, platforms should be less than 5 feet high, 6 feet for 4-to-6-year-olds and 7 to 10 feet high for school-age kids. Except at entrances and exits, any platform more than 2 feet off the ground should have guardrails 28 to 30 inches high around the perimeter. According to some play consultants, railings should be constructed with closely spaced vertical pickets that discourage climbing, but Rick Henke objects to the cagelike effect this creates. "Kids will climb the railings no matter what, so design them to be climbed, and make sure kids won't hurt themselves if they fall." He recommends a double horizontal railing made of 2 by 4s spaced a foot apart. Whatever the design, railings should not be set beyond the

edge of the platform decking, leaving a gap between the floor and rail that kids can slip through.

When a child falls, it is often not the landing but a protruding bolt or beam that causes an injury. Design the play frame so that any cantilevered or moving elements, such as monkey bars or swings, are set distinctly apart from the main structure. Kids won't fall on them, and the children on the ground will also be less likely to run under or in front of them. Use only round-head bolts and countersink the nuts so there is no protruding hardware to catch clothes or scratch tender skin; any moving parts that might shear, pinch or crush young fingers and limbs should be enclosed.

Falls can't be prevented altogether; children will always push each other, slip, lose their balance or over-estimate their ability. Nevertheless, parents can reduce the potential for serious injury by providing their children with a safety-conscious design – scaling the play frame to the child's size and ability, making sure platforms have guardrails, eliminating protrusions, providing soft landing surfaces and keeping heights within reason. Remember that kids enjoy low elevations as much as extreme height, as long as the means of getting there is challenging and fun. According to Joe Frost, "There appears to be no sound rationale for constructing play surfaces beyond the height required for kids to walk under them without knocking their heads on the beams." If the platforms are very high, prevent young children from climbing too far by making upper platforms accessible only to the older children capable of climbing hand-over-hand up inclined monkey bars or shinnying up a knotted rope. Otherwise, a toddler may be lured to the top of a climber and, like a kitten up a telephone pole, be unable to get down.

Playhouses

When I was growing up, my special place was a quilt tent – a ragged-edged blanket draped over the clothesline, spread-eagled corners pinned down with rocks. Here I passed long summer days curled up on a downy bed of pillows, reading stories aloud to a goggle-eyed audience of bears and dolls. Whether it is a tree fort, an appliance-crate cave or a miniature log cabin, kids appreciate a house they can call their own.

One study observed that children use play areas for quiet play and socializing as much as for active physical play, making the playhouse as important as the climber in a well-designed playspace. Commercial structures often attempt to meet both needs by combining the two concepts – setting a playhouse at the top of the climber – and although there is a strong temptation to follow suit in the backyard, where space and budget are usually limited, it may be a mistake. Admittedly, the platforms on a climbing frame are often used for dramatic social play, but it is of the full-bodied, active variety – platforms are primarily way stations where children make stopovers as they climb to or from somewhere else on the frame. Kids also need an intimate quiet spot where they can be alone with their own thoughts or with a few chosen friends, away from the hustle and bustle of physical activity. Such a retreat is not likely to be on top of a climber unless the child is the only one using the frame.

From the age of 2, kids love anything they can crawl into, though very young toddlers prefer not to be completely enclosed. When social inclinations start to flourish at about age 3, a playhouse makes a perfect meeting place to invent make-believe worlds, especially if loose

material props are stored nearby. A playhouse continues to be a social focus for elementary school children until the age of 10 to 12, when its appeal peaks; at this stage, the playhouse is usually changed into a clubhouse, designed and built by an exclusive membership. Teenagers continue to visit a favourite retreat long after they have given up all other vestiges of childhood, and in fact, some people never outgrow that craving for a cozy space set apart from the rigours of the world. Most settle for a rustic cabin in the woods or a cottage by the lake, but a few actually fill their need with an adult-sized hideout: one of the oldest oak trees in Oakville, Ontario, has a full-scale tree house perched in its branches, a solitary retreat overlooking Lake Ontario for a busy Toronto publishing executive.

Playhouses provide children with

privacy and a quiet place for imaginative play, but some parents worry that they will also be used as hideouts for unacceptable behaviour. The only possible response to that argument is that the benefits far outweigh any potential negative consequences. Giving a child privacy necessarily entails a measure of confidence and trust.

Make the playhouse design as generic as possible. If it looks too much like a fort, a castle or Hansel and Gretel's gingerbread cottage, it won't be flexible enough to fit into the full range of childhood fantasies. To be cozy, the retreat should be small, accommodating no more than two or three kids at a time: 3 by 6 feet is enough floor space for preschoolers, expanded to 6 by 6 for school-age kids. Interior furnishings should also be scaled to the child, though it is better to let the kids construct their

Just big enough for two or three special friends, a playhouse should be private and its design generic so childish imaginations have full rein. Although this elevated playhouse has a door, these brothers are sneaking in under the eaves, just one of many cutouts that serve as entrances and exits to their clubhouse.

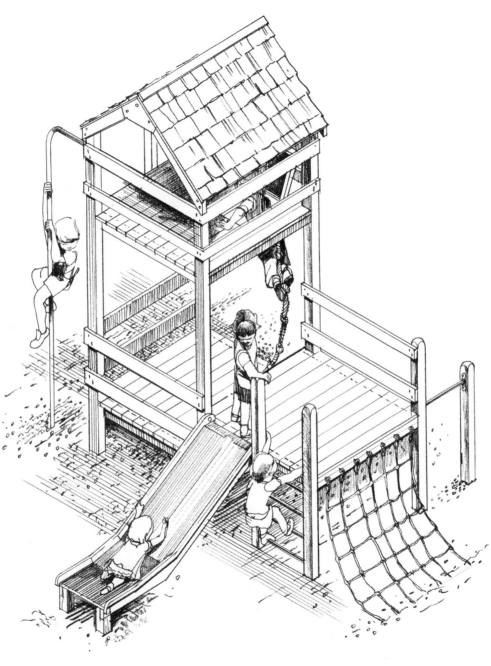

own tables and benches from the blocks and boards in a cache of loose material. Build shutters that work and extra-wide windowsills to double as store counters or ticket wickets. Whatever the design, the house should have a door – a place is hardly private if intruders can come and go as they please. A canvas flap, a slatted gate or a real hinged door encloses the space and gives kids control over who has access to their special retreat.

To enhance the impression of privacy, elevate the playhouse on posts, or follow the example of the Swiss Family Robinson and nestle it in the trees. Be careful, though – even if they are nicely camouflaged in summer, raised playhouses and other tall constructions stick out like sore thumbs when the leaves drop in the fall. If the new structure is likely to jut into the neighbours' panoramic view, consult them before construction begins.

A playhouse does not have to be elevated to be private. Tucked in its own corner of the yard or nestled among the honeysuckle and hobblebush, a ground-level playhouse can seem like a getaway hidden deep in the woods. If the floor is raised from the ground, the room will be more comfortable in cool weather, and the door should be designed so that it will still open when the playspace is covered with snow. In snowbelt areas, raise the door 4 inches and let the kids shovel the rest of the snow aside to get to their drifted-in hideout. Even an earthbound playhouse can give kids the pleasure of playing above ground: make the roof climbable by screwing cleats to a low slope or by adding a lookout deck on a flat roof.

If space or budget is limited, a big box is a good playhouse alternative for very young children. This is really just a permanent version of the cardboard appliance crate, painted to match the loose material. With loose material and a little imagination, a big wooden box can become Billy Goat Gruff's cavern, a cannibal's stewpot or the crow's nest atop a pirate ship. The exact dimensions are not important, as long as it is small and light enough that the kids can move it around and tip it on its side without adult help. As a guideline, 3-year-olds should be able to manage a box approximately 3 feet wide, 4 feet long and 2½ feet high.

Loose Material

How often have parents complained good-naturedly that they bought their offspring an expensive new toy and all the cute little tyke played with was the box? Yet few adults really take this observation to heart. The fact is that kids would sooner play with something they can shape and change than with a detailed plaything that comes with built-in expectations and limitations. If parents want to create a truly kid-oriented backyard, they must provide their children with what is collectively known as "loose material"—nondescript blocks and boards and bits of rope and cloth that kids can use to build their own play environment. In fact, according to Polly Hill, "A creative playground without loose material simply isn't one." In her experience, kids use physical play equipment to test and stretch themselves and to blow off steam, but only for short periods of time. If they have a choice, kids will spend more concentrated time with constructive, creative and social activities, all of which are stimulated by loose material.

With big, hollow blocks and a few boards, children can build a fort, then tear it down and build a better one, experimenting with the physical world, changing it, watching the consequences and effortlessly absorbing life's lessons.

It doesn't matter that the sawhorse has no wheels: turned upside down and grasped by the legs, it is a roaring, speeding motorcycle to an inventive child. These no-name props feed a child's fantasies more richly than any plastic replicas. Totally lacking in distinctive characteristics and open to the child's interpretation of what they are and what they should become, loose material adds the variety and flexibility that are so important in a creative play area. As well as stretching their imaginations, lugging these materials around and lifting them into position helps develop the large muscles, balance and coordination of young children.

While climbing frames, swings, slides and sandboxes can all be found on school and park playgrounds, loose material cannot. According to Joe Frost, "Such restriction of play opportunity is perhaps the greatest single error in playground design and use," but it is one that can be corrected cheaply and easily in the backyard playspace. Loose material is really a throwback to the adventure playground, and though concerns about safety and unsightliness

have kept the concept at bay in most of North America, parents can supply the necessary elements at home, encouraging their children to create and control their own environment.

It is important to remember that this kind of constructive play is not necessarily a family activity. When kids build from loose material, especially older children constructing fairly complex structures, parents should restrain their natural impulse to interfere, to show kids how to do it better. Don't forget that the purpose of loose material is to let children learn by doing, with adults being on hand to encourage, answer specific requests and show interest but not to take over the project. Whatever the kids make, let it be truly theirs, and as their skills improve, they will learn self-confidence and pride in what they do, as well as respect for the work of others.

Provide preschoolers with small homemade ladders or full-sized commercial models sawn in half, small sawhorses, small wooden nail barrels and sturdy boxes of any size, from appliance crates to mandarin-orange crates. The greater the variety of materials, the more creative kids can be when combining them. Add to these "found" materials a good selection of big hollow blocks and/or Swedish blocks, large-scale versions of the familiar indoor wooden building blocks that have been designed by education professionals to match the physical size and learning needs of preschoolers. Each set of hollow blocks consists of an 8-inch cube, a double cube (8 by 8 by 16), a half cube (4 by 8 by 8) and a double half cube (4 by 8 by 16). Swedish blocks are solid pieces of 3-by-6 hardwood cut to 1-, 2- and 4-foot lengths. Though they are easy to make at home, the material for these blocks is expensive: a single set can cost

Loose material such as these big hollow blocks is essential for a creative backyard playground. Stored where they are easily accessible to the kids, these nondescript raw materials will be transformed into forts, racing car ramps, dining room furniture for the playhouse or whatever props the play of the day demands.

$20, and a child needs several sets to build anything of consequence. However, financial outlay is more than justified by the creative potential of these blocks, and they will last far longer than the gaudy manufactured playthings that cost just as much. At Polly Hill's summer home on Sheep Island, Ontario, her original Swedish blocks, built more than three decades ago, are now stimulating the imaginations of her grandchildren.

Like Lego, Swedish and hollow blocks are designed in sizes that are all units of one another, fitting together to form modular systems. Unlike Lego, however, all the blocks as well as the loose parts must be the same colour. Adults are particularly resistant to this idea, unthinkingly assuming that children love bright primary colours. In this case, however, a rainbow of red, blue and yellow only lowers the play value of the material. All of Polly Hill's blocks and boards are painted a uniform hunter green, and whatever a child builds with them has a visual integrity that would be impossible with multicoloured parts. Also, they are interchangeable: the child is never left with a half-completed train because there are no more red blocks for the caboose. It is important to give the blocks a good weather-resistant finish because this is one backyard toy that will get year-round use; they will provide as much fun for mittened hands in the snow as they do for bare hands in the summer. Once they have been protected with a coat of good lead-free exterior paint, the blocks can simply be stacked against a wall or fence or kept in a storage shed handy to the play area.

Children should also have several wide boards to combine with the blocks or to make ramps and platforms on the

play frame. Because the boards need to be very strong yet light enough for kids to move, two or three 1 by 3s fastened together are better than a single 1 by 10, which would also have a tendency to warp: join them by nailing cleats on the underside. The cleats will double as a nonslip means of securing them to the play structure.

As children grow up, their need for blocks and boards does not diminish. In fact, loose material is the only type of play equipment shown to have equal appeal to children across all age and grade levels. However, older children need more materials and more variety, the monochromatic, controlled loose parts gradually giving way to the real-world construction typical of an adventure playground, where recycled materials are left as is for children to change as they see fit. Let kids gradually

add their own loose parts: old tires, lengths of rope and chain, salvaged lumber. The unsightly mess that is bound to result should not be discouraged, just confined to its own creative nook, well hidden behind a hedge if the kids' constructions offend the neighbours. Parents should limit their involvement to teaching the basics of tool use, giving kids their own tools, materials and a storage place so they will learn the responsibility of caring for their belongings and cleaning up after themselves. If salvaged materials are not available, a hardware store and lumberyard can supply everything a kid needs to get started for less than the cost of Castle Greystoke and a few Masters of the Universe: 2-by-4 boards, a hammer and a few pounds of 3½-inch nails — heavy enough to resist a neophyte's cockeyed wallops. Later, a 45-gallon barrel, a piece of canvas or tarpaulin with grommets around the edges and a few lengths of rope for lashing can be added.

Don't dump a vanload of raw materials into the backyard all at once – too much variety confuses and distracts kids. A better strategy is to provide a few boards and nails at a time, and when the possibilities of that offering are exhausted, add some rope or a barrel, items with their own play potential that will also add new dimensions to what is already a part of the adventure corner. After a few months, the kids will probably instinctively tear down their structure and start fresh; if not, parents should suggest a periodic dismantling. Some children may not have the nerve or heart to destroy their masterpieces, but without removing one structure, another can't be started, and kids will find themselves stuck in a play yard that has become stale and uninviting.

Storage

Although not a piece of play equipment per se, good storage strongly affects the "playability" of a creative backyard. If playthings are stored close to the action in a sturdy, weathertight cupboard scaled for kids and accessible to them, children find it easier to learn independence and responsibility, taking out toys and putting them away on their own, without constant pestering by their parents.

Playspaces need storage for loose material such as blocks, boards and outdoor dress-up clothes (firefighters' hats, Wonder Woman capes); large toys such as trikes and sawhorses; and smaller equipment such as the shovels, pails and funnels used in sand, water and winter snow play. These can all be accommodated in one large cupboard, but only if it has enough shelves and partitions to keep the playthings well organized. Otherwise, they will be jumbled together, broken and rarely used: no child wants to spend half the afternoon trying to find his favourite yellow truck buried in a heap of blocks, boards and cracked Frisbees.

The overall size of a storage cupboard will vary, but the shelves should be shallow enough (maximum 36 inches) that kids can reach right to the back. After the play area has been designed, make a list of the items that need to be stored – shelves, bins and hooks can be custom-fitted for individual playthings. Cupboard doors should be far enough off the ground that they will not freeze shut in winter and should open wide so the kids can easily see all the shelves – that way, they will be more inclined to put the toys back where they belong when they are finished. The storage cupboard itself should be weather-tight and solidly built, using standard house-framing techniques, but for safety's sake, be sure to make the doors and latches so children cannot accidentally be trapped inside.

Instead of one large storage unit, consider locating several smaller ones where the toys are most used. For instance, construct a loose-material cupboard on the back of the garage just a few feet from the playhouse, incorporate a sand toy bin into the sand table, or build a stall for the trikes and wheeled toys in the toolshed. If play storage is combined with other family storage – garden shed, toolshed, garage – be sure the children's area is distinct and is used only for toys. If kids have to climb over a lawn mower to get their hollow blocks or root around among the garden tools for a road-hockey ball, they may not bother.

In most cases, it is not advisable to combine storage with the climber or

A hammer, some nails and a few scrap boards piled in a kids' adventure area gradually replace the monochromatic loose material that toddlers use for constructive play. Add to the children's stockpile of building materials slowly, and provide storage space so that kids will learn to take care of their tools.

playhouse. If trikes, blocks and boards are stored in the playhouse or under the play frame, everything will have to be cleared out before the kids can play. Rather, design a cupboard specifically for storage, then make the exterior playable by nailing a ladder to the side or building a balcony on top. Be careful not to let playing interfere with the cupboard's primary function as a storage space. Kids should always have clear access to their toys without worrying about being jumped on as they pull the hollow blocks off the shelves. Whatever form the storage takes, it should be designed not only for convenience but, above all, for the kids. The extra time and energy absorbed by custom-designing a cupboard will be more than repaid in unbroken toys and kids who actually learn to pick up after themselves.

3 | Playscapes

The natural play environment

The natural environment creates its own context for play.

M. Paul Friedberg

In *Butter Down the Well*, journalist Robert Collins recalls his Saskatchewan boyhood: "Some days, happy in my solitude, I roamed among the farmyard poplars, maples and stubby caraganas or along pasture trails worn to dust by generations of horses and cows. . . . An outcropping of quartz thrust itself from a certain hill; I christened it my diamond mine. Beside the Long Slough – where spring runoff lingered long after other water holes had run dry – clung a stunted scrub willow. I scrunched under it and pressed my cheek to its gnarled trunk. . . . There were rocks so great that they defied all the pickaxes, crowbars, chains and straining teams of horses, and so they stayed, flinty, obdurate islands in the wheat fields. Sometimes, when the grain stood high, I hunkered down on a jutting rock, pretending it was a hut with a paved floor and bamboo walls."

A child experiences the landscape in a highly personal way, investing it with a meaning that has little to do with its physical façade. A trickle of spring runoff or an upended tree root is a trigger that sends the youthful imagination darting off into a labyrinth of wonder and delight. Designers work hard trying to build play equipment that is forever fresh and exciting, but nature does the job effortlessly and inexpensively, creating an environment which meets all the criteria of a good playspace. In fact, manufactured play equipment is largely an urban substitute for nature in the raw: a sandbox in lieu of the beach, a climber where there are no trees, a slide in the absence of hills. Although these constructed playthings are fun and are an important part of a child's development, a truly creative backyard playspace goes beyond a myopic preoccupation with specific structures and focuses on the total environment in which a child plays. The wisdom of this approach is now becoming apparent even to public playground designers. A decade ago, M. Paul Friedberg wrote *Handcrafted Playgrounds*, a book devoted solely to play structures, but he recently completed an innovative playground in New York's Central Park that has no perceived equipment, just an informal, natural environment shaped for play.

Constructed play equipment is important in toning the rapidly developing bodies of preschoolers, but as kids grow up, the natural environment takes on more significance. As American educator Edith Cobb observes, "There is a special period, the little-understood prepubescent, halcyon middle age of childhood – approximately from 5 or 6 to 11 or 12, between the strivings of animal infancy and the storms of adolescence – when the natural world is experienced in some happy, evocative way, producing in the child a sense of profound continuity with natural processes."

Berms, lush vegetation and natural elements such as sand and water transform a dull manicured yard into an exciting playscape, rich in diversity, ripe for exploration and learning. Aside from their play value, sculpted landforms and well-placed trees and shrubs can unobtrusively bar children from danger zones, such as busy streets, and can shape the microclimate so that kids enjoy playing outdoors year-round.

Gardening, pond building and animal husbandry are beyond the scope of this book, but this chapter will encourage parents to look seriously at landscaping solutions to children's play needs, taking to heart the advice of Swedish playground designer Arvid Bengtsson, a founder of the International Play Association: "Too much money and uninformed thought is often spent on

fixed play apparatus. It must not be forgotten that this is only furniture, and no matter how ingenious it may be, it alone does not make a playground."

Berms

In the suburbs of the city where I live, developers built a playground beside the four-lane highway that skirts the downtown core. To keep kids off the road, they bulldozed a huge mound of earth between the playspace and the pavement, installing typical play equipment in the flattened hollow at the base of the hill. I rarely see kids on the teeter-totters or roundabout, but the hill is always swarming with life. Legs poker-straight, arms pressed tightly to their sides and chins tucked in, kids torpedo down the grassy slope, then race each other to the peak to catapult down again. In summer, they play king of the castle, ragtag armies skirmishing to claim the crest of the hill, and in winter, they trade their stick swords for cardboard flying carpets that whiz and bump down the snow-covered incline. From behind the wheel of my Toyota, I can see the joy on their faces, but I can only imagine the icy wind that sears their cheeks or the furry tickle of fresh-mown grass as they tumble down the slopes.

Most North American homes, whether on the prairies or in the foothills, sit on property that – like the unused playground – is as flat as a pancake. This is for contractor convenience. Although it is not a conscious plot to undermine the local topography, the effect is the same: children are forced to play in backyards that have fewer contours than a cast iron griddle. Readers who plan to build their own houses can preserve the natural undulations that give a yard character simply by keeping a tight rein on the bulldozer, but most families must

PLAY AREA

PREVAILING WINTER WINDS

BERM & EVERGREENS

DRAINAGE PIPE

BUSY STREET

undo the developer's work and relieve the monotony of the typical home landscape by creating surrogate hills, or "berms."

A backyard berm creates visual interest – concealing a corner of the yard or shaping an unexpected nook – but it also has considerable play value. In contrast, a stepped terrace, which also changes backyard elevation, does not offer as many play opportunities as a slope. Whether play is physical, social or imaginative, kids become bored with a piece of constructed play equipment long before they run out of things to do on a simple rise of ground: rolling, running, climbing, sliding on the slopes, surveying the panorama from the peak or nestling in a cozy crook at the base. Aside from their play potential, berms also serve a practical purpose in defining backyard space. If the best play area flanks a busy street, a berm can act as a functional and visual barrier between kids and cars, as well as effectively buffering noise. Berms can also help control the microclimate of the yard, sheltering play and seating areas from

wind without blocking the sun.

Redefining the contours of the yard is a big job, though, requiring a considerable investment of time, effort and money. The disruption is worthwhile if the property needs a major face-lift and the family plans to be in the house long enough to enjoy the fruits of its labours. When embarking on a topographic overhaul, however, be careful to preserve some flat areas for games, quiet play and constructed components such as a playhouse or storage cupboard.

The entire property does not have to be reshaped to give kids the benefit of a slope or two. Half a dozen truckloads of fill dumped in one corner of the yard is enough to form a hillock 4 to 5 feet high with a base covering 200 to 300 square feet. Swimming pool companies, excavation contractors or municipal road crews may dump the earth for free or a minimal trucking charge, but make sure it is all loose fill. Rocks, pieces of concrete or metal bars may work their way to the surface of the mound, and organic debris such as stumps or boards can leave depressions after they decay.

The size and shape of a berm vary, but the vertical height is usually 2 to 5 feet. A slope cannot be too gentle, but it can be too steep—an incline of 1:1 erodes quickly, and even a 1:2 slope is hard to mow. A 1:3 slope is steep enough for rolling down but gentle enough that a riding mower can be used for maintenance. A 1:2 slope is a good incline for an embedded mound slide, but it is too steep for wheeled toys. Although no-maintenance wildflowers and perennial ground covers can be planted, grass is the usual surface for backyard berms. Even on a gradual slope, however, grass takes a beating from kids' pounding feet; plan paths at strategic points to reduce wear and tear on the lawn and lessen the possibility of erosion. Paths made of stepping stones or terraced timbers can also double as seating for quiet play. It is possible to lure kids off the driveway and into the yard by laying a hard-surface strip down the slope that is ideal for skateboards and tricycles, making it gentle enough that the vehicles do not pick up too much speed. Be sure to remove any obstacles from the run-out area at the bottom of the incline.

Instead of shaping a fully rounded berm, consider conserving space by banking the earth against a log or stone retaining wall. Such a design is used to advantage at the University of Guelph preschool play yard. There, one side of a 5-foot-high mound is gently sloped, with a slide embedded in the grass, but the other side is banked with timbers that support one end of a bridge that leads kids from the berm to a multilevel play frame. Children pedal their trikes on a path that curves under the bridge and around the hill to a playhouse in the far corner of the yard.

Whether one builds a half berm or a

Natural slopes are great for sliding at any time of year. Use toboggans or sleds on the snow-covered berm in winter, and in hot weather, spray a hillside path with water to create a slippery mud slide—messy but incomparable fun.

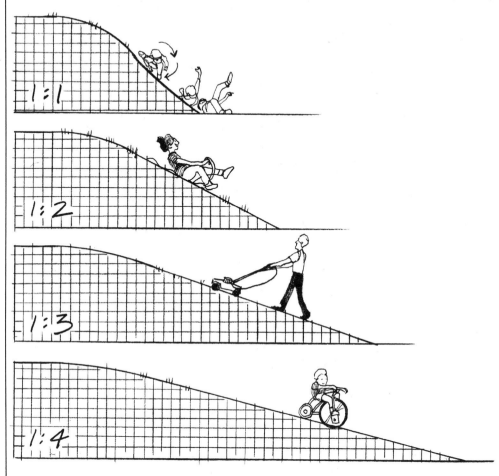

The incline of a berm affects both the type of play and the surfacing of the slope. A 1:1 slope is too steep for sliding and is prone to erosion. A 1:2 slope should be planted with perennial ground covers, but a 1:3 slope can be mowed. Only a 1:4 slope is gentle enough for tricycles and wagons.

fully rounded hillock, the challenge is to integrate the mound of earth smoothly into the backyard landscape. To be pleasing to the eye, artificial hills should mimic the fluid lines of the real thing, which was shaped by aeons of buffeting by wind and water erosion. Avoid symmetrical shapes and sudden or steep changes in elevation: a compound curve outlining a corner or an elongated ellipse along one fence looks better and is just as much fun as a cone of earth plunked in the middle of the yard. Start with a layer of gravel or rubble, and raise the berm gradually, compacting each layer to ensure it will retain its shape.

In public play yards, a buried culvert is sometimes used to incorporate tunnels and caves into mounds. This is expensive for a family backyard, for a concrete culvert requires special moving equipment and other materials may not withstand the pressure of the soil above. Instead of constructed tunnels, create cave-like niches with hedges, bushes and the drooping branches of trees planted close to the bottom of the slope.

In winter, the drifts that accumulate around berms are perfect for carving snow houses, and the slopes become handy toboggan runs, especially for preschoolers too small to trek unescorted to the local sledding hills. Preplan the toboggan run so it is clear of obstacles and delicate plants that could be damaged by compacted snow. Even if there are no natural or constructed berms on the property, winter can provide temporary mounds for children's play. In the backyard scheme, provide an open space near a deck or driveway (away from traffic), where shovelled snow can accumulate. At my younger son's country school, snowploughs clear huge areas for play at recess, but the youngsters ignore the open space and instead carve forts and caverns in the ploughed snowbanks. Malleable and totally ambiguous, snow converts the whole backyard into a giant winter sandbox, ripe with creative and dramatic play potential. Encourage winter outdoor play by storing hollow blocks and digging toys where they are accessible when the playspace is snowbound.

Modifying backyard topography can have negative effects that will not be immediately obvious. For example, trees and bushes will eventually die if their roots are exposed when topsoil is scraped away or if they are too deeply buried under the edge of a mound. Position the berm away from trees or construct large cribs around their trunks to protect the root systems. Reshaping the landforms may also disrupt drainage patterns in neighbouring yards as well as in one's own. Shape the berm to allow the sides to drain well, avoiding dimpled or flattened tops that could trap water. In a rainstorm, the base of a berm will be a catch basin unless the soil is very

berries; and in the fall, the leaves of the hardy bittersweet turn yellow just as its golden fruits burst to reveal crimson-coated seeds. The rosy red foliage of the Nanking cherry hangs on while the days grow cool, and when all the leaves have fallen, the stems of dogwood, willow and forsythia slash the monochromatic winter landscape with bold strokes of red, gold and green.

Some shrubs are not particularly distinctive but earn a place in the yard by attracting colourful birds. Eighty-six species of birds dine on the fruit of various kinds of dogwood, especially the red berries of the flowering dogwood. Chokeberry bushes draw songbirds such as the meadowlark and brown thrasher. Bobwhites, phoebes, flickers and chickadees are partial to bayberries, while cedar waxwings and evening grosbeaks love the crimson fruit of the American mountain ash. And to add a splash of blue, nothing works quite as well as a wall of sunflowers to draw flocks of screaming jays.

Aside from their obvious attraction to feeding and nesting birds, trees and shrubs also contribute valuable loose material for play. Generations of kids have twirled maple-key helicopters, whittled panpipes out of willow twigs and woven daisy-chain necklaces for their dolls. Backyard flora provide raw material to landscape sand cities and decorate mud pies, stout branches to fashion swords and bouquets to bedeck fairy princesses. Apart from feeding children's fantasies, fruit and nut trees also supply the needs of whole families of squirrels and chipmunks, wildlife that is a delight to watch and wonder at—as long as children learn from an early age never to approach even the tamest-looking rodent.

The natural landscape is a living laboratory where kids witness firsthand

Backyard plants provide an inexhaustible supply of loose material for children's play—dandelions and daisies to weave into flower chains, willow twigs to whittle into high-pitched pipes or honeysuckle berries to decorate mud pies and sand cakes.

porous or a drainage tile is installed to redirect water to a storm sewer or dry well. If in doubt, discuss the plans with a drainage engineer or landscape architect before building a backyard berm.

Plants

The kitten-soft bark of young sumac sprouts, the spicy scent of creeping thyme, Japanese lanterns rasping dryly in the breeze, black-and-yellow grosbeaks plucking crimson ash berries in the dead white of winter—whatever the season, plants embellish a child's world with a diversity, beauty and protean life that no hand-built contraption could ever duplicate. And if well chosen, the trees, shrubs, vegetables and flowers that beautify a landscape can also contribute to the recreational value of the backyard playspace.

Because their physical range is limited, young children need a fine-grained environment—one rich with minute detail—to stimulate their senses and provoke exploration. By tucking a few annuals in the flowerbeds, most people can produce a marginally colourful yard in the heart of summer, but with a little forethought, even those with underdeveloped green thumbs can design a natural environment with something to pique the senses all year round. Purple crocuses and sunny daffodils will poke through the last shreds of snow to brighten the bare spring landscape before honeysuckle, lilac or mock orange shrubs open their blossoms to softly scent and colour the lengthening days. In early summer, the dark, shiny leaves of the *Cotoneaster divaricatus* contrast sharply with its red flowers and then later with its carmine the cycle of life, death and renewal, a fundamental force that gains full significance if the child plants the original seed. Whatever other plants are part of the backyard landscape, give kids their own plot of land where they can grow herbs, flowers and vegetables. Many companies sell packages of mixed seeds just for kids, but if they want to select their own, suggest flowers such as violas and pansies, which bloom over a protracted period and thrive on repeated pickings, or fast-growing vegetables like radishes, carrots and peas, which are good finger foods. In addition to providing a private supply of on-the-spot summer snacks, gardening teaches kids to take responsibility for living things as they weed, water and protect the tender shoots from frost. In the process, they learn more about how things grow and begin to appreciate the food on their table. For preschoolers, a 4-by-6-foot plot is big enough, while about 10 by 15 is adequate for school-age children. Raised beds in which the soil is contained by timbers are best for small backyards and for young gardeners, so that they can better identify the boundaries of their mini-farms.

As children become intimate with their natural environment, they develop a strong affection for certain natural landmarks, usually a favourite tree or leafy retreat. While parents cannot predetermine which plants or places will be meaningful to their children, they can create a landscape ripe with potential. My own special hideaway was a fragrant clearing under the cedar hedge across from my grandmother's house, where I spent most of one summer sulking after the arrival of a new baby. My youngest son exhibits the same preference for conifers, having adopted as his refuge a needle-strewn cul-de-sac under a grove of blue spruces. According to Roger

Hart, who has studied the relationship between children and the urban landscape, many of the playhouses of children under the age of 8 are not built but found – nooks and crannies under hedges and low-hanging trees where kids act out their fantasies and escape from the real world. The best shrubs for such a cozy retreat are those with a lush canopy of leaves overhead and a relatively open network of branches underneath. Willows are an obvious choice, but among lesser known shrubs are the bottlebrush, a graceful member of the myrtle family with slender drooping branches bearing round spikes of white flowers, and *Photinia villosa*, a large deciduous shrub with spreading branches and clusters of hawthornlike flowers in early spring, colourful leaves in fall and bright red berries that survive into winter.

Aside from their play value, plants help shape the backyard microclimate,

controlling sun and wind for a year-round comfortable playspace. Lush trees and shrubs reduce summer glare and keep the yard cool, but they must be positioned carefully. Keep in mind that the sun's arc is low and narrow in January but high and wide in July: plant trees and shrubs where they will shade the playspace during the heat of summer without blocking welcome winter sunshine. Dense plants can act as windbreaks, diverting cold winter winds from the play area but funnelling summer breezes through the yard. Plant pampas grass, a tall-growing annual native to South America, as a novel summer windbreak, then cut and dry its long, silky plumes for indoor decorations. Some barberries are also good summer windscreens, growing over 3 feet tall with spiny dark green leaves that turn bronze in fall. These plants, like deciduous trees, are effective only in summer; plant evergreens to

Well-planned landscaping can influence the micro-climate of the backyard, making the home playground more inviting to kids all year round. A thick barrier of evergreens and shrubs will shield the play area from cold winds in winter without blocking cooling summer breezes.

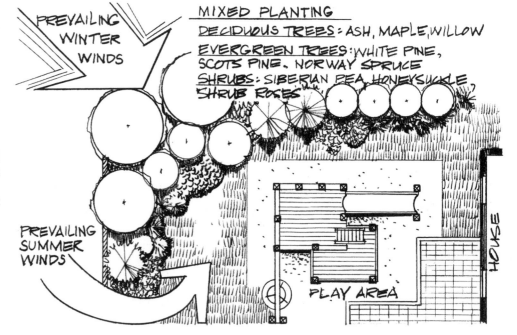

PREVAILING WINTER WINDS

PREVAILING SUMMER WINDS

MIXED PLANTING
DECIDUOUS TREES: ASH, MAPLE, WILLOW
EVERGREEN TREES: WHITE PINE, SCOTS PINE, NORWAY SPRUCE
SHRUBS: SIBERIAN PEA, HONEYSUCKLE, SHRUB ROSES

PLAY AREA

HOUSE

block prevailing winter winds.

Prickly shrubs make good barriers between the playspace and danger zones, such as a busy street or driveway, but plant a border of low plants in front to prevent kids from falling into the barbs. The hawthorn and other small trees and shrubs of the rose family are as decorative as they are effective, with showy flowers in spring and summer and small, red applelike fruits that cling to branches until midwinter. To screen the sandbox or separate the climber from the playhouse, trim unbarbed bushes into low hedges, choosing evergreens such as box and holly or deciduous varieties like buckthorn.

Although a workhorse among hedges, privet is not recommended for playspaces because the berries of several species are known to be poisonous and the leaves of some are suspect. In fact, many common landscaping plants are not appropriate for play areas. Young kids have a tendency to submit every plaything to the taste test, and while this can be a delightful experience with wintergreen leaves or nasturtium buds, many common species are toxic, particularly to children. For instance, all parts of the oleander are very poisonous: a single leaf or flower is enough to kill a child. Rhubarb stalks make a fine spring pie, but the leaves have caused death when eaten. Other common garden plants that have caused fatalities include yew, azalea, belladonna lily, foxglove, tansy and lily-of-the-valley. Although an animal or bird may eat a plant, it is not necessarily safe for humans—after all, horses and cows relish poison ivy. Teach kids at an early age not to put anything in their mouths before making a positive identification, and bar toxic species from the property.

Aside from internal poisoning caused by eating part of a plant, some

vegetation—poison ivy, poison oak, stinging nettle—irritates the skin, and the spines and thorns of rosebushes and hawthorns can cause painful scratches. Finally, many people are sensitive to the spores and pollen of certain plants, particularly ragweed and grasses. If there are allergies in the family, avoid plants that release heavy doses of pollen into the air. And don't spray plants, shrubs or trees with insecticides or herbicides, most of which are harmful to humans. (See plant lists on pages 138-39.)

In general, when selecting trees, shrubs and plants for the home playspace, consider the local climate, the hardiness of the species, its rate of growth and its height and shape at maturity. Judge these characteristics in the light of whether the plant is intended as a decoration, a traffic barrier or the future site of a tree house. Only by

knowing the plant well can one avoid the frustration of planting a 20-foot windbreak hedge that is killed in its first winter or that takes 10 years to rise even 5 feet. Look carefully at the entire growth cycle of the plant, noting when it flowers and sets fruit and whether the leaves drop in August or October. Through the orchestration of the seasonal personalities of a few species, the yard can abound with a variety of colours and textures year-round, from the slender red-gold stems of winter through the waxy flowering bulbs of spring and sprays of summer perennials or flowering shrubs to the taut, bright fruits and crisp, crimson leaves of fall. Consider the play potential of each plant so the yard will have a good mix of natural loose material, secret hideaways and learning experiences. If kids will be tempted to use the plants for play, either by climbing or by breaking off twigs and flowers, choose species that can survive such abuse.

Obtain the most mature trees and shrubs possible within budget limitations (the bigger the tree, the heftier the price tag). Large specimens are less prone to damage from rambling kids and will serve their function as barriers, borders and retreats sooner. This is especially true if parents plan to provide a climbing tree for their toddler; kids grow a lot faster than most trees. Protect small bushes and trees with low fences or by planting clumps of smaller vegetation around them. Never use guy wires where kids may trip over them.

Instead of planting formal beds of flowers and bushes, consider letting part of the yard go wild, sowing perennial or self-seeding wildflowers, and allow nature to take its course. Small children love to play in long grass, and it will attract a medley of butterflies, beetles and other bright-coloured insects,

Include a children's garden in the backyard playground, a small raised bed in which kids can plant seeds of their own choosing, enjoying the pleasure of harvesting flowers and summer snacks they grow themselves.

though the six-legged hordes may include such less welcome creatures as mosquitoes and blackflies.

Sand

A hundred years ago, the German sand garden was the inspiration for the North American playground movement, and families with preschoolers would do well to follow the same example today. For kids under 6, no other piece of play equipment is so well used or well loved.

Granular and abrasive, sticky and smooth, studded with diamond quartz and pink granite, a miniature zoo of millipedes and molluscs, sand heightens the sensual awareness of children by introducing a finely detailed world of colour, texture and shape. But the real value of sand is that it is simply sand and nothing more, a pure raw material to be moulded by a child's imagination. As they build and rebuild, shaping a child-sized environment that is totally under their control, kids give full rein to their creative expression and come to terms with the real world.

Children's reactions to sandboxes change dramatically as they grow up. Preschoolers prefer sandboxes over all other play equipment, but while kids under 2 like big sandboxes, older toddlers prefer enclosed sand areas that are smaller and cozier. Between ages 3 and 4, they shift from solitary sand play to building cooperatively with other children and incorporating sand into their make-believe worlds, baking sand cakes complete with moss icing and stick candles for a party of imaginary friends. Although school-age kids dig and build at the beach and may help younger siblings with a sand castle at home, the sandbox itself is viewed with some disdain, a symbol of bygone babyhood. In Marilyn Reid's Vancouver study of the play-equipment

preferences of elementary school children, the sandbox was at the bottom of the list of preferences at all schools and at all grade levels. Nevertheless, when we built our house a few years ago, the sand fill was a magnet for every kid in the neighbourhood. Toddlers brought their "diggers" and bulldozers, the 10-year-olds built intricate hamster mazes, and the teenagers buried each other, leaving only their disembodied heads poking up through what

eventually became the lawn.

The design of a sandbox greatly affects how much kids use it and how much of a nuisance it becomes to parents. A good size for a home sandbox is about 4 by 6 feet; expand those dimensions for a big backyard, but do not reduce them because anything smaller restricts the imaginative play that sand stimulates. The sand should be at least 8 inches deep—and preferably 18 to 20 inches—deep enough for kids to dig a major excavation without disturbing the underlying foundation. For good creative play, the sand should pack together when dampened; seaside sand,

thoroughly washed masonry sand or fine sand (not more than 1.5 mm) is appropriate as long as it is free of abrasive or organic material.

Sand is usually contained in a wooden box made of logs, timbers or boards, but stones and bricks make equally good borders for a sand garden. Set an 8-to-12-inch-deep sandbox on top of the lawn, or provide easy access for a deeper one by sinking it into the ground, with the edge barely rising above the grass. In either case, fill it only to within 3 or 4 inches of the top; that way, the sand won't spill over the edges and the wind can't blow it into kids' faces. Sandboxes are usually square, but the "box" can just as easily be a hexagon, lozenge, arrowhead or circle. Public playgrounds often use gigantic tires as sandboxes, but they are so heavy and cumbersome that they have to be moved with a crane and flatbed. Unless there is already a tire in the backyard, stone or wood is a cheaper and more attractive alternative.

Typically, children use the corner seats and edges of a sandbox as tables to hold their creations, spilling sand into the surrounding grass. Discourage kids from using the borders as a ledge by rounding off the tops with a half log, then build them a sand table in the centre to use as a work surface for making sand cakes. Be sure, though, that the sandbox is large enough for both the table and an expansive sand city. Consider incorporating a storage bay in the table for the small rakes, shovels and pails that are essential to creative sand play. A sand table effectively controls spillover, but some grit still manages to escape the sandbox by clinging to the kids. A rim of cobblestones or pavers acts as a buffer between the lawn and sand garden where they can stomp the sand off their shoes and clothes, minimizing the amount that gets tracked across the yard and into the house.

At the beach, a child's first instinct is to burrow his hands in the sand, cup the crystals high in the air, then spread his fingers to let the grains sift back to earth. Dry sand flows like a liquid, but add a little water from the lake and it becomes wonderfully plastic, a gritty sculptor's clay to be scooped and shaped into sand cakes, castles or fanciful cityscapes. Sand and water belong together, teaching kids the magic of synergy – two familiar materials fusing to create an exciting new substance. Most backyards have an outdoor water source, and with a little planning, this can be adapted to bring the full complement of seaside pleasures to the sand garden.

Sand inevitably gets wet, but it only becomes sour and unfit for play if it does not dry out quickly; therefore, good drainage is essential. The sand can simply be spread over soils with good natural percolation, but if the soil does not drain well naturally, lay a 4-inch layer of gravel or crushed stone over a foot of granular fill, then line the bottom of the sandbox with bricks, laid close together without mortar so the sand can drain. (If the sand is so deep that kids can't dig up the gravel even with deep excavations, the bricks can be eliminated.) In rock or heavy clay soils, lay a perforated 4-inch drain tile from the centre of the sandbox to the nearest ditch, dry well or catch basin. Slope the gravel slightly toward the tile, and be sure it is covered with a layer of filter cloth to prevent sand from clogging the holes.

Good drainage helps keep it fresh, but sand also needs to be exposed to the purifying rays of the sun for at least part of every day. Locate the sandbox where it will be in direct sunlight, though preferably not at noon when it can get too hot for kids to play. Turn the sand

occasionally to ventilate it and to bring deeply buried layers to the surface. Sunlight and good drainage discourage microscopic life forms, but there is no foolproof way of barring larger animals, especially cats that delight in this king-sized litter box. Solid lids and tarps make the sandbox too dark and dank; a screen made of nylon netting or chicken wire effectively keeps out animals and debris without blocking fresh air and sunlight. Install the sand garden near a solid wall

or fence that can support the screen when the kids are playing.

Since the sand garden is designed primarily for preschoolers, locate it close to a main entrance of the house, with seating nearby for parents to share in the pleasure of their children's creations. Tuck the sand garden out of the flow of active play, and above all, avoid the temptation to make a sand ground cover under physical play equipment double as a sand play area. Though the material

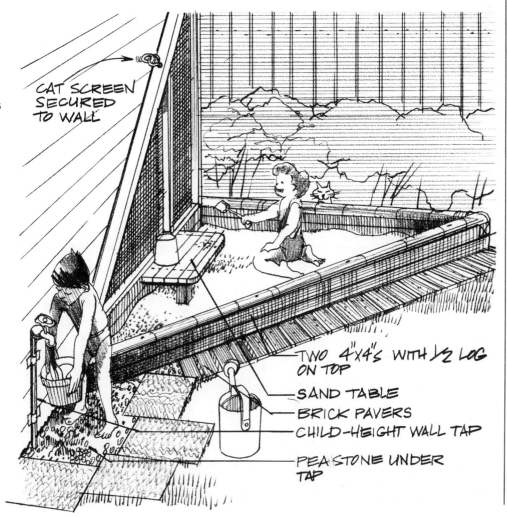

CAT SCREEN SECURED TO WALL

TWO 4"x4's WITH ½ LOG ON TOP

SAND TABLE

BRICK PAVERS

CHILD-HEIGHT WALL TAP

PEA STONE UNDER TAP

Sand and water are natural companions. Position a child-size tap or hand pump near the sand garden and provide good drainage underneath. To keep the sand clean and fresh, be sure it is exposed to direct sunlight every day and protect it with a cat-proof screen cover when not in use.

51

Water is indispensable in the backyard playground, though sources like streams, ponds and pumps are more fun and have more play value than sprinklers and wading pools where kids can do little more than get wet.

is the same, the design, maintenance and use of each space is entirely different. Even if the yard is used by only one child, a separate sand garden that she associates with quiet, contemplative play is likely to promote more imaginative sand sculptures.

Water

Water is one of the four basic elements of life, yet a child's experience of this fundamental substance is often limited to the bathtub and the kitchen sink where, harnessed and subdued, it trickles from stainless steel to porcelain with little of the magic of water in its natural habitat. Glistening over stones or casting rainbows in the sunlight, a haven for frogs and mayflies, lily pads and cress, water can add more joy and learning to a backyard than any other single play material. Through the animals, insects and birds that water attracts and the plants it nourishes, children come to understand the intricate balances of the natural world, forging a bond with the environment that can last a lifetime. With a simple hand pump, a container and some stones, kids learn many of the basic principles of physics – displacement, suction, gravity, pressure – but although it invites such intellectual inquiry, water can also provide a purely sensory experience, dribbling slowly through cupped fingers, splashing and flowing, even babbling to those who take the time to listen.

Water is one of the seven elements that, according to Roger Hart, children value in a landscape, yet it is rarely part of our built environment. When it is, kids and adults alike are irresistibly drawn, doffing shoes and socks to wade in city fountains on parched summer days or searching out puddles to splash in after a rain. There are many ways to incorporate the unique pleasures of water into playspace design, from buying a $10 garden hose to installing an elaborate stream and fountain complete with recycling pump. In general, water systems that kids actually play *with* – damming a stream to float walnut-shell ships or pumping a cupful of water to moisten mud pies – are more fun and have more developmental value than those they play *in* – sprinklers and wading pools.

Water play is usually excluded from public playground designs because of health and safety concerns. With large groups of children, pollution is a problem unless expensive filtration devices are installed, and without close supervision, there is always the fear a child may drown. Because fewer children use the water at home and adults can exercise more control, parents should not be reticent about providing water-play opportunities for their kids. Swimming pools are much more dangerous and difficult to maintain than a simple play stream, yet they are a common fixture in family yards.

For the lucky few who already have a natural water source on their property, a little grooming – moulding of a slippery or steep shoreline with stones or a timber retaining wall to ensure safe access – may be all that is needed to improve its play value. If there are no natural streams or ponds, consider excavating an artificial one and stocking it with a variety of plants and fish to fascinate kids.

For very young children, water need not be a permanent part of the backyard ecology. Preschoolers get as much enjoyment and education out of a play stream that is filled and drained on demand. It can be as simple as a trough of rocks that begins under the outdoor tap at the side of the house and

Few backyards are blessed with natural streams, but an artificial one can be constructed by pouring a reinforced concrete streambed and embedding rocks around the rim. Provide a tap or hand pump to fill the stream and a drain with an attached plug at the lowest point.

meanders across a corner of the yard to drain into a hollow pool of flat stones. For a stream that holds water until the kids pull the plug, excavate a streambed and trowel reinforced concrete over a granular base, making the stream no deeper than 6 inches. The actual shape and size of the stream can be as simple or as complex as imagination and budget dictate: it can flow past the sandbox or loop around an island complete with footbridges. Mortar stones into the sides and top edge to give it a natural look, but make the bottom relatively smooth – though nonslip – for safe wading. Slope the streambed toward a drain as far from the water source as possible, and the stream will have a current to float boats from one end to the other. Connecting the drain to a dry well or storm sewer and chaining a screw-in

plug to the bottom or edge of the streambed will allow kids to drain it like a bathtub. A screen mesh over the drain keeps it from getting clogged by sand and debris. Establish a family rule from the outset that the play stream is always drained when not in use, especially if there are very young children at home.

The play stream can be filled using a garden hose, but a separate water source in the play area is a good idea, especially one near the sandbox, so that kids can mix the two materials. Fasten an outdoor water faucet to a 6 by 6 set in porous backfill topped with smooth pebbles or sand and dished slightly under the spout. Connect the faucet either to an underground pipe from the main house water supply or to a hose fastened to an existing outdoor faucet, and at the foot of the post, install a 6-inch perforated drain tile to direct seepage to a dry well or storm sewer.

The drawback to taps is that kids get involved in their play and leave the water running, but a hand pump spews water only long as the kids keep working the handle. Besides being practical and fun, a hand pump is a great demonstration of the laws of cause and effect: I still remember my own delight when, at the age of 4, I stretched up with both arms and wrestled down the wooden pump handle at my grand-parents' house, to be rewarded by a rush of water gurgling out of the spout and tumbling down a moss-stained trough. These old-fashioned hand pumps can still be bought quite inexpensively at hardware stores and set on a well cap or reinforced concrete platform, textured to prevent slipping. Some retailers sell hand pumps that have enclosed tops to prevent kids from dumping sand into the mechanism, but they are expensive and unnecessary as long as kids understand they should not put anything in the pump. If the pump can't be hooked up to a well, connect it to the municipal water supply through a regulating valve that reduces the pressure. A much cheaper option is to bypass the house water supply altogether and mount the pump or tap on a rain barrel or outdoor cistern fed by eavestroughs.

Animals

In his delightful memoir *My Childhood and Yours*, Robert Thomas Allen recalls the four-footed friends that shared his youth: "We talked animals, thought animals and dreamed animals, and were always pestering our parents for pets. . . . If we couldn't have a rabbit, we visited some other kid who was on a winning streak and had a rabbit or maybe a white rat. He'd let you hold it and let it go up your sleeve and out the

collar of your shirt, and you'd stand there laughing at the pleasure of feeling its cold nails digging into your skin."

Animals put kids in touch with the world of nature in a very special way, responding to loving care as no cucumber or dahlia ever will. The excited drumming of a puppy's tail or a kitten's gravelly purr makes a child feel uniquely loved and needed. Animals are even infiltrating public playgrounds, at least in Europe: several Amsterdam elementary schools have a section of the yard reserved for raising goats, chickens and rabbits, teaching kids the responsibilities and rewards of feeding and caring for living creatures.

Dogs and cats are the traditional family pets, but rabbits, chickens, guinea pigs, gerbils, goats and even de-scented skunks make good companions for kids. Last spring, our neighbours adopted a

newborn otter that had been abandoned by its mother, and the sleek swimmer has since become a faithful family friend, playing water polo with the kids and greeting visitors by rearing up on its hind legs and emitting low, questioning growls. Municipal bylaws may restrict the kind of animals allowed, but whatever the species, house them appropriately, remembering that most animals cannot tolerate direct exposure to either summer sun or winter cold. Put food and water within easy reach of the young caretakers, and give the kids sole responsibility for looking after the animal—but supervise their efforts to make sure the animal stays healthy. Don't make a spur-of-the-moment decision to buy, say, a mink, then spend years trying to figure out how to get rid of it without breaking the kid's heart; research the prospective pet thoroughly, and understand the kind of care involved before making a commitment.

Wildlife brings much of the joy of pets to a backyard without so much responsibility. Help the children set up a birdbath, or build birdhouses and feeding trays they can keep well stocked with seeds year-round. Dozens of species of songbirds—jays, cardinals, chickadees, sparrows, juncos, phoebes—will flock to a backyard feeder, even in the middle of a city. Some will even become quite tame: one summer day when my son was practising his violin near the bird feeder, a particularly bold chickadee landed on his bow, as if in appreciation for the dinner music. Learning to recognize the different species, their favourite foods and feeding and nesting patterns is a fascinating and rewarding hobby for the whole family.

Those same feeders will likely attract seed-eating rodents like squirrels and chipmunks, which can be discouraged with metal collars around the feeder posts or welcomed as extra guests. Roger Tory Peterson, author and illustrator of the famous series of field guides, buys extra seed and sets the feeder low to the ground so bushy black squirrels and tufted titmice can share breakfast. As tame as they seem, however, these furry creatures are not extras from a Walt Disney movie: teach children of all ages that animals in the wild are not pets.

Borders

Children's play is only one of many priorities vying for space in the family backyard; flower and vegetable gardens, patio and barbecue, toolshed and greenhouse, doghouse and birdbath all need a piece of the property. A border is a good way to separate the sandbox from the asparagus and the preschooler from the street, but its effectiveness depends on how high it rises and how it is made. Properly designed, a border can even make a small contribution to the play value of the yard.

Low borders, 2 or 3 feet high, are best suited to defining activity areas and guiding children's movements in the yard. For instance, plant a knee-high hedge around the patio to discourage kids from extending their soccer game beyond the lawn or a border of Icelandic poppies to direct kids to the front door of the playhouse; or build a balance-beam border to distinguish the active-play climber from the more subdued sand garden. A 3-foot-high border is enough to confine toddlers, blocking access to the woods, the street or a neighbour's yard, and although not physically restraining, a low border can even be an agreed-upon barrier to limit an older child's range ("I promise I won't go past the rail fence"), eliminating the need for constant parental nagging. Low borders make good climbers for young

An attractive and effective way of differentiating the play area from the rest of the backyard, a border can also become a play element in itself. These upright logs separate a berm from a tricycle path and serve double duty as a challenging climber for preschoolers.

children, who can test their balance by walking the rails, though parents should ensure there are no pitfalls – hawthorns or jagged stones – on either side. Squat borders of stone or squared timbers can double as benches and retaining walls for raised growing beds, effecting small but significant changes in elevation. Even a 2-foot rise is enough to make young children nestled at the base of the border feel snug and private as they play, without blocking them from adult view. Remember, though, that small children see the world from a very low perspective, and while parents may be able to see their kids over a knee-high panel fence, the child's view of both mother and house may be blocked. Furthermore, if fences are too high, the child will be hemmed in by a blank wall instead of the varied landscape that the family has worked so hard to create.

High borders, 5 to 6 feet tall, are useful for manipulating the microclimate of the yard, blocking cold winds, providing shade at certain critical times of day and acting as a snow fence to shape drifts for winter fun. They are also good for keeping older children out of sight. This is not as heartless as it sounds: after a certain age, kids prefer to be walled off from the world. When Polly Hill's children were young, she planted a thick hedge along the back third of the property, and behind this low border, her kids happily built a succession of make-believe worlds, conveniently out of sight yet within earshot of home. A high, solid fence is ideal for enclosing an adventure play area for school-age children, shielding the unsightly mess from neighbours' eyes and from the more carefully manicured parts of the family landscape while giving kids the

55

privacy and independence they crave at this stage.

For planted borders, choose species which are dense, hardy and sturdy enough to withstand kids' play but which will add interest and variety to the playscape. Children readily incorporate natural borders into their play, picking dusky Nanking cherries to decorate sand cakes, snapping off bayberry twigs to build tiny lean-tos and crouching under the branches of a cedar hedge to play hide-and-seek, and with some advance planning, constructed borders can also fit into kids' projects. If they are not intended as barriers, space

A backyard tricycle path keeps preschoolers off busy streets and sidewalks. Design it to meander around the yard, with storage for wheeled toys at one end and a widened section that can serve as a parking lot or mechanic's pit stop.

the horizontal bars of fences so they are climbable. See-through rail fences have the added advantage of giving children a feeling of enclosure while letting parents unobtrusively watch what is going on, and if the rails are set at the same height as sawhorses, kids can incorporate the fences into their constructions, using boards to create platforms or roofed hideaways. Instead of bordering their preserve with a predictable square or rectangle, surround the kids' adventure

area with a zigzag fence reminiscent of the original split rail, or create an unusual polygon with many angles and corners. For older children or parents who want to shield the yard from prying eyes, a solid fence is more appropriate. Soften the visual impact of a solid, high border by planting vines such as scarlet runner beans that add both colour and a source of easy-picking snacks.

Paths

Beside the house where I spent most of my childhood years runs a ravine, an overlooked crevice in the landscape where nature was left to its own devices. Revisiting the little gully now, I realize it is only a 30-foot swath of stunted willows and knee-high weeds, but when I was 5, it was an alluring, forbidding wilderness that stretched as far as my imagination. A dirt path sagged from the lawn's crisp edge down a steep incline, curved past the gnarled-root entrance to a rabbit's burrow, through the lilac bushes where a Hallowe'en-hued oriole nested every spring, to . . . well, to nowhere in particular. This path had no real destination, yet I spent countless hours exploring its sandy trail, sliding down the little hill on my snowpant-padded bottom in winter, building leaf houses between the trees in fall and sucking lilac nectar as I checked on the progress of newborn orioles.

To the adult eye, a path is no more than a means to an end, a route between where one is and where one wants to be, but as Roger Hart observed, kids often find as much enjoyment in getting places as they do in being there. Backyard paths exploit this natural inclination by giving children avenues of exploration through the varied environment created by berms, plantings, water and sand. Paths become accessories to the child's imaginary world as she hides in

the chrysanthemums to ambush passersby or bravely strikes off the beaten path in search of adventure in the forsythia grove.

For families with very young children, backyard paths also serve as safe alternatives to the street. From the age of 2 or 3, kids love to ride, push and pull wheeled toys, searching out the best "highway" to drive on, often a driveway, sidewalk or road where they are in danger of being run down by real cars. A backyard path will suffice until the child graduates to a two-wheeler, at around age 6 or 7, and even these school-age kids use old trike trails as roller-skate and skateboard runs. Furthermore, there are some games – hopscotch, skipping and bouncing balls, to name a few – that simply work better on a hard-surfaced path. Aside from their aesthetic and play value, paths serve a practical purpose, delineating play areas and preserving grass and plants by offering predetermined routes through the backyard.

Make paths and walkways at least 2 feet wide, with occasional widenings to create small oases for playing pit-stop mechanic or turnarounds for backing up and parking. If designed primarily for trike traffic, make the path a continuous loop so children can ride to their hearts' content without interruption, and incorporate low hills to give cyclists an extra thrill.

Integrate kids' paths visually into the overall landscape. If they are too prominent, paths become treadmills, demanding to be used in a prescribed, boring way that limits rather than expands the play potential of the backyard. Design serpentine paths that meander throughout the yard, tying the disparate activity areas together visually while creating an interesting route for kids to manoeuvre by "car" or on foot.

Soften the edges of the paths with plants, bushes and benches to give the traveller a refreshing change of scenery and to lend each special little stretch of road its own distinctive character.

The choice of materials helps a path blend into the landscape. Concrete and asphalt are fine for heavily used playgrounds, but sand, gravel and paving bricks are more appropriate for the backyard. Paving bricks are attractive but expensive; washed gravel confined between timber borders is cheaper but more difficult to bike on. Whatever the surface, it should be comfortable enough for walking yet hard enough for play and easy pedaling. Since none of these surface options is very resilient, the child will inevitably end up with a scraped knee or two, a time-honoured badge of childhood.

Seating

Wendy Walton's backyard playspace began with a lawn swing – one of those wood-slat platform rockers built for whiling away summer afternoons – gently swaying in the shade of some towering pines. "When the kids were little, we would rock together on the swing, but now that they are bigger and have their own swings and playthings, I can sit in the sun and read, keeping an eye on them without putting a damper on their play."

Adult seating is an important part of any yard, but in a playspace, it can keep adults within sight of their kids without being obtrusive – close enough to participate or assist when invited but not hovering over the kids at play. Children, particularly the very young, enjoy the security of having an adult nearby while they dig in the sand or clamber over the jungle gym.

Kids make their own tables, chairs and benches from their hollow blocks and

boards, but it is a good idea to incorporate permanent child-sized seating into the play area. Small tables and benches provide a place for kids to paint, draw and read – quiet, traditionally indoor activities that take on an entirely different quality out in the fresh air.

According to architect Joan Simon, child-sized picnic tables are a boon to play areas: kids use them not only as intended – as tables – but also as another element in their stockpile of loose material, turning them upside down to use as boats, on edge for forts or crawling into the natural "cave" underneath. Older children are less likely to tip over the family picnic table, but it will be a focal point for social gatherings, especially for teenagers who, given a comfortable place to lounge in the backyard, may manage to absorb some sunshine along with their endless soul-searching.

Encourage quiet, creative play as well as the rough-and-tumble variety by adding benches to the backyard playspace. Reading and drawing take on a new perspective when a child is tucked in a favourite corner of the yard, surrounded by the stimulating sights and sounds of outdoors.

4 Planning for Play

Layout and design

Live life as play.
Plato

When Adam Walton was 3, his father Raymond built him a sandbox just outside their back door by sinking 6-by-6 hemlock from a nearby northern Ontario sawmill into the ground and filling it with sand from the shores of Ruth Lake, located just a mile or so down the country road. Adam loved his personal square of beach, bulldozing mountains in it with his Tonka earth-moving equipment and grading superhighways for his Matchbox racers, but on hot summer days, the sun was too much for him. An irrepressible handyman, Raymond started sketching a shade canopy for the sandbox. He quickly realized that by making the supporting posts just a little heavier, the roof could become a play platform. As his son grew, so did the playspace – a swing was cantilevered off the side, a balcony jutted from the front, and the platform was closed in and roofed with boards salvaged from a demolished cottage. When Adam started school, he relinquished the sandbox to his younger brother Ian, and Raymond added monkey bars to keep his eldest entertained. When the baby of the family grew into the sand-shovelling stage, Raymond designed a swinging bridge that zigzagged from the balcony to the ground, supported midway by a cast-off swing-set frame. The playspace was sold when the Waltons moved recently, but Raymond is already sketching plans for a new one – Adam is ready for a cable ride, Ian needs a playhouse, and young Andrew . . . .

As the Walton family discovered, a good playspace is never finished: it continues to evolve as long as kids grow and develop. By planning ahead and designing each element to adapt to kids' changing needs, the transition from hollow blocks to cable ride can be a smooth one, disrupting the yard only marginally and leaving few pieces of play equipment discarded in the dust of a child's passing interest. Choosing the right combination of natural and constructed elements to stimulate kids through childhood is only the first step in the planning process. How they are arranged in the yard is equally important: a sandbox in the sun just a few steps from the kitchen deck is healthier, safer and more fun for toddlers than one tucked out of sight in the shade of the spreading oak behind the garage. A good layout will take into consideration the property, the other activities claiming space in the yard and the personal needs and preferences of the family. While there is no single "right" solution, this chapter will help readers avoid costly and inconvenient errors, guiding them step-by-step through all the stages of developing a master plan: selecting a site, choosing the components, designing a layout, drawing plans, building a model, costing the project and deciding whether to buy or build the equipment.

American playground designer Paul Hogan always included children in his projects by staging design contests and incorporating the best play-equipment ideas. As he notes in *Playgrounds for Free*: "Children need not only to be presented with playgrounds; they need to be invited to help build playgrounds. . . . I've yet to meet a child who wouldn't rather build his own plaything than have others do it for him." At Ottawa's Century School playground, designed by Hogan in 1978 for the 7th World Conference of the International Playground Association, two of the components were designed by kids, including a cable-reel tower that came from the drawing board of a 6-year-old girl. Parents with very young children have to base their design decisions on

Asked to draw an ideal playspace, many kids will outline the swings, slides and metal jungle gyms they see in schoolyards and public playgrounds. Instead, have them paint pictures of what they like to do outside and design the backyard to suit these preferences.

Playgrounds are for kids, and they should be involved in the planning process right from the start. For some children, a playhouse and a sandbox will take priority, but others, like this young Tarzan, **previous page**, will insist on challenging climbers to test their skills.

observations of the kids at play, but this is not difficult; one hardly needs a Ph.D. in child psychology to differentiate the monkeys, who prefer swinging from the highest tree, from the Michelangelos of sandbox sculpture. Older children, however, should be included in the planning right from the beginning. Even in the home setting, the play area is one of the few places that really belongs to kids, and it is only fitting that they have a say in its design.

Unfortunately, kids can visualize only what they know. When I asked a class of grade 5 and 6 children to draw a dream playground, they handed back pages of traditional swings and slides—they had never been exposed to anything else. Instead of asking kids what they would like in their personal playgrounds, ask them how they like to play, and develop a layout based on those preferences.

Once introduced to the possibilities that lie beyond a swing set, children have the imagination and flexibility of mind to help develop a unique and exciting playspace. And apart from the skills they learn by helping to plan their personal playground, kids who have been actively involved in the decision-making process are more likely to use, maintain and improve the playspace.

Priorities

When Norman MacDonald designed his child's backyard playspace—with the help of his father-in-law—he knew exactly what he wanted and why. Both he and his wife work, so their daughter Ashley and her friend Stephanie are cared for by a sitter who comes to their house on a tree-lined street in Toronto. Having just turned 3, the girls needed a challenging outdoor place to play.

''There are several good public playgrounds nearby,'' admits MacDonald, ''but we can't always take Ashley. Neither can the sitter, and the girls are too young to go alone. Besides, we want to encourage our daughter to bring her friends home—that way, we not only know where she is but who she is playing with. Even when she is 10 and going to the park herself, I want the yard to be enough fun that she'll want to come home to play too.''

MacDonald's playspace is designed specifically for two preschoolers, with ladder climbers, low swings, a slide, a sandbox and a jungle gym with movable platforms. The ladder rungs are spaced comfortably close together near the bottom but farther apart near the top so the girls can climb higher as they get older, and there are rope rungs waiting for the day they get bored with a stable ladder and want to risk a surface that moves under their feet. To design a playspace that suits children this well, it is important first to identify who will use it. Start by listing the children in the family, then branch out to their usual friends. A 10-year-old living in the country six miles from his closest classmate and dependent on a parental shuttle service probably plays with one friend at a time, unlike an urban child growing up in a subdivision where there are as many kids on the street as kittens in a barn. Note the ages of the kids who will frequent the playspace, since it affects both the choice of components and their scale. It is also important to know whether kids of different ages will use the playspace at the same time. Will three toddlers play while the big sisters are at school? Or will kids from ages 4 to 10 descend on the yard at once? If it turns out that the children's best friends all live on adjoining properties and seem likely to stay there for several years,

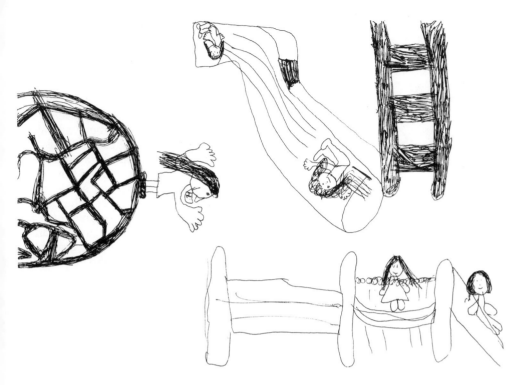

A kid's drawing may not yield detailed plans for a backyard playground, but it is an ideal way to discover how kids really like to play. The energetic, uninhibited lines will also be a source of inspiration, reminding parents of their children's own sense of playfulness.

do with play. How important are aesthetics? What are the financial limits of the project? Will this be a major overhaul of the backyard or just a few pieces of play equipment and some marginal landscaping? Is low maintenance a personal priority? What adult activities demand backyard space: gardening, car repair, sunbathing, birdwatching, socializing around the patio barbecue? A playspace is essential for children, but since it exists within a family context, it is equally important for parents to come to terms with their own personal priorities.

Figuring out what the family really wants and needs is not quite as easy as it sounds, especially since there is little to show for this collective navel gazing except endless lists. However, as parents and children proceed to the more practical and rewarding phase of mapping the site and drawing layouts, it is important to keep these priorities in focus to ensure that the evolving plan does not stray too far from the family's original goals.

Site

Unlike the tabletop flatness of most backyards, the terrain behind James Calhoun's house drops steeply into a treed ravine. "When we set out to buy outdoor play equipment for our son, it quickly became apparent that off-the-shelf swing sets, jungle gyms, slides and so-called custom-designed play equipment couldn't be used on such a site," he writes in *Popular Science*. Instead, he designed his own playspace, using the hill to advantage by building a split-level play frame that is just a few feet off the ground on one side but elevated dramatically on the other. A long cantilevered beam suspends a rope climber and swing over the deepest part of the ravine, safely separated from a

consider approaching the other families about building a joint playspace that straddles two or three property lines. This complicates the decision-making process but increases the budget and, with a good set of ground rules, can be an enjoyable and worthwhile cooperative venture.

Because kids continually grow and change, it is not enough to think of the playspace only in the present tense. Look to the future, plotting the ages and stages of the children 5, 10, even 15 years into the future. Although long-range plans are subject to change too, consider whether or not the family intends to remain on the property until the children are grown. A design developed only to keep toddlers stimulated and happy until they reach school will not need the same built-in flexibility as one intended to adapt to

kids' changing needs from preschool to high school. Likewise, if a playspace is designed to last until the grandchildren arrive, it justifies a greater financial investment in more permanent landscaping features, sturdier equipment and more durable materials. Whatever the projected life span of the playspace, be sure to divide those years into the major phases of childhood: preschool, early elementary school, late elementary school and adolescence. This helps the family choose the most appropriate components, both natural and constructed, and it also provides the framework for a phased implementation of the playspace design.

Since parents will be doing much of the work of building and maintaining the playspace and will be footing the bill for its construction, they need to set some priorities of their own that have little to

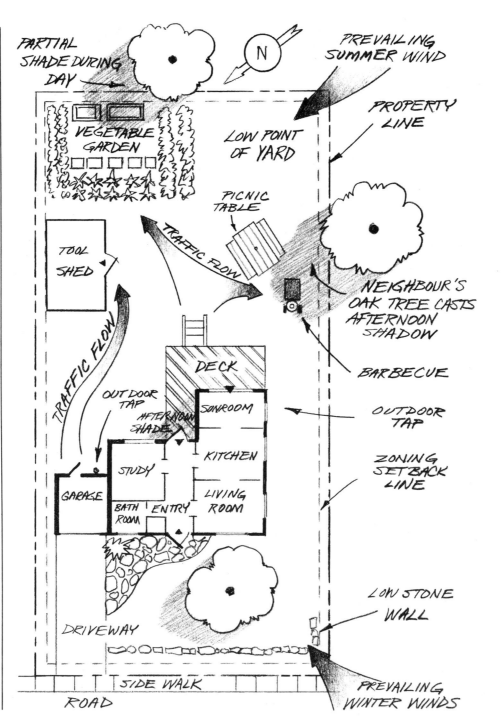

PARTIAL SHADE DURING DAY

N

PREVAILING SUMMER WIND

PROPERTY LINE

LOW POINT OF YARD

VEGETABLE GARDEN

PICNIC TABLE

TOOL SHED

TRAFFIC FLOW

NEIGHBOUR'S OAK TREE CASTS AFTERNOON SHADOW

TRAFFIC FLOW

BARBECUE

DECK

OUTDOOR TAP

OUTDOOR TAP

AFTERNOON SHADE

SUNROOM

ZONING SETBACK LINE

STUDY

KITCHEN

GARAGE

BATH ROOM

ENTRY

LIVING ROOM

LOW STONE WALL

DRIVEWAY

SIDE WALK

ROAD

PREVAILING WINTER WINDS

slide, tunnel and steps.

Some yards, like Calhoun's, are particularly challenging, but with a little imagination, any property can be developed for play. There are several important considerations in selecting the best part of the yard for a playspace: its relationship to the house, the quality of the soil and its exposure to wind and sun. Kids will not appreciate a sand garden blooming with emerald fungus or a playhouse mired in a soggy swale, but with some forethought, these blunders – and worse ones – are easy to avoid.

To get a feel for the play potential of the property, begin by drawing a site map. Trace the property plan, if one is available, or measure the lot and draw it to scale on graph paper. Be sure to make the site plan large enough: a standard 8½-by-11-inch sheet is adequate, but a 24-inch-wide piece of graph paper, available by the yard from office suppliers, makes it easier to visualize the space and accommodates a scale of 1:100 (roughly ⅛ inch to 1 foot). Mark the outside dimensions of the property and the location of north (using a compass), then place the house and other buildings (garage, shed, greenhouse) on the map, drawn roughly to scale and positioned accurately within the boundaries of the building lot. Indicate all the existing landscape features: trees, walls, paths, steps, fences, patio, swimming pool, gardens and general ground surfaces (grass, asphalt, bare earth, gravel). Although it is impossible to be perfectly accurate without a transit, show variations in contour, using arrows to point down the slope. Note any underground hydro and telephone wires, water and sewer lines, well and septic system – if you are uncertain about what is under the lawn and where, check with local utilities, neighbours or previous owners. Mark any features

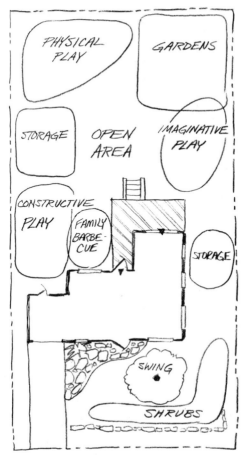

outside the property boundaries which could be significant to the playspace site: large trees or buildings that cast shadows into the yard, busy streets, dangerous swamps or deep woods that should be out of bounds for children.

Reducing a slab of real estate to a single sheet of paper gives family members a new perspective on their yard, one that usually makes it easier to contemplate adding a mound here, a hedge there or moving the patio to make room for a playhouse. Thus far, though, only the physical space is represented. Now shade in the areas currently used for various family activities—

barbecuing, playing badminton, sunbathing—and the traffic patterns that flow through the yard and around the house. These may change when the space is rearranged, but it is often useful to take advantage of well-worn routes when planning the space.

With all the "givens" laid out on the site map, it is possible to consider how the yard can be restructured for play. Don't dismiss any part of the property without careful consideration. Many families forget about their front yards, using them only as a buffer between the house and the sidewalk, yet Roger Hart's studies show that, at least in summer, kids prefer playing out front where they can be seen by friends and be close to the action of the street. In winter, the pattern changes, with kids reverting to their backyards, possibly because there are fewer people out and about in cold weather.

The front yard is especially attractive if it flanks the main entrance. Several studies confirm that kids like to play close to the most frequently used door. Very young children need to maintain close ties to the house when they go out to play, balancing their desire for freedom and independence with their need for a secure touchstone. The distance a child ventures from home is a direct function of age, so while a toddler happily plays by the front stoop, older kids prefer to be out of sight, where they can sustain the illusion that they are entirely on their own. The house-playspace connection is also a strictly practical concern. Make it convenient for kids to go out to play, storing jackets and boots in a closet or mudroom near the door closest to the playspace. If possible, position the playspace where children have access to an indoor playroom so that trucks, dolls, dishes and dress-up clothes can be used outside

as well as in. Likewise, place it where parents can supervise the kids (especially young ones) without actually patrolling the yard. The Waltons' play area is just 20 feet from the back door, which, according to Wendy Walton, is "close enough for the kids to feel secure about going out on their own when they are really little and to be within sight of the kitchen window so I can keep an eye on them."

To establish the relationship between the indoor living space and the play area, mark all exterior doors on the site map, putting a star on the most frequently used family entrance. Note the position

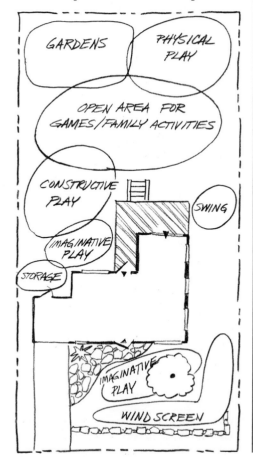

Lay tracing paper over the site plan and experiment with different arrangements of activity "bubbles," linking complementary play elements like loose material and the playhouse and isolating conflicting ones such as the sand garden and climber. Remember that young children prefer to play close to the house but older kids enjoy some privacy.

Consider the sun when positioning play equipment. For maximum use, it should be shaded during the hottest part of summer days but exposed to warm sunshine the rest of the year, especially during fall and winter.

play equipment in the yard—front or back.

The weather also has an effect on where the playspace should be. The conventional image of play is a summer one: kids in t-shirts scrambling up a climber or intently scooping sun-warmed sand. The truth is that the Canadian climate is one of extremes, with blazing summers and bone-chilling winters separated by long transition periods of cool, often damp weather. When choosing a playspace site, maximize the good weather and minimize the bad by paying close attention to the microclimate of the yard.

In Sweden, residential developers are forced by law to locate playgrounds where they receive maximum sunshine, and indeed, in cool northern climates, the sun is a welcome play companion. Nevertheless, at high noon on a midsummer's day, it can be too much of a good thing. Ideally, locate the playspace on the south side of the house where it receives full summer sun only in the morning and late afternoon but remains unshaded all day in winter when the sun is low in the sky and less intense. The best combination of sun and shade depends on when the play area will be most used: an east-facing site that is sunny only until mid-afternoon is a good choice for toddlers but not for 9-year-olds who want a sunny place to play after school. Check the site map to see where shadows will fall in summer and in winter, then eliminate areas that are dark most of the day. Fences and trees can be added to shade a sunny spot, but nothing will bring sunlight back to a corner dark-ened by a neighbouring barn or apartment building.

Like sun, wind is also a mixed blessing, pleasantly cooling in summer but chilling in winter. Fortunately, in

of windows that overlook the yard, as well as the function of the rooms they serve. If parents and kids are both home during the day, it would obviously be best to have the playspace just a glance away from the office, kitchen or workshop. Also, mark on the map the doors of outbuildings that can be pressed into service as storage areas, and note the location of outdoor water taps.

Certain parts of the yard may be off-limits because of legal restrictions. In Walkerton, Ontario, the parents of 8-year-old Heather Eidt built a two-storey Victorian-style playhouse in front of their house, not realizing that it violated a zoning bylaw prohibiting structures on front lawns. The Eidts moved before the issue was settled, taking their playhouse with them, but because they had built it without a building permit, they could have been forced to tear it down. Check with local planning officials before constructing many parts of the country, the prevailing wind direction changes with the seasons; for instance, in much of Ontario, the winter winds approach from the north and northwest, while summer winds blow from the southwest. This makes it possible to erect windbreaks that block only unwelcome cold-weather winds. The weather office can supply information on local wind patterns, but they may not apply to a specific site. Skyscrapers and stretches of hot asphalt make dense urban areas particularly prone to complex, erratic wind patterns, but even a rural yard with a barn on one side and a row of poplars on the other has its own distinctive breezes. Take note of the wind directions on the property, and add the information to the site map. Though a windy spot should not be ruled out, understanding the winds that buffet the playspace will help to determine where to plant trees, build fences or shape mounds to improve the microclimate.

Drainage is another important consideration in choosing the playspace site. As much as kids like to muck about in mud puddles, an unintentional slough in the middle of the play area is a definite deterrent to play. Do not dismiss a site simply because it is damp, however. Water-trapping hollows can be filled in and graded to improve drainage, and clay soil can be dug out and replaced with porous sandy loam. Kids who have been cooped up on a rainy day should be able to go out to play as soon as the thunderclouds clear, without waiting two days for a soggy lawn to dry.

With the site map complete, the family can now get down to the serious business of choosing the playspace site. There are basically two approaches to locating the playspace: one specific part of the property can be set aside for play, or the components can be scattered

around the lot—front, back and side yards—and integrated into the overall family landscape with borders and paths.

If the playspace is one distinct area, it does not have to be large. Rural and suburban yards may offer more room for play, but with careful landscaping and positioning of equipment, even a small urban yard can have a playspace that seems wonderfully large to a child. One play consultant suggested that the public playgrounds designed for children 4 to 8 years old should provide 50 to 100 square feet of space for each child, an estimate so broad that it is all but meaningless. Admittedly, it is difficult to set size guidelines, and this is especially true for a family play area because it depends entirely on the age and number of children who will use it and the priorities of the family involved. Keep in

mind that bigger is not necessarily better: children are half the size of adults, so scale the playscape to their young bodies.

Components

The choice of specific creative-play-space components depends on the age and interests of the kids using it. A play yard for preschoolers is the most specialized, for children develop rapidly at this age, maturing within the space of a few years from incoherent toddlers barely able to stand on their own two feet to expressive and agile young people. Physical play equipment predominates: the Canadian Institute of Child Health suggests devoting up to 40 percent of the available space to muscle development and coordination. This includes a hard surface for wheeled toys, body-building equipment (swing, slide,

Opportunities for physical play are especially important for preschoolers, since muscles and coordination develop rapidly at this age. Include body-building equipment like jungle gyms or balance beams and open grassy spaces for running and rolling.

65

climber, balance beam) and open grassy areas for running or playing ball. Youngsters between the ages of 3 and 5 also need a playhouse or "big box" and tables and benches for social and imaginative play. Sand, water and loose material are essential for promoting creative play among kids of this age, but they also need hideaways for their pensive solitary moments. Because pre-schoolers like to maintain close contact with home base, position the play area close to the house and locate seating nearby so parents can watch and participate. At this age, borders and barriers are important for safety and for controlling children's access to other parts of the yard.

This intense social, intellectual and physical development continues in the early school-age years between 6 and 10. As they become more independent and adventuresome, kids need more privacy, so extend the play area farther from the house and let trimmed hedges grow from low borders into visual barriers. At this stage, kids gradually abandon the sand garden and convert trike paths to skateboard runs or hopscotch and skipping courts. Since children's bodies are still growing and developing rapidly, the climber remains important – keep it challenging by adding flexible climbers, monkey or chinning bars and Tarzan swings. Toward the end of this period, kids become attracted to games with rules and begin playing court and field sports. While most yards cannot accommodate a baseball diamond or soccer field, they do have room for a backboard where kids can practise tennis strokes or basketball foul shots.

Interest in organized sports increases in the late school-age years from 11 to 14, but this is also the peak of what Edith Cobb called the "halcyon middle age of childhood," when kids forge

lasting bonds with the natural world. Although parents are often aware of the need to stimulate preschoolers, the creative and cognitive development of older kids is generally left to the school. Pique the curiosity of these budding biologists by giving them their own gardens and pets, perhaps excavating a living pond with pollywogs and lily pads, and by planting vegetation that attracts insects, birds and wildlife. To give kids an increasing independence and to let them learn by doing, isolate part of the yard as an adventure construction area. Physical-play equipment is still important for this age group, though it must be properly scaled for continued challenge. With components such as Tarzan swings, trapeze bars and cable rides, older kids can take thrilling risks and test the agility of bodies that are rapidly approaching adult size.

The emotional turbulence that marks the transition from childhood to maturity peaks in adolescence. Kids at this age act like 2-year-olds one minute and 20-year-olds the next. As the craving for privacy and independence that began

during the late school-age years reaches its zenith, the play area functions mainly as a cozy, quiet niche where the teenager can brood undisturbed in soothing, natural surroundings. Although probably no longer interested in building a tree house, adolescents may still be attracted to a lofty perch where they can revel in being aloof from the world in which they are struggling to find their place. These years are marked by extremes. Teenagers may spend hours in isolation, but they are also a gregarious lot, and if there is comfortable seating in the yard, it will become a gathering place for friends. For this age group, playground "equipment" is largely passé – their playground is more likely to be the local hockey arena or library – but home turf continues to be important as a safe, secure retreat.

The preceding information will not be entirely accurate for any individual child, but it should help the family select the most appropriate components for their yard (see chart on page 137). Many of the elements can be adapted for children with special needs: ramps, widened paths and an elevated sand garden for kids in wheelchairs, a cinder track for a future Abby Hoffman or a high wire to keep the young daredevil from running off to the circus. Since they may not all fit the site or the budget, the not-so-essentials may have to wait for another summer.

Layout

The tire swing, the hollow blocks, the hawthorn hedge and the red brick path all function as separate entities in the play area, yet together they create an environment with more total play value than the individual parts. Although a child cannot be on the climber and in the sand garden at the same time, the arrangement of those elements determines how comfortable, stimulating and safe the playspace is. In fact, the organization of a play area is just as important as the choice of its components.

The first step in developing a layout is to arrange the clusters of physical, intellectual and imaginative play equipment so they enrich rather than conflict with each other. Link related activities, locating the sand garden next to the playhouse where sandcakes will be served and storing the loose material between the playhouse and climbing frame, enabling kids to use the boards and blocks to make tables and chairs or movable ramps and platforms. On the other hand, try to separate activities that are potentially antagonistic. For instance, if the sand garden is built beside the climber, kids are tempted to use the soft sand as a landing pad, jumping over the heads of younger brothers and sisters bent over their bucket-and-shovel play. Because they stimulate such different activities, physical and imaginative play areas should be distinct, though setting them too far apart may disrupt the child-sized scale of this part of the yard. Use paths and borders to help define and connect play areas, encouraging a natural flow of movement from one activity to another within the playspace as a whole. The separation of conflicting zones is less critical in a very small playspace designed for only one or two kids, but associating related activities remains important whether the yard hosts 2 or 20.

There are few restrictions on the layout of equipment for constructive and imaginative play, but the physical play zone is a challenge because of the numerous elements involved and the safety concerns raised by robust play. Isolate equipment such as swings and

Physical play equipment like these climbing logs should be kept distinct from quiet corners reserved for imaginative play. Resist the temptation to have the sand ground cover around the logs double as a sandbox: kids jumping off these perches would disrupt youngsters intent on creative bucket-and-shovel play.

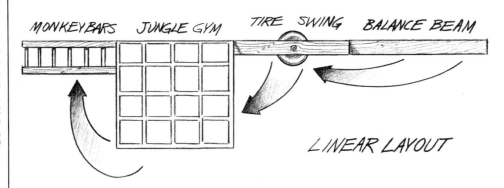

MONKEY BARS JUNGLE GYM TIRE SWING BALANCE BEAM

LINEAR LAYOUT

mound slides, but design a complex and stimulating layout for the physical play area by linking as much of the rest of the equipment as possible. Play that is strictly physical usually does not last long, but when the slide, cargo net, monkey bars and platforms are tied together functionally, kids use them for games and dramas that would never be possible if the bits and pieces were scattered around the yard.

A play frame is often central to the physical play area. Whatever individual accessories are added to the frame, the flow of movement within and around the overall structure is important. If the layout provides a variety of play options that blend into each other smoothly, with multiple choices at every turn, play is never repetitious or boring. Furthermore, kids of a wide age range can all play safely on the same equipment if the layout is designed for graduated challenge, making lower levels approachable by ramps, for instance, but having high platforms accessible only by knotted ropes or steps too widely spaced for young children to negotiate.

The simplest layout is linear. However, by lining up the swing, slide, jungle gym and balance beam much as

they were in traditional playgrounds, the physical play area becomes an easily mastered obstacle course that soon loses its appeal. By splitting the arrangement into two short lines, play possibilities more than double. Instead of moving in sequence from one activity to the next, the child crisscrosses the equipment, and if the two sides are joined by a cargo net, clatter bridge or monkey bars, traffic patterns begin to zigzag, loop and swirl. Arrange the equipment in a closed circle or square and opportunities multiply further, with kids moving around the structure, into the centre and back out to the yard. Experiment with different arrangements of platforms and accessories, drawing arrows to indicate the flow of movement into, out of and around the proposed structure. In general, the more complex the physical layout, the more fun it is and the longer it sustains the kids' interest.

Play value is a major consideration in layout, but so is safety. Each piece of physical play equipment exerts a "field of influence," that space into which a trapeze bar can swing or a child can jump from a platform. In general, the field of influence extends as far in the direction of movement as the unit is tall. Remove any obstacles—rocks, benches,

birdbaths—within the field of influence, and to further minimize the risk of injury, protect the ground surface below with a material that cushions falls. Also, design the layout to encourage kids to approach equipment from the safest direction: swings from the front and freestanding slides from the back.

The Plan

Developing an overall plan is a lot of fun and allows families to toy with the design variables, arranging and rearranging them on the site map until all the playspace jigsaw pieces fit. Norman MacDonald put his plan together in a matter of days, but a family can also savour the process, whiling away the winter in front of the fireplace, graph paper and pencils in hand, until warm weather and swing fever send them outdoors with lumber, saws and bolts. Because a design usually goes

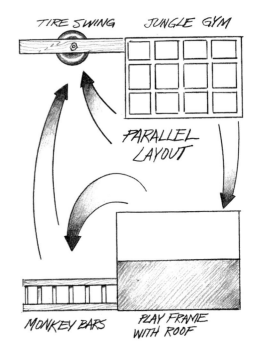

TIRE SWING   JUNGLE GYM

PARALLEL LAYOUT

MONKEY BARS   PLAY FRAME WITH ROOF

through many transformations before it is finalized, develop the plan on a series of sheets of tracing paper rather than sketching directly on the site map. Begin by drawing large circles to indicate roughly the size and location of the areas to be incorporated in the yard: physical, constructive and imaginative play, gardens, natural areas, pet enclosures and so on. Pencil in the borders and paths that link and separate these zones, anticipating traffic patterns between the house, the playspace and other parts of the yard. Be conscious of potential conflicts and ways that different zones might work together to improve children's play.

Having broadly defined the functional areas, focus on the layout within each, deciding exactly where to put specific play components for maximum play value and safety. As details fill in, the amount of space allotted to each area may have to be adjusted, reducing garden size to give the climber more room or combining several types of storage to create more open lawn for games. It will not take long to discover that designing is a spiral process – the refinement that solves one layout problem creates a whole new set of considerations. Each adjustment ripples through the design, improving some features and distorting others, which then have to be brought back into focus. Refer often to the original list of priorities and to the criteria for a good playspace; the final design will not only be fun and fulfilling but will be uniquely suited to the family members and their backyard.

Instead of consuming reams of tracing paper reworking the layouts, try drawing the play components roughly to scale on cardboard or heavy construction paper (use dimensions from manufacturers' catalogues or from actual

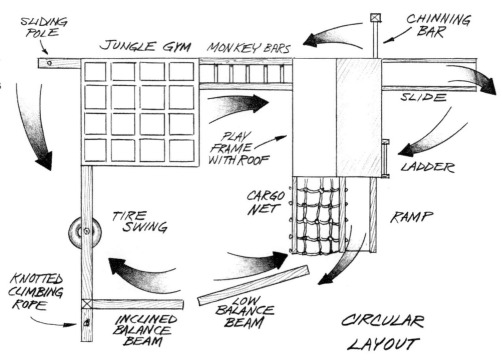

measurements of neighbourhood playground equipment). Move these cutouts around the tracing sheet to create clean new layouts without having to redraw the whole plan. If the swing is smack in the middle of the natural path between the back door and the side gate, a flick of the finger can nudge it safely into the corner by the currant bushes. When the components are positioned to everyone's satisfaction, trace or glue them onto the paper and pencil in natural features, such as paths and borders, and nonplay fixtures like seating and storage.

This final rough layout represents phase one of the playspace, a workable, attractive design that meets current family play needs. One layout might be enough if the family has 20 kids – the youngest outgrowing the jungle gym just

as the eldest is bringing home the first grandchild – but with today's small families, the playspace needs to be flexible, able to grow and change with the child. Refine the rough layout further by thinking through the projected life span of the playspace and assessing whether the location of each component makes future as well as present sense. For instance, a sandbox built behind the shed will have to be dismantled when the kids outgrow it, but located beside the deck, it can be converted to a raised-bed perennial planter.

Furthermore, as the kids develop, the playspace will need new equipment – a cargo net at 5, a cable ride at 8 and a Tarzan rope swing at 10. Earlier in the planning process, the family established phases for the playspace – now develop a

The best play-frame layout is a closed circle or square that kids can play around, moving into the centre and back out to the yard again. In this arrangement, the components blend smoothly together, providing several choices at every turn so the play frame never becomes boring.

separate rough layout for each. Phase one, just completed, becomes the site plan for phase two. Lay a sheet of tracing paper over top and incorporate appropriate elements from the first phase into the second, removing or adapting those the kids have outgrown and adding components to suit their new ages and interests. This process may reveal shortcomings in the initial layout that can be corrected to give the plan greater longevity. The completed phase-two layout then becomes the site plan for phase three, and so on. Develop phased layouts for as long as the family expects to live on the property, continually adjusting all prior phases as the master plan evolves.

By the time the last phase is completed, the rough layouts may be almost indecipherable. Before translating these rough sketches into clean final drawings, look again at the overall site and decide what needs to be done to make the leap from backyard to playspace. Then draw the new site plan for phase one, indicating the features that need to be removed with a dotted line, and fill in the final design details of the natural and constructed play environment, drawn to scale. Prepare these drawings for each phase of the playspace; together, they form the master plan.

Drawings can be as formal and detailed as the family desires, but they are not cast in stone. The final layout may still change if someone gets an inspiration during construction or if the kids' interests do not develop as anticipated. In fact, given that a good playspace is continually evolving, a final design is, by definition, impossible. Nevertheless, it is useful to think through the entire design before construction begins. The process uncovers many potential problems and conflicts that can be solved easily and inexpensively before the family starts planting begonias and setting posts in concrete.

Some families may want to take the design process even further and build a model. Aside from the fun of con-structing a miniature version of the family estate, projecting the plan into three dimensions may give an important new perspective on the design. At the very least, it sustains family interest at a high level until the real thing takes shape. Build the model on a base of plywood, particleboard or other strong, lightweight material that will not warp. Mark the edges of the board at 1- or 2-inch intervals to help establish the correct scale and spacing. Begin by shaping contours with salt paste, sand and white glue or with stiff paper that holds a curve. Then add permanent existing features such as trees, house, garage and sheds. Build models of the constructed play equipment and set them up in the play area, then add the natural landscaping features. Use "found" materials wherever possible: green-cloth grass, rubber-washer tires, string cargo nets, necklace chains, a balsa wood and toothpick jungle gym, a cardboard-box playhouse, pebble paths, *Lycopodium* shrubs and Play-Doh or real rock boulders. Don't glue down the elements; leave them loose so the design can continue to evolve as the family visualizes the scaled-down playspace in use.

Costs

Norman MacDonald did not set out to build play equipment for his daughter Ashley—he intended to buy it. He expected to pay more for modular

wooden components than for the usual metal swing set, but he was not prepared for the price list that came with the manufacturer's catalogue he ordered. "I was shocked," he recalls. "They wanted thousands of dollars for what I knew I could build for a couple of hundred." In the end, his play structure – a frame with two swings, a set of rings, movable platform, portable roof, slide, monkey ropes, ladders and a sandbox – cost a grand total of $325, even though he

bought swings and a slide. "I described what I built to a manufacturer, and he said they would have charged $3,000 for a setup like that."

Finances play a part in the design process right from the beginning. After all, there is no point in designing a $5,000 playspace if the budget limit is $500. Parents establish a rough budget when they set their priorities, but now is the time to figure out exactly what the playspace plan will cost to build. Be

forewarned: outdoor play equipment is not cheap. Very little can be built for less than $100 – even a good supply of hollow blocks runs into three figures – so don't expect the price tag to be competitive with a department store swing set. Instead of comparing a creative playspace with a swing set, consider how much the family spends on indoor toys and entertainment. Add up the cost of all the Lego, Tonka trucks, Masters of the Universe, Care Bears and

71

To reduce costs, build simple equipment first. For example, this inexpensive chinning bar, made with two short posts, two flanges and a length of pipe, provides hours of fun and challenging exercise. Likewise, natural play components are labour-intensive but require little capital outlay.

Cabbage Patch Kids in the playroom, and the cost of an outdoor playspace begins to pale by comparison. And unlike the faddish plastic gewgaws crammed on toy-store shelves, backyard playthings entertain and educate kids for decades. Furthermore, a well-designed playspace will likely add to the value of the property. While it may initially be expensive to convert these plans into reality, it is a very small price to pay for such vital, long-term benefits.

Building the playspace in phases helps minimize its financial impact. If funds are limited, start with those parts of the project that are labour-intensive but require little capital outlay: reshape the contours of the property and move existing sheds or bushes. Then build components that offer the most play value for the least money, such as loose material that provides maximum flexibility and variety at relatively low cost. The most expensive item is a play frame, which is used for relatively short periods of time considering its cost. Keep the kids busy and happy with a balance beam, climbing wall or mound slide until the family can afford a more ambitious climber.

Landscaping is also inexpensive in terms of its play value. Friends and neighbours will gladly contribute perennials culled from their own flowerbeds, and many rural landowners willingly give permission for digging up a few saplings to thin their woodlots. As well as being free for the hauling, these native species are more likely to survive the local climate than nursery-bred trees and bushes. Our own yard is landscaped with potentilla, wild rose, mountain ash, nannyberry, black cherry, hawthorn, spruce and red and white pine, all transplanted from local forests. It is a good idea to make trees an early priority and to transplant the most mature specimens possible, since they take a long time to produce the shade, berries and climbing branches so valuable to the play yard.

To figure out an accurate budget for the playspace, list all the components, break down their costs into materials and labour, and call a local building supplier for estimates. If the family undertakes construction, labour is free except for the services of specialists such as a backhoe operator to create a mound or a plumber to hook up the play stream.

The family will likely discover, as Norman MacDonald did, that in most cases, it is a lot cheaper to build creative backyard play equipment than it is to buy it. For instance, Paris Playground Equipment Inc. of Paris, Ontario, sells a roofed play platform with a half-tube slide, a horizontal climber and two baby swings built to public-use standards for $4,000. Playworks! Recreational Equipment Limited of Canning, Nova Scotia, sells a two-level fun centre with a swing extension for just under $1,000, which is about as inexpensive as ready-made equipment gets. Most systems are modular, consisting of a basic structure of posts and decks with attached play accessories, and although buying one is quick, convenient and secure (the industry is commendably sensitive to safety issues), they meet only a fraction of children's play needs. Parents still need to shape a stimulating natural environment and provide the loose material and creative elements that are essential to well-balanced development. Most manufactured equipment is designed for public, not private, use. Engineered to provide maximum durability with minimum maintenance and to withstand the antics of hundreds of kids and the perversions of vandals, it is overbuilt for family use. Expensive and mass-produced, rather than custom-

tailored to the site, purchased play equipment robs the family of the unique pleasure of working together to build something of lasting value.

However, individual components are sometimes worth buying, and most companies sell parts such as slides, swing seats and cable-ride assemblies to individuals. Children's Playgrounds Inc. of Unionville, Ontario, sells an 8-foot climbing net for $55 and a 7-foot slide for $135. MacDonald estimates he could

have built a metal slide for about $50 but still considers the slide he bought good value in terms of the time it saved him. If the family opts to buy instead of build, assess the units critically for both play value and safety. Those intent on doing their own design and construction will find manufacturers' catalogues a gold mine of ideas for play-frame layouts and a useful source of specialized hardware and hard-to-build accessories.

Playspace Principles

Whatever its final form, the playspace should meet the basic criteria that appear below. Refer to this list frequently as the design evolves to ensure that original goals remain in focus.

• Include play opportunities for all ages of children using the playspace.

• Choose components that stimulate a well-balanced mix of physical, cognitive and imaginative play.

• Scale equipment and design to the physical size and developmental ability of the children.

• Provide graduated physical challenges so children gain confidence from mastering new skills and can progress at their own rate.

• For maximum physical stimulation, provide facilities for large- and fine-muscle development as well as for the full-body movement that develops coordination and balance.

• Diversity and choice lead to exploration and learning: include as much variety as possible in the selection and design details of natural and constructed components.

• Nurture curiosity by providing flexible, changeable components kids can manipulate and have an impact on. If they cannot be modified or moved, playthings must be complex enough to sustain a child's interest.

• Stimulate the child's senses with a variety of colours, textures, contours, smells and sounds.

• Include a mix of open expanses and private, womb-like enclosures.

• Organize components to link related activities and separate conflicting ones.

• Control the microclimate to encourage year-round play.

• Provide convenient access to the house and storage areas to encourage responsibility and independence within a secure context.

• Design, build and organize equipment to encourage children to stretch their personal limits and to allow them to take calculated risks without suffering serious injury.

• The simplest things are often the most fun: a playspace need not be sophisticated and expensive, just well planned.

Consider safety as well as play value when laying out the home playground. For instance, even a Tarzan swing can be quite safe if it is installed where little children are unlikely to run in front of it and if there is sufficient clearance so the child will not collide with the swing frame.

Layout Specifications

Swings

•Choose location carefully: swings are a permanent fixture throughout childhood.

•Isolate swings, especially traditional single-axis types, from other play equipment; locate them out of the main traffic flow, at the edge of the yard or against a fence or garage wall; encourage mounting from the front by building or planting a low border to restrict access to the danger zone behind the swing.

•If swings are attached to a play frame, suspend them away from the main flow of physical play.

•Traditional and tire swings may be in the sun, but suspend infant swings and adult hammocks in summer shade.

•To avoid collisions, provide adequate clearance (30 inches) between swings and between the swing and its frame; there should be 6 feet between the maximum extension of the swing and nearby surfaces (walls, fences, trees).

•Remove any obstacles (rocks, stumps), and install a resilient protective surface under the full arc of the swing.

•Suspend Tarzan swings for older children over stream, pond or ravine (remove jagged hazards).

•With a multiple-swing frame, provide storage for alternate swing fixtures.

Cable Ride

•Ideally, select a gently sloping site (1:25) with trees for support posts and a clear run between.

•Remove obstacles underneath, and lay a resilient ground cover along the entire length or at least under the landing area.

Slides

•Install the slide on a mound for maximum safety and/or bumpy ride; the mound should have a 1:2 slope; provide

optional paths to the top of the slide.

•A play-frame slide should be one of several optional exits from a platform.

•Do not run a slide bedway into a sand play area.

•Face a metal slide north or shade it to prevent skin burns; position winter slides for maximum sun.

•Remove obstacles from the run-out at the base of mound slides and sledding paths.

•Provide a soft, 6-foot, obstacle-free surface in front of slide and on either side.

•There should be no structural components within 5 feet above the sliding surface and no equipment or moving parts that come within 3 feet of the sides of the slide. Do not place any component from which a child can swing (chinning bars, horizontal ladder) near the slide.

Climbers

•For fixed physical play equipment over 2 feet high, provide a soft, obstacle-free landing surface that extends 6 feet from the apparatus in all directions.

•Isolate climbing components from quiet, imaginative play areas.

•Climbers installed close to constructive play areas allow kids to use loose material to make platforms and ramps.

•Link physical play components with each other for maximum play value and a balance of individual and whole-body muscle development.

•Lay out the play frame and accessories for maximum variety, choice and graduated challenge; avoid linear layouts and encourage complex traffic patterns.

•Install the sliding pole at least 18 to 20 inches away from the platform, deck or structural member that supports it and outside the traffic pattern of ground-level activities so that the slider does not land on a friend. Barricade the space under the sliding-pole platform.

•Use a sloped site to advantage with bridges and play elements that kids cannot fall from. (A slope cannot hold a resilient ground cover.)

Playhouse

•Locate the playhouse on a flat area as near as possible to the sand garden and loose material.

•Buffer it from active play areas.

•Control access with borders to allow privacy and to direct guests toward the entrance.

•Provide storage nearby for imaginative play props such as costumes and pots and pans.

Loose Material

•Locate loose material on a flat area near the playhouse.

•It should be separate from but close to the active play area so boards and blocks

can be used to extend and modify the play frame or jungle gym.
• Include adequate, accessible storage.
• For older children, provide a visual barrier to isolate the construction area from neighbours and the house.

Storage
• Position separate storage near loose material, sand garden, water, swings (if multiple frame) and paths (wheeled vehicles).
• Alternatively, locate one large central cupboard where it is accessible to related play components.

Berms
• Position changes in elevation for aesthetic interest.
• Locate berms to act as barriers to danger zones.
• Design them to be used for sledding.

• Position berms to improve the micro-climate, creating warm south-facing slopes to block north winter winds.
• Integrate constructed hills smoothly into the landscape.
• Do not locate berms where they might disrupt current drainage systems or create future problems.
• Build cribs around trees so added soil does not suffocate the roots.

Plants
• Position tall, thick bushes and coniferous trees to block prevailing winter winds and control snow drifting for play; avoid creating winter shade.
• Position deciduous trees for midsummer shade, especially for quiet play areas and sand gardens.
• Position dense, thorny bushes as barriers to danger zones such as heavily used streets or dense woods.
• Plant low hedges or flower borders to control traffic between activity zones in the yard.
• Do not locate plants where they will be subject to damage (in the path of mound slides or at the base of hillocks where early frost is likely to settle).
• Position plants that attract birds, provide loose material and create cozy retreats near quiet play zones.
• Position gardens for the best growth conditions.

Sand
• For purification, expose sand to the sun during part of every day.
• Locate it for summer shade at high noon but full sun all day in spring and fall.
• If several children use the yard at once, position the sand garden outside active traffic paths.
• Isolate the sand garden from active play zones.
• Do not use the ground cover under the

play frame as a sand play area.
• If sand is located near water, kids can more easily mix the two materials.
• Provide storage nearby for sand toys, accessible in winter so the same toys can be used with snow.
• Locate it close to the house and near seating so parents can join their toddlers without crouching in the sandbox.

Water
• Position water source close to the sand, with provisions for the two to be mixed.
• Locate taps or play stream near a main water source to reduce plumbing.
• Provide storage nearby for water toys.

Borders
• Locate low borders (fences or hedges) to enclose the playspace and to define and separate play zones.
• Locate high borders to protect children from danger zones, to control the microclimate, to give privacy and to shield their constructions from sight.
• Locate fences where they can be incorporated with loose material (boards and sawhorses) in constructive play.

Paths
• Locate paths to link related activities.
• Lay out serpentine paths through "wild" natural areas.
• Design continuous-loop paths for wheeled vehicles, with storage nearby for trikes, et cetera.

Seating
• Orient benches to the sun.
• Cradle benches with bushes to protect them from wind and snow.
• Locate adult seating near the sand garden and toddler play areas for supervision.
• Locate children's benches in quiet areas for reading, drawing, et cetera; they can also double as steps or walls.

Design physical play equipment so it continues to challenge children as they develop. This 3-year-old girl can climb up the jungle gym with ease but has yet to master the rope ladder suspended from the cross beam. Incorporating such graduated challenges keeps the play equipment stimulating and makes it appropriate for children of several ages.

75

Play-Frame Plans

Designed to suit the kids and the site, each play-frame layout should be unique, but to give families some idea of the possible combinations of platforms and play elements, two sample layouts are presented on the following pages. Each is a phased design developed to be easily adapted to children's changing needs as they grow from toddlers to adolescents.

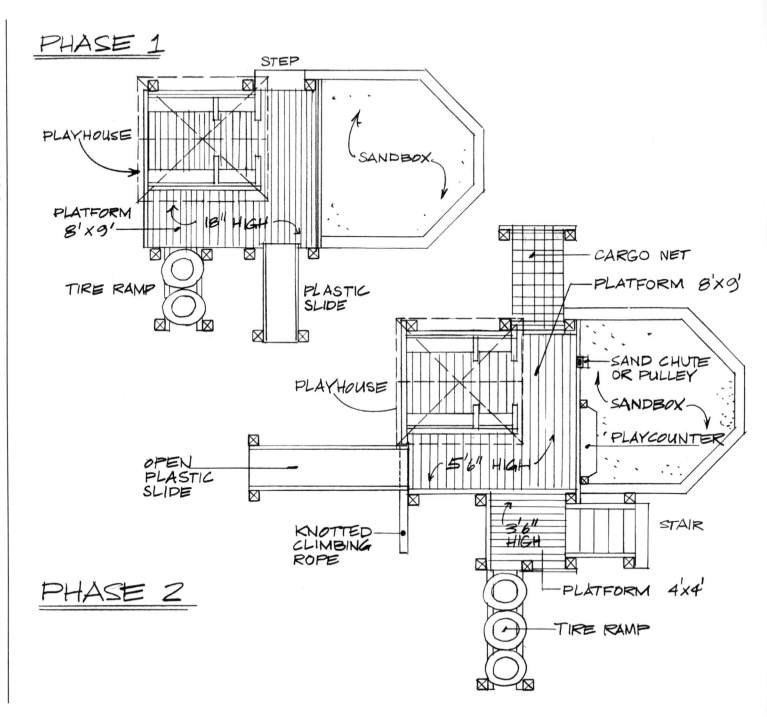

PHASE 1

STEP

PLAYHOUSE

SANDBOX

PLATFORM 8'X9'

18" HIGH

TIRE RAMP

PLASTIC SLIDE

CARGO NET

PLATFORM 8'X9'

SAND CHUTE OR PULLEY

SANDBOX

PLAYHOUSE

PLAYCOUNTER

OPEN PLASTIC SLIDE

5'6" HIGH

KNOTTED CLIMBING ROPE

3'6" HIGH

STAIR

PHASE 2

PLATFORM 4'X4'

TIRE RAMP

The basis of this layout is an 8-by-9-foot platform supported by posts that extend 8 feet above grade. In phase one, designed for very young children, the platform is only 18 inches high, but it is raised to 5 feet 6 inches as the children reach school age. The playhouse that dominates one corner of the platform remains unchanged: it will appeal to 10-year-olds in search of a clubhouse as much as to 3-year-olds playing house. In phase one, the low platform is reached by climbing steps or crawling up a tire ramp installed beside a gentle plastic slide. For preschoolers, the large sandbox is a major attraction, and it can continue to be part of the layout if the family includes both toddlers and school-age kids. Phase two adds a smaller low platform and a play counter under the high platform so both age groups have a private hideaway. The slide is raised and repositioned and the tire ramp extended. To challenge the older kids, a cargo net is added to one side and a knotted rope is suspended from a cantilevered beam. Depending on the materials used, the entire unit can be built for under $1,500.

This layout is more elaborate but is likewise built in stages, distributing the total cost of $2,500 over several years. The first phase (top right), built when the children are 2 or 3, includes a low platform and a large sandbox with a central "cake table." The back two-thirds of the platform is roofed and has built-in benches along both sides. The front third, reached by low steps, is a balcony overlooking the sandbox. If big hollow blocks and boards are stored under this platform, kids will combine them with the steps and platform in imagination-expanding constructive play. As the kids get older, add a crawl tunnel (centre) from the sandbox to a second low platform. This tunnel can be a plastic tube purchased from play-equipment manufacturers, a clean metal drum with the edges safely capped or a series of tires suspended vertically between two 4-by-4 rails.

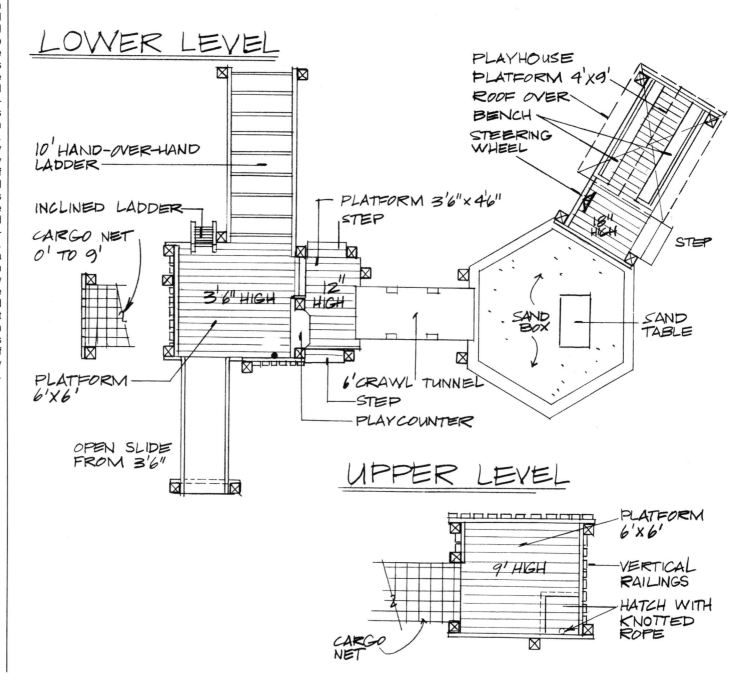

LOWER LEVEL

10' HAND-OVER-HAND LADDER

INCLINED LADDER

CARGO NET 0' TO 9'

3'6" HIGH

PLATFORM 6'X6'

OPEN SLIDE FROM 3'6"

PLATFORM 3'6"X4'6"
STEP

12" HIGH

6' CRAWL TUNNEL

STEP

PLAY COUNTER

PLAYHOUSE PLATFORM 4'X9'

ROOF OVER BENCH

STEERING WHEEL

18" HIGH

STEP

SAND BOX

SAND TABLE

UPPER LEVEL

PLATFORM 6'X6'

VERTICAL RAILINGS

HATCH WITH KNOTTED ROPE

9' HIGH

CARGO NET

The final phase of this layout is a two-storey play tower. The lower platform—3 feet 6 inches high—is overlooked by a play counter and has steps leading up from the tunnel platform, as well as a slide off one side and inclined monkey bars off the other. Because the upper platform is 9 feet high, it is restricted to older children and can only be reached by a rope cargo net or a knotted-rope climber that leads from the lower level to a hatch above. Both this layout and the one on the previous page lack swings, which should be suspended from their own frame set away from the running and climbing play.

Playspace Plans

Instead of plunking a play frame in one corner of the yard, play elements should be incorporated into the overall design of the backyard. On the following pages, a small urban yard and a large suburban yard are each shown in three phases of development, the layout of the yard evolving as the family grows.

Urban Yard

This design makes maximum use of space and adds interest to a small backyard. The sun deck that overlooks the yard has storage cupboards underneath for tricycles (near the path) and for loose material (beside the constructive play area). Flowering vines trail from the deck railing to the brick play patio below, where kids build with blocks and boards. In its first phase, designed for preschoolers, the centre of the yard is dominated by a jungle gym and a sand garden, with an outdoor tap just a few steps away on the side of the deck. The back corner of the yard is a small wild area planted with flowering ground covers and two deciduous trees. The dogwoods across the back attract birds while the honeysuckles add spring colour as well as secret hiding places. These shrubs nestle the swing frame so kids are not tempted to run behind.

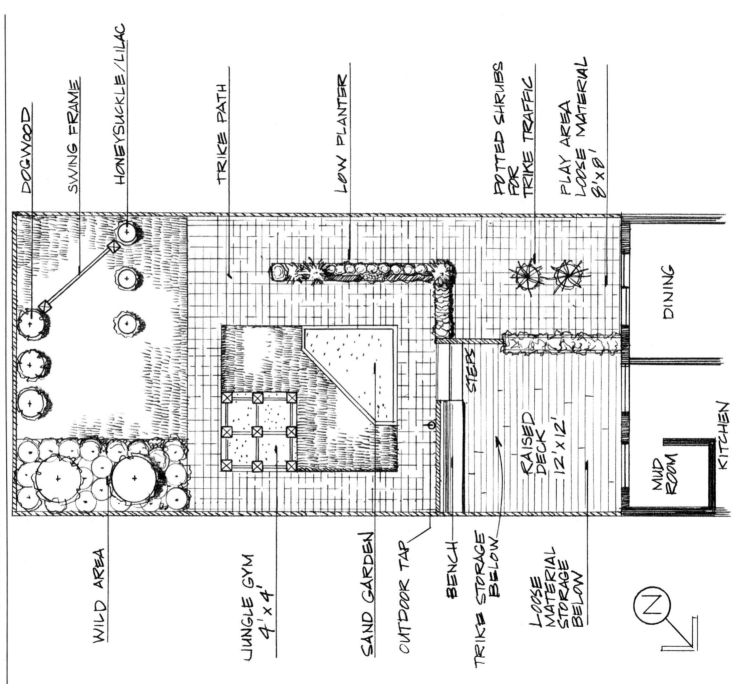

DOGWOOD

SWING FRAME

HONEYSUCKLE/LILAC

TRIKE PATH

LOW PLANTER

POTTED SHRUBS FOR TRIKE TRAFFIC

PLAY AREA LOOSE MATERIAL 8'x8'

DINING

KITCHEN

MUD ROOM

RAISED DECK 12'x12'

STEPS

BENCH

LOOSE MATERIAL STORAGE BELOW

TRIKE STORAGE BELOW

OUTDOOR TAP

SAND GARDEN

JUNGLE GYM 4'x4'

WILD AREA

N

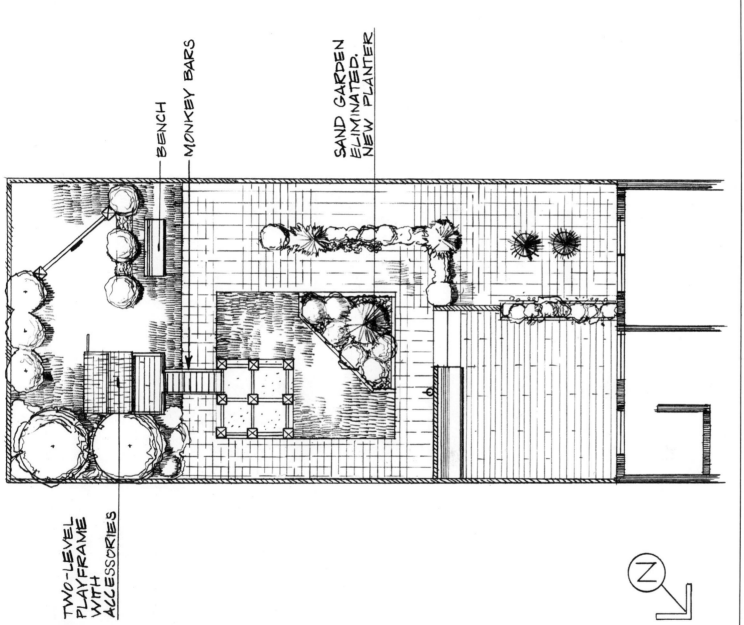

BENCH

MONKEY BARS

SAND GARDEN
ELIMINATED.
NEW PLANTER

TWO-LEVEL
PLAYFRAME
WITH ACCESSORIES

As the children grow older, the sandbox converts to a shrub garden and monkey bars lead from the jungle gym to a two-level play frame where a sliding pole, knotted rope and cargo net provide access to a playhouse at the top. Although the kids will have outgrown their trikes, they will still use the brick paths for skateboarding, hopscotch and ball games.

N

Even a small city lot has room for a backyard playground, especially if the design spreads up instead of out. The jungle gym provides a lot of fun and exercise in a relatively small space, as does the two-level play frame. Concentrating the robust play on the jungle gym leaves the play frame, with playhouse above and play counter below, mostly for dramatic, imaginative pursuits.

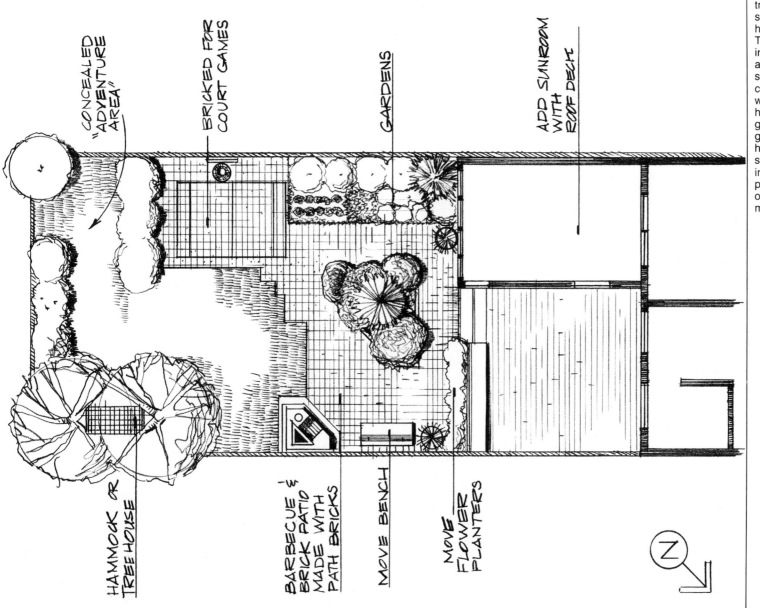

CONCEALED "ADVENTURE AREA"

BRICKED FOR COURT GAMES

GARDENS

ADD SUNROOM WITH ROOF DECK

HAMMOCK OR TREE HOUSE

BARBECUE & BRICK PATIO MADE WITH PATH BRICKS

MOVE BENCH

MOVE FLOWER PLANTERS

N

As the kids approach their teens, the climbers and swing frame are dismantled, and the mature backyard trees are pressed into service to support a hammock or a tree house. The brick path is recycled into a ball court, and an adult patio is built around the shrub garden. The constructive play area gives way to a sun room for the house, fronted by a kitchen garden of herbs and salad greens. The honeysuckle hedge is now high enough to shield a kids' adventure area in the back corner, offering privacy to both adults and offspring, despite the minimal space.

Suburban Yard

A large suburban lot has enough space to develop a separate children's play area that evolves as they grow. In this design, a berm angled across the back third of the yard creates a sunny playground with a playhouse and a jungle gym built into the retaining wall on one side of the mound. Kids can roll down the hill, slide down the slide or hide in the nooks created by the bushes at the base. When the kids are small, the top of the berm is protected with railings or a barrier hedge of thorny *Rosa rugosa*. A trike path with a wide turnaround at one end leads from the house to the active play area or back around the vegetable garden and onto the brick patio where there is storage for wheeled vehicles and loose material. Both the constructive play area and the sandbox are close to the house for easy supervision, and a water tap is installed where it is handy to the sand and the gardens.

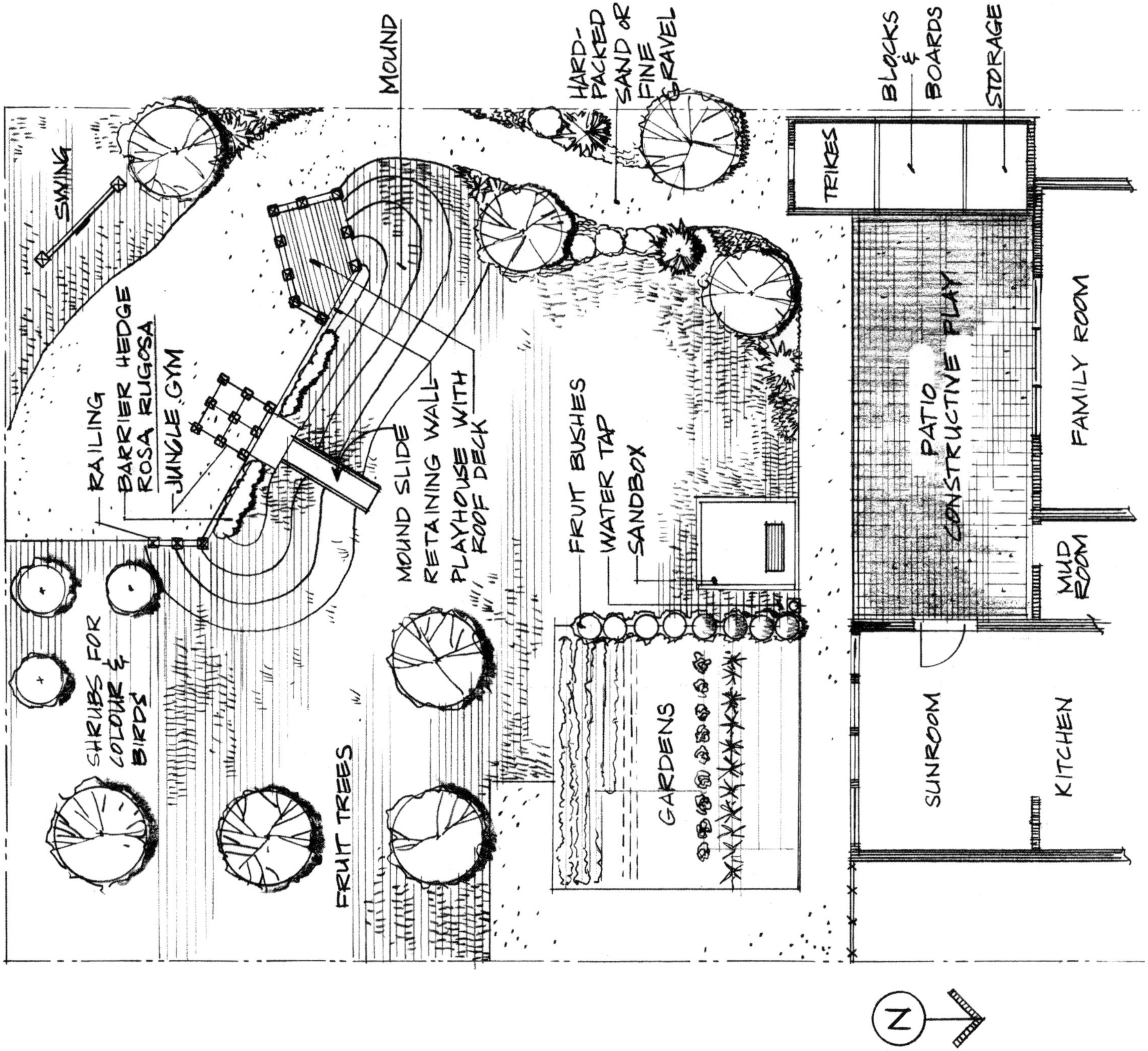

MOUND

HARD-PACKED SAND OR FINE GRAVEL

BLOCKS & BOARDS

STORAGE

TRIKES

FAMILY ROOM

SWING

RAILING

BARRIER HEDGE ROSA RUGOSA

JUNGLE GYM

MOUND SLIDE

RETAINING WALL

PLAYHOUSE WITH ROOF DECK

FRUIT BUSHES

WATER TAP

SANDBOX

PATIO CONSTRUCTIVE PLAY

MUD ROOM

SUNROOM

KITCHEN

SHRUBS FOR COLOUR & BIRDS

FRUIT TREES

GARDENS

N

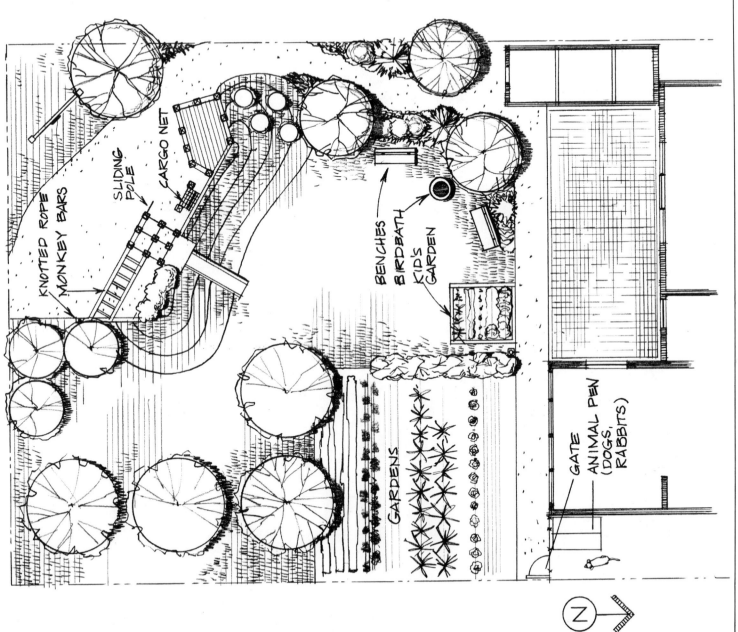

As the kids grow, the sandbox is converted to a children's garden and the vegetable garden is enlarged to absorb the trike path around it. On the east side of the house, a fenced dog or rabbit run has a gate to the backyard. For school-age kids, the railings at the top of the berm are removed and some of the bushes are transplanted so the active play area can be expanded to include monkey bars, knotted ropes, sliding poles and cargo nets attached to the retaining wall.

KNOTTED ROPE
MONKEY BARS

SLIDING POLE

CARGO NET

BENCHES
BIRDBATH
KID'S GARDEN

GARDENS

GATE
ANIMAL PEN
(DOGS, RABBITS)

N

The retaining wall that supports the half-berm in this design cradles the playground in a private sunny nook and also provides a solid surface for attaching play elements such as a cargo net. Using the change in elevation to good effect, the circular layout gives kids a wide range of options: they can climb up the knotted rope, across the monkey bars and the jungle gym to come down the sliding pole or cargo net back into the playground; they can cross to the hilltop and slide down the mound slide; or they can run to the roof deck, open the hatch and climb down into the playhouse.

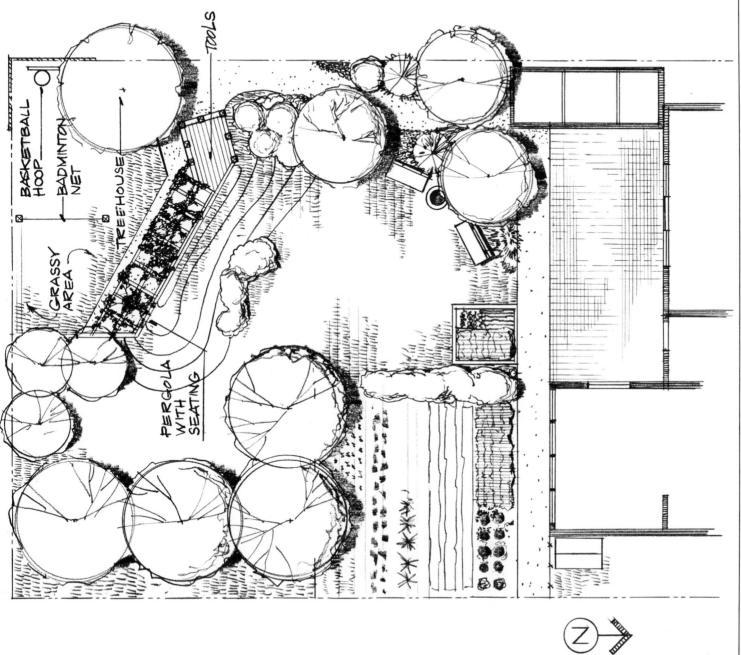

TOOLS

BASKETBALL HOOP

BADMINTON NET

TREEHOUSE

GRASSY AREA

PERGOLA WITH SEATING

In its final phase, the back corner becomes an adventure-games area fully shielded by the tall bushes that now flank the berm. The playhouse becomes a storage shed for tools and construction materials, and the climbers are recycled to create a trellised seating area where children congregate. The path remains, but the turnaround is expanded into a court for badminton, volleyball or basketball.

N

5

The Right Stuff

Play-equipment materials

Sweet childish days, that were
    as long
As twenty days are now

William Wordsworth

The first public playground equipment was made almost exclusively of iron and steel, not because metal is best to play on but because it is easy to mass-produce and is virtually immune to the ravages of children and climate. Wooden play structures have invaded schoolyards and parks in the last decade, but this may prove to be just an aberration in the evolution of large-scale play apparatus. Major manufacturers are again promoting metal as their material of choice, updated with brightly coloured plastic coatings. They maintain that their eye-popping orange-and-blue climbers have more "kid appeal" than natural-wood models, which they claim have gone the way of macramé and hand-thrown pottery, but the switch back to steel has probably been directed by those who buy the equipment rather than by those who use it. At least one Canadian playground builder admits that his new line of metal equipment was developed not because kids prefer the material but because municipal employees complained that wooden play structures were hard to maintain and were easy targets for vandals.

Parents, with no need to worry about hooligans or the wear and tear of hordes of unsupervised children, are free to choose materials for the benefit of the kids, rather than for the convenience of the manufacturer or maintenance supervisor. Nevertheless, there are other considerations in choosing materials for the constructed components of the playspace: they must be safe, compatible with the skills and tools of the average homeowner, easily maintained, reasonably priced, readily available and an asset to the home landscape. This chapter reviews the relative merits of wood, plastic, metal and rope for building play equipment, as well as the best material options for finishes, hardware and ground covers. It closes with the pros and cons of using recycled materials in the home playspace.

Wood

I always wondered why "FROST" was embossed on the steps of every slide I played on. To be sure, the metal frame was finger-numbing cold from September to May, but the label did not explain the sizzled skin of summer. Wouldn't "FROST-FRY" be more appropriate? It was years before I realized the word identified the slide's manufacturer and even longer before it dawned on me that play equipment didn't *have* to be so uncomfortable. Metal may be acceptable where temperatures hover in the comfort zone year-round, but in a climate of extremes like Canada's, metal is far too effective a conductor of heat and cold to be much fun to play on.

Wood, on the other hand, has much to recommend it. Because it has some insulation value, wood feels cool in summer and warm in winter. Compared with the hard, slick surface of metal, wood is almost soft to the touch; certainly it is more resilient if kids fall against it. Whereas metal requires special tools and skills to shape it into a piece of play equipment, working with wood is within the capabilities of most adults, even those whose experience is limited to building a birdhouse in grade 7 shop class. The tools, hardware and raw material are relatively inexpensive and are as accessible as the nearest lumberyard. Furthermore, the muted hues of wooden play equipment blend unobtrusively into the backyard landscape, never overpowering the natural components of the playspace.

"In an urban setting, kids need to feel natural materials," says Rick Henke, owner of Children's Playgrounds Inc.,

Wood is an ideal material for home play structures. Most homeowners possess rudimentary woodworking tools and skills, and they have access to good-quality lumber that is relatively inexpensive. Also, wood's natural tones blend unobtrusively into the backyard landscape, and it is both resilient and comfortable.

In public playgrounds, material is chosen for its ability to withstand neglect, vandalism and hard use by thousands of children. A home playground, **previous page**, is subjected to less wear and tear and can be more diligently maintained. As a result, play value can be the major criterion of material selection.

one of the few play-equipment manufacturing companies that design and build equipment for backyards as well as for municipalities. "But most people are not prepared for the way wood behaves when it is exposed to the elements."

Although wood is unquestionably the structural material of choice for backyard builders, it does have drawbacks. When a 4-by-4 post is still part of a living tree, its cells are bloated with moisture that begins to dissipate as soon as the tree is felled, and as the drying cells collapse, the wood shrinks. If this process takes place unevenly – the outside layers of wood drying faster than the centre – tension develops between the fibres, causing hairline cracks, or "checks," that radiate out from the heartwood. If the check extends right through a piece of wood, it is called a "split." Wood may also develop "shakes," or cracks between the annual growth rings, a characteristic of some tree species that is accentuated by uneven shrinkage. If the crack is large enough in relation to the size of the lumber, shakes, checks and splits compromise the structural strength of the wood.

Kiln-drying wood under controlled conditions makes it less prone to checking, but, by nature, some species are more susceptible to the problem than others. For instance, both red and white cedar and red and white pine dry with relatively little shrinkage, whereas western larch checks noticeably as it seasons, and shakes are common in eastern hemlock. As the outside surface wears, some species are also likely to splinter, a hazard worth avoiding on play equipment. Although redwood is a weather-resistant outdoor wood, Henke says it becomes brittle and disintegrates into slivers within three years, making it unsuitable for play equipment. Fir also splinters, and prolonged weathering will even raise a rough grain on cedar.

After its initial shrinkage, wood continues to expand and contract with the fluctuating moisture content of soil and air. As a result, a joint that fits tightly during the hot, humid summer months gradually loosens as the relative humidity drops in winter. The same phenomenon explains why exterior wooden doors that stick in July gape in January. Inspect joints periodically and retighten them to prevent the play structure from becoming wobbly.

It takes more than a wrench to solve the most serious consequence of exposing wood to the elements. An organic material, wood is the staff of life for many species of primitive plants, some consuming only the food stored in the wood cells but others attacking the very fibre of the material. In most parts of this country, fungi are the primary cause of wood decay, and given the right combination of conditions, they can reduce wood to pulp within three years. Fungi require air, water and warmth to survive. As a result, only wood that is found in the Arctic, the desert or under water is immune to their destructive appetite. Exposed to normal outside conditions, it is impossible to keep wood cold, dry or wet enough to stop fungal growth. Some species are more naturally resistant than others, but all succumb eventually. Wood with less than a 20 percent moisture content – kiln-dried or thoroughly air-dried – is too dry to support fungal life, but any lumber exposed to consistently damp weather or in contact with soil inevitably rises above that level.

For play equipment that will survive through a childhood, build all vulnerable parts with a naturally decay-resistant wood or one that has been treated with preservatives to kill destructive fungi and bacteria. Only certain softwoods are naturally immune to fungi: redwood, cypress and – the most common species – cedar. The totem poles on Canada's West Coast are prodigious proof of cedar's durability, for despite enduring the wettest climate in the country, they remain sound after two centuries. Cedar's resistance to decay comes from natural fungicides that form as the tree grows and which are deposited in the outer heartwood. The inner heartwood near the pith has a relatively low resistance to fungal attack, and the light-coloured sapwood between the core of the tree and the bark is as vulnerable as any other wood.

Unfortunately, the rot-resistant heartwood of redwood, cypress and cedar has become increasingly expensive and hard to find. The only alternative is to mimic nature by impregnating cheaper, more common species with a chemical preservative. Ancient Egyptians used cedar oil to extend the life of vulnerable wood, but today the most common preservatives are creosote, pentachlorophenol and inorganic arsenic salts. The first two are sold as paints for home application, while the third is used primarily in commercial "pressure-treated" wood.

The terms pressure-treated and preserved sound innocuous enough, but the chemicals involved are potent pesticides formulated to repel termites, bacteria and fungi for decades. Although homeowners want their backyard swings and slides to last, the thought of children playing on poisoned wood is repugnant. It is not surprising, then, that as wood gained popularity as a play-structure material, preservatives came under close scrutiny. These chemicals are practical and convenient, but are they safe?

Ultimately, all preservatives pose some risk, although the health hazard varies from potentially serious to negligible, depending on the chemical in question. Creosote, the smelly black goo smeared on railway ties and telephone poles, is the oldest industrial wood preservative and has been in use for almost 150 years. In laboratory animals, creosote causes skin irritation, cancer and genetic damage; in humans, it has been linked to skin cancer and causes eye and skin irritations, dermatitis and burns. It remains potent for years, moving easily through the wood to affect the soil—and the skin and lungs of anyone who touches it or breathes its vapours.

Pentachlorophenol (PCP) is a cleaner alternative to creosote, but it is equally suspect from a health standpoint. A member of the same chemical family as 2,4,5-T, it contains dioxins and has

caused cancer and birth defects in laboratory animals as well as short-term effects such as skin, eye, nose and throat irritations. It is easily inhaled and absorbed through the skin and continues to give off toxic vapours for as long as seven years. In the United States, the Environmental Protection Agency (EPA) controls the use of both PCP and creosote and recommends sealing wood contaminated by these preservatives with two coats of urethane, shellac or

latex epoxy enamel. Shellac, which is slippery when wet, is inappropriate for outdoor play structures.

The pressure-treated wood sold in lumberyards is preserved with inorganic arsenical compounds, either chromated copper arsenic (CCA) or ammoniacal copper arsenate (ACA). CCA was developed by Karl Heinrich Wolman in 1913 (hence Wolmanized wood) and has been used for 50 years as an inexpensive alternative to creosote. Associated with rats and lace-trimmed old ladies diabolically doing in unsuspecting boarders, "arsenic" strikes a note of uneasiness in most people, but it is a

common element in the environment. The form of arsenic used in treated wood is in the pentavalent state—the same as that found in shrimp, mushrooms, rice and sardines. In laboratory animals, inorganic arsenical compounds cause cancer, birth defects and genetic mutations, as well as short-term effects such as headaches, dizziness and muscle spasms. But, unlike PCP and creosote, the arsenical preservatives bind tightly to wood fibres. Studies show that the chemicals do not migrate into surrounding soil and plant tissue and are not absorbed through human skin. The EPA concluded that pressure-treated wood is "safe for frequent contact because absorption through the skin is negligible."

The preservative process sometimes leaves a bloom of chemical residue on the lumber, and while children cannot absorb the arsenic directly by touching it, their fingers often end up in their mouths. To assess this danger, the California State Department of Health conducted a study in which a researcher repeatedly licked his hands after rubbing them over treated wood surfaces. After several days of testing, his urine showed no increase in arsenic even though the measuring device was sensitive enough to reveal the effects of a single sardine. The authors of *Evaluation of Risk to Children Using Arsenic-Treated Playground Equipment* concluded that kids have as much chance of getting skin cancer from the CCA-treated play equipment as they do from playing in the sun.

CCA is probably more of a health risk to parents than to their children since minute amounts of preservative-laced sawdust may be inhaled or swallowed during construction. Wear a dust mask when sawing or machining arsenic-preserved wood, and do the work outdoors to avoid contaminating indoor

Most wood species cannot survive prolonged exposure to the elements, yet many wood preservatives have questionable health consequences for humans. Studies indicate that pressure-treated wood is safe, but the only chemical-free solution is to build play structures with a naturally decay-resistant wood such as cedar.

air with preservative dust. Because the incineration of treated wood releases arsine, an extremely poisonous gas, wood scraps should never be burned; bury them or take them to an approved dump site.

Pressure-treating the wood does not inject preservative right to the core of the lumber; thus, drilled or cut surfaces have to be brushed with at least two coats of liquid preservative. Wear rubber gloves during these applications, avoid dripping the chemical on plants, and wash hands thoroughly after skin contact to remove any residue. After the structure is built, hose it down with soap and water to remove the surface deposits of chemicals.

Though these three account for the bulk of preservatives sold in this country, there are alternatives: low-toxicity preservatives such as copper and zinc naphthenate, copper-8-quinolinolate, polyphase, bis [tributyltin] oxide (TBTO) and TBTO/polyphase. These are not known carcinogens, are not herbicidal or poisonous in the concentrations used for preserving wood and are relatively stable. All effectively prevent damage from mould, mildew and rot by keeping wood dry enough to discharge fungi and bacteria. Copper naphthenate, the active ingredient in Cuprinol, has been on the market the longest (since 1948). Often used to treat lumber for greenhouse growing beds, copper naphthenate is the only one of the above chemicals rated to withstand constant ground contact. Because it can be difficult to paint over and must be reapplied if the wood cracks, it is better to use copper naphthenate below ground and zinc naphthenate or one of the other water-repellent finishes above ground. However, these chemicals are not sufficient to protect wood against

termites, a serious problem in parts of southern Ontario. Termites dine on copper naphthenate as readily as they do cedar, leaving CCA-treated wood as the only alternative in infested areas.

Playground books written 15 years ago often advocated recycling salvaged utility poles and railway ties for play equipment, questionable advice in light of what is now known about creosote's health risks. Still, it seemed like a good idea at the time. Since creosote had been around for more than a century, it was presumed safe, and the same argument might be made for CCA or copper naphthenate: any major problems would surely have surfaced by now. New chemicals, buttressed by reassuring toxicological studies, are continually being introduced to consumers, but homeowners who are concerned about contamination should limit the use of

any chemical preservative to structural members in contact with the soil, choosing untreated wood for the railings and decks that children will touch. Better yet, pay the tithe for peace of mind, and build exclusively with cedar.

Prolong the life span of outdoor wood by using construction techniques designed to minimize its contact with water. Wood that sits on or in soil is always wet enough to rot, and since the air near ground level is usually humid, the closer wood is to the ground, the more likely it is to rot. Keep wood well ventilated by raising platforms, playhouses and storage cupboards at least 6 inches off the ground so air can circulate underneath. Design above-ground parts of the structure to shed rainwater quickly: round the tops of posts and space deck boards a nail's width apart to allow water to drain through quickly. Because the end grain of lumber readily absorbs water, cover it wherever possible, extending handrails over support posts and finishing platforms with a nosing, or edging, to conceal the end grain of decking. Protect wood that is intermittently wet and dry with water-repellent finishes.

Obviously, wood species vary considerably in their natural resistance to decay, their ability to absorb preservatives deep into their fibres, their reaction to paint and stain and their tendency to splinter and check as they weather. Whether one is felling woodlot timber or trucking lumber from the local builders' supply, these characteristics are important to the strength, durability and safety of an outdoor play structure. In general, the decay-resistant cedars (white, red and yellow) are the preferred woods for outdoor construction. Douglas fir, western larch and tamarack, though moderately resistant to decay, do not take preservatives well and are prone to

Rope adds a new dimension to play structures that cannot be duplicated with wood. Knotted into climbing ropes, bridges or cargo nets, rope is a flexible material that "gives" under the weight of the child, teaching balance, coordination and the effect of other children's movements on the surface he or she is trying to negotiate.

surface splinters, rendering them inappropriate for play equipment. The pines, on the other hand, absorb preservatives easily and become smoother with wear. The woods to avoid are those that have no natural resistance to decay and are difficult to treat with chemical preservatives, particularly the eastern spruces. When purchasing preserved wood, try to find out what species it is, though this may not be as easy as it sounds: the retailer may not know, and most laymen can't tell. "All preserved wood is not created equal," warns Henke. "Be sure it is not poplar or spruce but red pine. It will last much longer."

These softwoods are suitable for the structural parts of the equipment – the posts, beams, joists and decking. (The terms "hardwood" and "softwood" refer to the lumber from deciduous and coniferous trees, respectively, and are not necessarily related to the physical hardness of the woods. Aspen, for instance, is a hardwood that is softer than Douglas fir, a softwood.) For railings, rungs and sliding poles, choose a strong, dense species that can be shaped and finished smoothly, such as maple, ash, red oak, birch or southern yellow pine. Lumberyards sell dowels made of ramin mahogany, which is as strong as maple, but according to Henke, it will not last under outdoor conditions. Plywood is used for solid railings on high platforms, for enclosing playhouses and for storage cupboards and also as a firm support for sheet metal or Arborite on slide bedways. Special plywoods, such as Duraply, that have a smooth paper coating bonded to one side, make good slides and outdoor tabletops. Buy only exterior-grade plywood, seal the edges with a water repellent, and inspect the panels regularly for wear, especially at the edges where the layers may

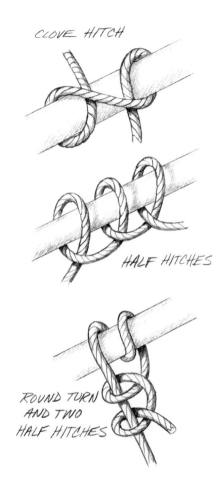

CLOVE HITCH

HALF HITCHES

ROUND TURN AND TWO HALF HITCHES

delaminate and chip.

Whatever the species, buy No. 1 grade, kiln-dried lumber with as few knots and defects as possible in order to minimize twisting and warping. Children's Playgrounds Inc. builds its backyard play frames with 2-by-3 and 2-by-4 yellow pine that appears delicate compared with the robust 6 by 6s used in commercial play equipment, but according to Henke, the smaller dimensions are possible because the wood is dense, extraordinarily clear and

twice as strong as cedar. A few kind words may persuade the local lumber dealer to allow homeowners to sort through the stacks for the clearest boards, but they still have to resort to heavier timbers to counteract the inevitable knots and other wood defects. However, as Al Potvin of Hilan Creative Playstructures in Almonte, Ontario, cautions, "Wood doesn't have to be as massive as in public play equipment. Even the wildest activity in the backyard won't be a quarter as wild as in a schoolyard." Individual plans give lumber specifications, but under most circumstances, 4-by-4 posts, 4-by-6 or 4-by-8 beams, 2-by-6 or 2-by-8 joists and 2-by-4 or 2-by-6 decking can be used, as long as they meet the load requirements of the local building code. It is dangerous to use wood too small for the job and expensive to overbuild: if in doubt, consult a professional builder or engineer.

Rope

The most important rope of my childhood dangled 30 feet from the rafters of my best friend's barn. Lazily snaking back and forth through the mote-specked sunlight, this rajah of ropes was our Tarzan swing, our ladder to the loft and a pendulous weapon to let fly in the face of a real or imagined intruder. Redolent of tropical jungles, motor oil and manure, the earthy hemp of my memories has now been largely replaced by sunflower-yellow synthetics. But whatever the fibre, rope remains a flexible, versatile material that is indispensable to the backyard playspace. Knotted into cargo nets, ladders, railings and chains, ropes push a play structure beyond the squared-off world of posts and beams into a realm where the earth really does move.

Select ropes for play equipment on the

By learning some basic, time-honoured knots, a family can convert a few lengths of sturdy rope into a bridge or a flexible climber. The hitching knot shown here can be used to make railings and to tie off the loose ends of rope used to anchor the tarpaulin roof over a play-frame platform.

A mainstay of macramé crafts, the square knot can be used to create flexible surfaces such as nets and bridges, although the quantity of material required will make tying a plant hanger seem like child's play. The bowline is best for fashioning a secure loop of rope for a swing seat, a set of flexible rings or a Tarzan-swing foothold.

basis of durability, strength, elasticity, weight, ease of maintenance, smoothness to the touch and the lack of propensity for inflicting skin burns. Manila hemp, sisal and jute ropes are all made from plant fibres, but only high-grade manila rope is appropriate for play equipment. Properly called abaca, manila is the strongest natural-fibre rope, roughly equal to the strength of the same diameter of mild steel. Hard, pliant and fibrous yet neither prickly nor slippery to the touch, manila rope has enough body that kids can grip it firmly with their hands or knees, making it a good choice for a knotted rope climber. Furthermore, manila is not susceptible to rot when exposed to the elements, which accounts for its popularity with sailors. Although increasingly hard to find (try farm and marine suppliers) and more expensive than synthetics, natural rope has a unique smell, feel and look that is worth a few extra cents a foot.

Synthetic ropes—nylon, polypropylene and polyethylene—are derived from the chemical by-products of coal and oil. Although strong and smooth to the touch, they tend to be slippery and can cause rope burns, making them ideal for traditional swing supports but not for Tarzan swings or a shinnying rope. Nylon is more than twice as strong as manila and wears two to four times longer, resisting abrasion, mildew and rot. The other synthetic rope commonly available in lumber and hardware outlets is polypropylene, a petroleum derivative. The weakest of the synthetics (½-inch polypropylene supports only 715 pounds compared with nylon's 3,000 pounds), polypropylene is also sensitive to sunlight, fraying and splintering after only a few months in the sun, according to Henke. He recommends polyethylene rope, which is almost as strong as nylon and is immune to the destructive power

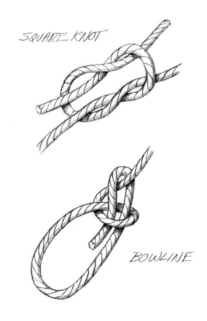

SQUARE KNOT

BOWLINE

of ultraviolet radiation but is generally difficult to buy in Canada. Where polyethylene is unavailable, nylon is the next best choice.

Because synthetics have a relatively low melting point, they must be protected from friction-generated heat, but the constant rubbing produced by the pendulum motion of a swing is hard on any rope. When using rope for suspension, line the loop or eye with a steel thimble that protects the fibres from abrasion. The thimble is much cheaper and easier to replace periodically than is an entire rope ladder. When the rope has to hold a child's weight, it is not safe to create an eye by just lashing or clamping the cut end back against the rope: separate the strands, and splice them securely into the rope to prevent them from unravelling. Melt the cut ends of

synthetic ropes so they will not fray, but make sure the rope itself is not heated so much that it loses its elasticity, breaking instead of stretching when a child climbs on the seat.

Kids need a few unadorned 6- and 10-foot lengths of natural-fibre cord for their cache of loose material, but for most other playspace uses, ropes have to be knotted. With a few twists of the wrist, you can transform coils of rope into ladders, railings, nets and bridges—a skill that Harry Bruce eulogizes in his essay "Love Letter to the Art of Tying Knots": "You can find few things as elegantly unequivocal, beautifully functional and clearly correct as a properly tied knot. In a world that seethes with hopelessly confusing values, a knot is always a simple moral declaration." Whole books are devoted to this time-honoured skill, but there are a few basic knots applicable to playspace construction.

The bowline—Bruce's "King of Knots"—creates a safe loop of any size to use as a swing seat, foothold or climbing ring. Use the clove hitch for railings, fastening the rope alternately to an upper and a lower wooden support. Or make a railing by tying continuous loose half hitches along both the top and the bottom railings, then weaving them together with a third rope crisscrossed between the upper and lower loops. A round turn and several half hitches secure the rope at either end of the railing. The reef, or square, knot makes a good bridge, a project well within the skills of anyone who has done some basic macramé. Be forewarned, though: sorting out the strands for a plant hanger is child's play compared with the rope spaghetti of a 6-foot bridge. Ropes can be woven into a cargo net using eye- and side-splices, although most play-equipment manufacturers sell polyethylene and polypropylene cargo nets as separate components.

Plastics

When Ed Attlebery, vice president of Paris Play Equipment, boasts that kids slide down Paris slides in the Sahara and above the Arctic Circle, he offers the information as proof not of his marketing skill but of the quality of modern plastics. A relatively new addition to play equipment, plastics are hard-wearing and strong, they do not conduct heat and cold as metal does, and they are more resilient than either wood or steel. They are, however, vulnerable to weather: in extreme cold, most plastics become brittle; exposed to the ultraviolet rays of the sun, they deteriorate. When buying plastics for outdoor use, be sure they contain ultraviolet inhibitors and stabilizers and are formulated to withstand low temperatures.

Sheet plastic can be moulded into interesting shapes and the edges can be smoothly rounded, but since this requires special equipment and skills, homeowners will likely purchase rather than make their own plastic play equipment. Slides are the most common plastic component, usually made of polyethylene or, occasionally, fibre-reinforced polyester resin (fibreglass) and sold as tubes, half tubes or long moulded ramps. The big orange polyethylene tubes that slope like giant proboscises from municipal and school play structures were adapted from industry, which uses them to slide raw materials from one end of a factory to another. Although play-equipment manufacturers will sell these slides to homeowners, they are prohibitively expensive for most families, costing around $400 for a 7-foot tunnel. Children's Playgrounds Inc., however, markets a 7-foot slide – designed

specifically for home use – that is moulded from ¼-inch polyethylene and sells for only $135.

Metal

Traditionally, slides have been made of metal, but those who have scorched their thighs on a summer slide are painfully aware of its major drawback. The surface of a metal slide can reach a sizzling 185 degrees F when exposed to the sun, unlike a plastic slide, which stays at body temperature. Trees can shade the searing ramp in summer, but nothing short of a chinook tempers the mitten-stealing cold of a metal slide in winter. Besides being uncomfortable, metal is potentially dangerous: it is a hard and unyielding surface to fall against, and its joints and edges are lethally sharp if not carefully sealed and capped. As a general rule, unless

strength and durability are primary concerns, choose plastic, wood or rope over metal for both safety and year-round play comfort.

Although metal is very durable, corrosion can cut short its life span. Use only galvanized metal parts, hot-dipped in zinc to protect them from rust, or rust-resistant metals such as aluminum and stainless or chrome-plated steel. If recycling metal parts for play equipment, sand off any corrosion, and paint them with an outdoor rust-resistant paint.

Make slide bedways of sheet metal thick enough that it will not tear or puncture – for instance, 22-gauge stainless steel installed over a solid plywood base. Avoid any hazardous sharp edges by sandwiching the sides of the sheet metal under handrails, folding seams to the inside, sealing them

Unlike metal, plastic neither freezes the skin in winter nor sears it in summer, but because the material requires specialized forming equipment, homeowners will likely buy rather than make their own plastic play accessories. Tube slides like the one shown here are prohibitively expensive for most backyards, but several manufacturers sell less costly models for home playgrounds.

securely and rounding the top and bottom edges to prevent kids from scraping themselves when they are getting on or off the slide.

Some manufacturers use metal bars for ladder rungs, monkey bars, sliding poles and chinning and trapeze bars, though a good nonsplintering hardwood dowel sanded to a smooth finish works just as well and is more comfortable in cold weather. File metal bars smooth to remove any burrs that might catch clothing and scrape tender skin. Wherever there is an opening, there is a tiny finger to probe its darkened depths, so be sure all pipe ends are covered, capped or plugged with a dowel or cork. Use bars that are narrow enough for kids to grasp easily – ¾ to 1½ inches in

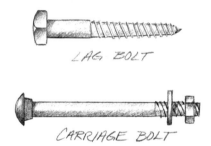

LAG BOLT

CARRIAGE BOLT

diameter – and fasten them to wooden supports with pipe mounting flanges.

Metal chains for swings need to be only half an inch in diameter; 2/0 chain is usually sold for backyard swings, but parents may want to install the heavier-gauge 4/0 specified for standard public swings. In either case, check the bottom and top links periodically, as these are the first to wear. One of the biggest drawbacks of metal chain is pinching: choose a design with small links that will not trap little fingers, or avoid

this hazard altogether either by sheathing chains in narrow garden hose or by substituting ropes or steel cables for the chains.

Use ⅜-inch galvanized steel cable for the cable ride, but where children are likely to touch the cable, use a plastic-coated type (⅜ inch or larger) that will not fray. The needlelike wisps of steel that jut from a worn cable are extremely dangerous, so inspect it regularly to ensure that the coating is intact and that the cable has neither frayed nor rusted. Clamp cable ends tightly, or wrap them and sheathe the joints in garden hose to make them inaccessible. Because cable usually stretches, attach it with a turnbuckle that can be tightened from time to time.

Hardware

Like all metal components, the hardware that fastens play equipment together must be able to withstand outdoor conditions without rusting or staining the wood. Buy only screws, bolts, brackets and specialized hardware made of noncorrodible materials: aluminum, stainless steel and cadmium-

plated, chrome-plated or hot-dipped galvanized metals. Be sure that any hardware subject to wear, such as a swing-bearing hanger, has grease fittings to help eliminate rust and to extend use through the cold months.

Lumber can be fastened with nails, screws or bolts, though nails are only recommended for platform decking and other places where the joints are unlikely to loosen. To fasten flooring, use hot-dipped galvanized spiral nails three times as long as the thickness of the board being fastened but not so long that the tip protrudes. Inset the nail heads ⅛ inch. Screws have better holding power than nails, though they require the extra work of drilling pilot holes and countersinking the heads flush with the surface of the wood. Use flat-head screws that are ⅛ to ¼ inch shorter than the combined thickness of the materials being joined or long enough that the screw penetrates the second piece of wood at least 1½ times the thickness of the first piece. Drill the pilot hole half the length of the threaded part of the screw.

Stronger than either nails or screws,

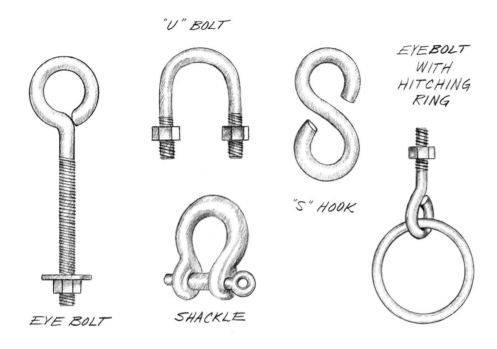

"U" BOLT

EYEBOLT
WITH
HITCHING
RING

"S" HOOK

EYE BOLT

SHACKLE

bolts are heavy-duty fasteners for large-dimension lumber. Because they can be disassembled, bolts are especially good for joints that will need periodic tightening. Carriage bolts, available in $^3/_{16}$-to-$^3/_4$-inch diameters and ½-inch to 10-inch lengths, are best for play equipment because their smooth, round heads will not catch on clothes and skin or poke into children's eyes. Pound the bolt into a prebored hole barely large enough for the shaft, and secure it on the other side with a countersunk washer and nut. Buy bolts exactly the same length as the thickness of the joint, or precut a longer bolt so it is flush with the wood. Al Potvin recommends coating the end of the bolt with a thread-locking compound that increases the amount of torque needed to remove the nut and reduces the chance of the nut loosening through wood shrinkage or vibration. If

one side of a joint is inaccessible, fasten the wood with lag bolts. Drill a pilot hole about half the bolt's diameter, and countersink the head so it does not protrude.

Several play-equipment manufacturers have developed their own fastening systems aimed at making wooden play structures stronger, more resistant to vandals and easier to maintain. For instance, Hilan uses a bracket system fastened with lag and carriage bolts that eliminates periodic tightening, and Children's Playgrounds Inc. installs a tamper-proof nut which can only be loosened with special tools. Both use a "load distributor" designed to take the weight off bolts at the vulnerable joint between the post and deck beam where heavily used structures often start to loosen. Although backyard equipment is subject to neither the stress nor the

vandalism of public play structures, manufacturers are willing to sell these specialized fasteners to individuals on request.

Play-equipment manufacturers are the only source for some specialty hardware, namely the cable ride assembly and the universal swivel joint for multiaxis tire swings. The swivel joint should rotate on roller bearings with grease fittings and have forged eyebolts for the suspension system. Be sure that the wheels or pulleys of cable-ride hardware are enclosed and inaccessible to small fingers and that the unit is designed so it cannot jam or jump off the cable. Play-equipment manufacturers also supply mounting brackets for tires, chinning bars and sliding poles. Although some of these can be homemade with standard off-the-shelf parts, it may be worth paying a few dollars extra for hardware designed specifically for maximum safety and rugged outdoor use.

Finishes

Because outdoor play equipment has to survive children's scuffling feet in addition to the driving rain, blazing sun and bitter cold of this northern climate, its finish has to be both durable and safe, containing no poisonous compounds and offering a nonslip surface for kids to play on. Wood can be finished in at least three different ways, depending on its exposure and on family preferences. Naturally decay-resistant wood such as cedar needs no finish at all—unprotected, it bleaches to a soft barn-board grey with a silvery sheen—but any species other than cedar, cypress or redwood that is in constant contact with soil needs to be treated with a preservative finish, either factory-injected CCA or copper naphthenate, both of which impart a greenish tinge to the wood.

Consider safety when choosing and using hardware in play-equipment construction. Be sure it is sturdy enough for the job and install it securely, clinching S-hooks tightly and deforming the threads on bolts so the nuts cannot work loose. Avoid protruding hazards by countersinking the nuts and cutting the threaded end of exposed bolts flush with the wood.

Protect structural parts that are only intermittently damp with a clear, water-repellent sealer to prevent decay and to keep wood from cupping. To protect concealed surfaces, brush the sealer liberally on all wood members before fastening them together.

Clear sealers maintain wood almost in its original condition, but some people prefer to add a little colour by painting or staining the play equipment. Paint coats the surface of the wood and tends to peel as it weathers; stain soaks into the wood fibres and wears away unobtrusively with time. The depth of colour depends on the kind of stain: semi-transparent stains tint the wood without hiding the grain, but solid, heavy-bodied stains completely obscure the tone and texture of the material underneath. Before brushing on the stain, let the wood dry thoroughly so it is able to absorb the pigment. The stain can be applied over or under a sealer or mixed half-and-half with a water repellent, depending on the product. Although a stained surface does not have to be scraped and sanded before it is refinished, the wood will likely have to be recoated every few years.

When it comes to stains, consumers usually get what they pay for. Good-quality materials last longer, and the price of the stain is a pittance compared with the investment in time it takes to apply it. It is also wise to read labels carefully: some outdoor stains contain pesticides to help protect wood against decay-promoting organisms, so avoid those that promise to keep termites, fungi or bacteria at bay. And be sure the decorative or protective finishes used on play structures do not contain lead, antimony, arsenic, cadmium, selenium, barium or mercury.

To obtain poison-free moisture protection, a family can make its own wood sealer. The recipe below, developed by the U.S. Forest Service Forest Products Laboratory in Madison, Wisconsin, uses paraffin wax to repel moisture, linseed oil as a drying agent and turpentine as a solvent. In laboratory tests, window frames treated with this mixture showed no signs of decay even after 20 years, while untreated frames rotted within six. The formula extends the longevity of wood not in contact with the ground, but like all wood sealers, it has to be reapplied every few years to maintain the protection. Its main drawback is that it leaves a thin, waxy film on the wood which may prevent proper adhesion if another type of stain is applied later.

If mould or mildew appears on the wood, clean it off with a chlorine-bleach solution, let the wood dry for a few days, then recoat with the water repellent. If the mould recurs within a short time, look for an underlying cause – surrounding soil may need to be sloped or the wood reshaped to drain water more effectively.

Water-Repellent Finish

1 oz. paraffin wax
1½ cups boiled linseed oil
Solvent to make 1 gallon (room
  temperature, 60 to 80 degrees F)

Melt the paraffin wax in the top of a double boiler. Slowly pour the melted paraffin into the solvent, stirring vigorously. When they are well mixed, add the linseed oil and continue to stir until the mixture is uniform. This water-repellent finish can become a preservative by adding 1¾ cups copper naphthenate after the linseed oil. It can also be made into a stain by adding tints available from a paint store: about 6 ounces each of burnt sienna and raw umber produces an acceptable cedar-brown stain. Be sure to make enough stain to do the whole structure at once to prevent variations in colour. To keep the pigment in suspension, add half an ounce of zinc stearate (available from drugstores) to each gallon of stain.

Because the solutions are volatile and flammable, the Forest Products Laboratory recommends doing all the mixing outdoors. Wear gloves, avoid breathing the vapours, do not expose the mixture to flame or sparks, and keep the liquid away from the eyes and face. Before construction, dunk precut pieces of wood in a shallow trough containing sealer, or apply the sealer with a brush, flowing the mixture on heavily so it seeps into joints and the end grain of the wood. The ingredients in this homemade water repellent may separate if it cools. To redissolve, just warm the mixture to room temperature and stir.

Ground Covers

Today's parents would never consider paving their children's private playspace with asphalt or concrete (the original playground surfacing materials), yet the hard-packed earth uncovered where grass wears away is almost as dangerous – a child can sustain a concussion if he falls on packed earth from a height of only 2 feet. Select the ground cover around the playhouse, sandbox and loose material on the basis of personal preference, cost, ease of maintenance, durability and play value, but make safety the priority in choosing the surface under active play equipment. After good equipment design, a resilient ground cover is the second line of defence in preventing play injuries. If a swing chain breaks or children slip off a platform, the material they fall on may make the difference between a goose egg and a blow to the head that sends them to the hospital. In an effort to unearth

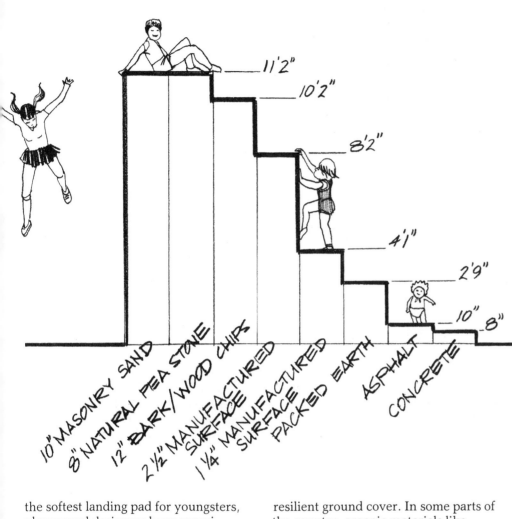

10' MASONRY SAND — 11'2"

8' NATURAL PEA STONE — 10'2"

12" BARK/WOOD CHIPS — 8'2"

2½" MANUFACTURED SURFACE — 4'1"

1¼" MANUFACTURED SURFACE — 2'9"

PACKED EARTH — 10"

ASPHALT — 8"

CONCRETE

as bacteria and fungi, insects and even small rodents.

An occasional visiting vole may be preferable, however, to the animals that sand attracts. The family feline considers a sand ground cover its own personal litter box, a problem that has no easy solution. Even disposing of the cat will not dissuade the neighbours' pets from wandering over to use the facilities. There is also the danger in large families that toddlers will play in the sand under, say, a jungle gym while older siblings romp boisterously overhead. Unwashed pit-run sand contains a range of particle sizes, and after a few rainfalls, the small grains roll between the large ones, settling to the consistency of hard-packed earth. Even masonry sand, which is composed of relatively uniform particles that are not easily compacted, has to be raked regularly to keep the material loose and resilient.

Sand and pea stone have a comparable cushioning capacity, and roughly a foot of either one will protect kids from falls of up to 12 feet. Pea stone is a naturally occurring gravel with particles uniformly about ¼ inch in diameter. Because all the stones are the same size, they do not interlock and compact, unlike unsized crushed gravel that eventually settles to one solid mass. Although pea stone is quite a bit more expensive than sand, it will not attract cats, dogs or shovel-wielding small fry. For safety, durability and weather resistance, pea stone is the best overall resilient ground cover, but even it must be raked regularly to prevent it from compacting as dirt accumulates between the tiny crevices.

Extend the ground cover at least 6 feet in all directions from the perimeter of fixed play equipment, and contain it within borders to prevent it from being scattered throughout the lawn. In public

Surfaces vary in their ability to cushion falls. For instance, a child could be hurt falling from an 8-inch height onto concrete but can safely fall as far as 11 feet onto 10 inches of masonry sand. Whatever the ground cover material, it should extend at least 6 feet in all directions from the edge of a play frame.

the softest landing pad for youngsters, playground designers have experimented with a bizarre array of materials, from cocoa shells and grape seeds to rice hulls and pea stone. Fortunately, the best options are neither expensive nor exotic, though they do require the most maintenance.

For a safe surface, dig up the sod under active play equipment and replace it with one of four options: wood chips, sand, pea stone or a manufactured resilient ground cover. In some parts of the country, organic materials like tanbark and wood chips are cheap and available, but although very resilient, they have several disadvantages. Wood chips swell when they get wet, displacing the air trapped between fragments that gives them their cushioning capacity. Dampness leads to decay, and the ground cover gradually compacts as it decomposes. Organic materials harbour microorganisms such

Recycled tires, a staple of community-built public playgrounds, are also appropriate for home play equipment. Even bald tires make good swing seats and sand cranes, though steel-reinforced models should be scrutinized to ensure that no metal strands protrude from the rubber casing.

playgrounds, the ground cover should also extend 6 feet beyond the maximum extension of the swings, but at home, a 20-by-60-inch swath under the swing's path is sufficient. The continual landing of small feet kicks the ground cover away from the base of slides, sliding poles and swings, thinning it dangerously. For these vulnerable spots, manufactured ground covers are ideal, though they are too expensive for large areas. Water-permeable and designed to withstand both the heat and cold of the outdoors, these resilient squares are anchored permanently in place. They are especially useful under swings, where kids' dragging feet otherwise wear ruts that become mud holes after a rain. Available as tiles or interlocking pavers, they require some subsurface preparation; set them just below grass level where they will be unobtrusive and will not interfere with the lawn mower.

Grass is the best surface for the rest of the playspace, especially in the quiet play areas near the loose material and playhouse. Within a very short time, however, kids' feet can wear paths across the lawn and pummel delicate green blades into a wasteland. Consider planting tougher varieties in play zones: wide-leaved, thick-stemmed grasses are not as soft on the feet, but they wear better, and the creeping varieties rejuvenate better than the tussock-forming types. Or drastically reduce wear and tear on plant life by designing brick or gravel paths for high-traffic areas or by laying down stepping stones embedded just below grass level for easy mowing. Where traffic is especially low, plant interesting flowering ground covers such as myrtle, creeping thyme, sedum or moss.

Bricks are excellent low-maintenance materials for paths, though they are expensive and can be abrasive if a triker takes a spill. Install them carefully on a well-prepared subsurface so they drain properly and don't heave with the seasons—loose or uneven bricks are an annoyance and a hazard. Asphalt is also a good material for wheeled-vehicle paths and court games or as a base for shallow pools and play streams. Although not slippery when wet, it can be very hot in summer, making a yard uncomfortable if much of the dark surface is exposed to the sun. Concrete is more durable than asphalt, but unless it is given a textured surface, it can be dangerous in water-play areas, since it is slippery when wet or when covered with sand.

Recycled Materials

Many of the community playgrounds of the 1960s were built with reclaimed materials: worn tires, cast-off utility poles, cable spools, railway ties, conveyor belts and even dead trees. The motivation was based not only on finances but on the belief that citizens could lighten civilization's load on the environment by recycling some of its useful garbage. The principle is still sound, but homeowners who opt for salvaged materials must exercise caution. Initially cheap or even free, secondhand goods have a hidden cost, usually exacted in increased labour for transportation and preparation. Often a design has to be reworked to fit the freebies, and more importantly, the materials may already be well used, increasing the maintenance and shortening the life span of the equipment. But if the materials are in good condition and the family has the time and inclination to clean them up for construction – to remove nails, refinish rusted metal and chip mortar off reclaimed bricks – recycling does indeed lower the cost of the backyard playspace significantly. If using recycled wood or rope, be sure it is sound, with no dark fibres or soft spots that indicate decay, and beware of materials such as railway ties and telephone poles that may have been treated with poisonous pesticides.

The most common recycled material in playgrounds is tires. In an attempt to use up at least a fraction of the half-billion discarded tires heaped in dumps and garages around North America, tires were suspended as swings, stuck in the ground as tunnels and sandboxes, fastened together into lumpy cargo nets and tacked to poles to make climbers. One Japanese playground, the Rokugo Tire Park in Tokyo, was constructed with more than 3,500 tires, several hundred of which were joined to form a giant dragon that towers above children's heads. Recycling tires for play gradually spread from community-built playgrounds to municipal and school playgrounds, but ironically, the salvage

rationale was lost in the transition. None of the tires used on Canadian playgrounds today has ever kissed pavement: they are brand-new, often with factory defects that keep them off the roads but do not affect their safety as play equipment.

New tires may be more convenient for public playgrounds, but there is no reason homeowners can't use the good-as-new tires that have been languishing in the shed since the VW Bug expired. Even blowouts can be recycled, provided the rest of the tire still has reasonably good tread – bury the damaged portion below grade to create stepping-stones or tunnel-climbers. Kids need some tread on climbing tires for hand- and footholds, but bald tires can be recycled by cutting them into belt- or hammock-style swing seats. Steel-reinforced tires are the only type that

may not be acceptable for play equipment: be sure that the tire still has enough tread that no metal strands protrude from the casing.

Although tires are too unrefined for some backyards, they are relatively clean once the road dirt is washed off. They also trap rainwater, so drill one or two drain holes in the bottom of the tire with a 1-inch auger (a high-speed drill bit stretches and tears the rubber rather than cutting a clean hole). Suspend tires with rope, cable or chain, and fasten them to posts or to each other, but always insert an internal support – blocks of wood or a metal plate available from play-equipment manufacturers – so the tire does not tear at its fastener or cave in under the children's weight. Al Potvin recommends installing side-mounted tire climbers with a ¼-by-4-inch steel reinforcing spine that covers at least a third of the tire's circumference, and he includes three "spreaders" in a horizontal tire swing to keep the tire carcass from collapsing.

Bolting tires together tread-to-tread to create bridges or cargo nets is a difficult, time-consuming job best done with a pair of helping hands. Although the tires may be free, the hardware is expensive – each joint needs a ½-inch-diameter carriage bolt, two nuts, two hardwood blocks, washers and a ratchet extension or deep-well socket wrench to reach the nuts.

Tires can also be used without hardware. For kids strong enough to manoeuvre them without getting hurt, they make good loose material, especially in an adventure play area. Similarly, inner tubes, sometimes available at little cost from local gas stations and trucking companies, make cozy seats and effective sleds for snow berms in winter and water slides in summer.

Tires make good flexible climbers, but unless they are securely fastened, they will sag and collapse. Bolt each tire to a wooden frame using a large metal washer or a block of hardwood to distribute the load on the rubber.

6

Nuts and Bolts

Playspace plans

For a playground to succeed, its ultimate users must be its builders.

Paul Hogan

In their 1909 textbook on play, Arthur and Lorna Leland wrote of homemade equipment: "We consider that such playgrounds will be much more valuable than the ready-made ones, so that if the apparatus were more expensive when made by the children, we should still advise that they make it and receive the training it would give. The same principle also applies to the landscape gardening of playgrounds, which should be done by the children as much as possible. . . . Let the children make the apparatus and then have the fathers and big brothers come to put it up, and the mothers can come and furnish the luncheon." The quaint sexism of their remarks aside, the Lelands were ahead of their time in suggesting that parents involve their kids. Unlike most of their contemporaries, they understood that when one is building a playground, just as when one is playing, the process is as important as the product.

The plans in the following pages are intentionally simple to encourage parents to include their children in the construction as well as in the design of the backyard playspace. The chapter begins with some building basics – how to shape, join and anchor wooden play structures – followed by detailed plans for the equipment discussed in Chapters 2 and 3. Wherever possible, options are included to stimulate the family to create its own distinctive playthings, custom-fitted to its site and circumstances.

The designs are based on discussions with play consultants and equipment manufacturers, but since there are no mandatory standards for home playground construction, prefabricated equipment may not always conform to these specifications. The dimensions suggested for certain age groups are intended as guidelines only – as any parent who has ever visited a classroom knows, age and size are not necessarily related. The recommended step height for a 6-year-old may be dangerously high for a Lilliputian offspring and no challenge at all for a Brobdingnagian one. Parents are advised to use their own judgment to adapt the information to their children's needs.

The plans are based on the use of clear No. 1 cedar as the building material, so be sure to recalculate spans when substituting other species or grades of lumber. Although based on common construction practices, the plans may have to be adjusted to meet local conditions or codes. If in doubt about any of the details shown, consult a construction or playspace specialist.

Foundations

"Flying the moon" was one of the rites of passage at the elementary school I attended. When the teachers were safely out of sight, we would coax a fresh-faced grade 1 student, eager to join our gang, to prove his mettle by standing up on the swing and pumping for all he was worth until the front right leg of the metal frame began to heave. We cheered and egged him on until the leg reared above the grass, hoisting high the round concrete collar that was supposed to anchor the swing to the ground. Although it never actually tipped over, the frame would lean steeply into the arc of the swing, teeter precariously on three legs, then thump back to earth with a bone-jarring shudder that reduced the young swinger to screams and tears.

The foundation under that swing frame was clearly inadequate, but although swings and cable rides need an anchoring system designed to withstand extreme lateral forces, not all play equipment is subjected to such stress. Depending on their design and local soil

Free-floating structures, **left**, rest on the surface of the soil, though the bottom plate is often buried under the ground cover. This system is appropriate for equipment such as playhouses and platform climbers that are not subject to racking and that have a square, solid base. Lightweight structures can be anchored with hardwood stakes, **right**, provided there is adequate horizontal and diagonal bracing to keep the unit from tipping.

In the absence of established play-equipment standards, parents must rely on common construction practices and their own good judgment of their children's needs and abilities when designing and building backyard playground structures, **previous page**.

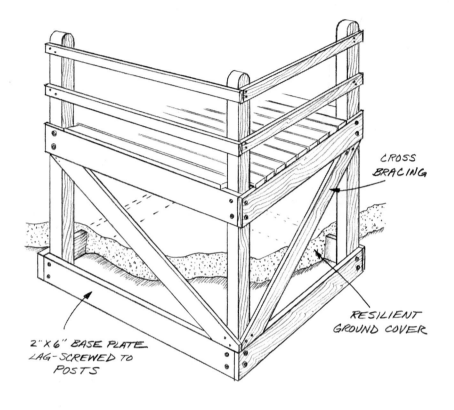

CROSS BRACING

RESILIENT GROUND COVER

2"X 6" BASE PLATE LAG-SCREWED TO POSTS

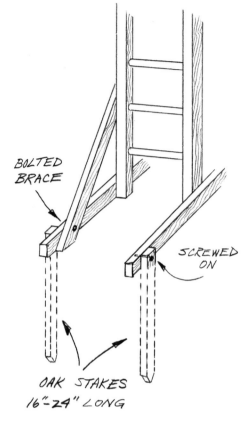

BOLTED BRACE

SCREWED ON

OAK STAKES 16"-24" LONG

and weather conditions, constructed play components can be free-floating or secured to the ground with stakes, buried posts or concrete foundations. Whatever the system, it must support the weight of the structure as well as the weight and motion of boisterous kids at play—not only the lightweight 3-year-old running around the backyard now but the strapping 12-year-old she will soon become, throwing all her weight into making that rope swing "fly the moon."

Finnskoga Play Systems Inc. of Winnipeg, Manitoba, installs only free-floating play equipment, with no anchoring system at all. According to

owner Richard Gillespie, this approach makes particular sense in Manitoba where the subsoil is a rich clay gumbo that heaves massively with the freeze-thaw cycle, lifting even the deepest concrete foundations. A structure resting on the surface of such soil moves as a unit, so it is less likely to be pushed out of square. Freestanding structures are also easy to relocate within the playspace or to dismantle if the family moves. However, only equipment that is not subjected to racking—climbers, sandboxes, playhouses, slides—can safely free-float, and even it must have either a solid, square base at least as

wide as the structure is tall or a system of braces to prevent the structure from tipping. Chipmunk play equipment, a series of climber-playhouses designed for preschoolers by Hilan Creative Playstructures, is also free-floating, its broad base and low height providing adequate stability. Before allowing kids to play on it, test free-floating equipment to make absolutely sure it will not tip; if in doubt about the stability of a design, ask an engineer for advice.

Children's Playgrounds Inc. anchors its backyard equipment with stout oak stakes, 16 to 24 inches long, driven into the ground and screwed to each corner

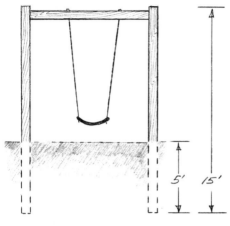

HALF OF EXPOSED
UPRIGHT IS BURIED
(MINIMUM 4')

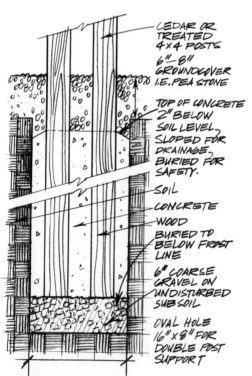

CEDAR OR
TREATED
4×4 POSTS

6"-8"
GROUNDCOVER
I.E. PEA STONE

TOP OF CONCRETE
2" BELOW
SOIL LEVEL,
SLOPED FOR
DRAINAGE,
BURIED FOR
SAFETY.

SOIL

CONCRETE

WOOD
BURIED TO
BELOW FROST
LINE

6" COARSE
GRAVEL ON
UNDISTURBED
SUBSOIL

OVAL HOLE
16"×8" FOR
DOUBLE POST
SUPPORT

of the play structure. Because there are no holes to dig and no concrete to pour, installation takes only a few hours. According to Rick Henke, the play equipment is secure because the horizontal ground supports, tied to the uprights with diagonal bracing, are as long as the structure is tall.

Only Children's Playgrounds' backyard models, constructed of lightweight 2-by-3 lumber, are anchored with stakes; their public playground designs, built with 6-by-6 timbers, are supported by foundations. If equipment is heavily built (monkey bars, climbers) or is subjected to severe lateral stress (swings, cable rides), it should be firmly anchored below grade, with concrete piers or wooden posts that extend deep enough to stabilize the structure. Frost penetrates only 1 or 2 feet into the ground in the warmer parts of this country but as deep as 6 feet in some locales, so consult the local building inspector to find out how deeply play-equipment foundations must be sunk to give them immunity from the repeated freezing and thawing of the soil. Dig the holes by hand or with a posthole digger — an 8-inch-diameter hole is adequate for 4-by-4 posts, expanded to 12 inches for 6 by 6s — but keep the sides as straight as possible. The bottom of the hole should be undisturbed soil covered with 6 inches of coarse gravel for stability and drainage. A poured footing is necessary only in unstable soil.

Most manufacturers anchor play equipment simply by sinking the wooden uprights deeply into the soil. To avoid decay, the uprights must be naturally rot-resistant, commercially preserved with inorganic arsenicals or treated with three or four coats of copper naphthenate (treat only the wood that will be in contact with the soil). Do not install posts in frozen or partly drained

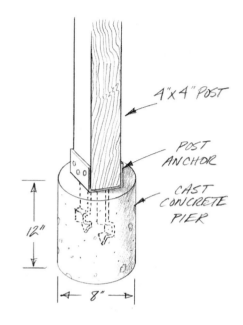

4"×4" POST

POST
ANCHOR

CAST
CONCRETE
PIER

12"

8"

soil or when temperatures are below freezing, since they may settle when the ground thaws or dries. Stand each post in its hole, rocking it slightly to seat it firmly. Make sure it is plumb and square, then secure it with temporary diagonal braces that are sturdy enough to withstand some jostling.

To stabilize the posts, fill the holes with concrete or tamped earth. The drawback to concrete is that the wood expands as it absorbs moisture from the freshly poured mix, then shrinks after the concrete dries and becomes slightly loose in its concrete collar. According to Henke, a 6 by 6 shrinks enough to leave a ⅛-inch space between the wood and the concrete, a potential water trap and cause of decay if the post sits on a footing instead of on free-draining gravel. An alternative is to backfill the hole with earth, a few shovelfuls at a time tamped solid with a 2 by 2 or a narrow pole cut flat on the bottom — a

If equipment is built with heavy lumber or is subjected to severe lateral stress, it should be anchored by extending the posts below grade to the frost line. For swing and cable-ride frames, **top left**, bury one-third of the posts. Stabilize them with well-tamped earth or concrete, **bottom left**, that is rounded on top so water drains away from the wood and that is low enough to be buried by the ground cover. Wooden uprights can also be fastened to concrete piers with post anchors, **right**, a system most appropriate for playhouses.

Post-and-beam construction is ideal for play structures because the airy, boxy shapes make it easy to add handrails and to close in cozy playhouse spaces, **right**. In general, the posts and beams are fastened together with carriage bolts; countersink the nut to avoid a protruding hazard. Because the end grain has little holding capacity, however, butt joints should be fastened with metal connectors, **left**.

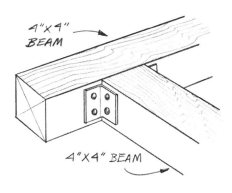

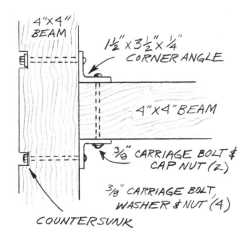

wide tamper spreads the force out too much and does not compact the earth as effectively. Continue tamping small amounts of earth into the hole until it is filled and the post is rigidly in place. Be sure the soil contains no wood scraps or large roots that will decay and compromise the stability of the backfill.

Most play-equipment manufacturers stabilize posts with concrete. Brace the post well, then pour the concrete around its base, sloping the top surface to encourage water to drain away from the wood. Leave the surface of the concrete just below soil level so it can be well buried under a resilient ground cover;

exposed concrete is a tripping hazard and a dangerous surface to land on if a child falls. After pouring the concrete, recheck the posts for plumb, let the mix set overnight, then cut the uprights to the required height, using a line level to determine the exact height.

For well-braced play frames and playhouses (though not for swings), an alternative to burying posts deeply below grade is fastening them to galvanized-metal post anchors set in concrete piers that extend below the frost line. Pier foundations keep wood out of contact with damp soil, minimizing decay; however, it is best to treat any wood in contact with the ground cover. If the soil is firm enough, use the hole itself as a form for the concrete pier; otherwise, pour the concrete into a homemade wooden form or a fibre tube that is plumb and secured in well-tamped earth. In unstable soils, add a 12-by-12-inch concrete footing, 6 to 8 inches deep, under the pier. The top edge of the pier should be about 2 inches below the soil level and 8 to 10 inches below the ground cover. While the concrete is still malleable, insert the post anchor and taper the tops of the piers so water will not pool at the base of the wooden post. After the concrete sets, seat each post in its anchor and fasten securely. Whether concrete is used in a pier or as a stabilizer for wooden posts, be sure it is completely cured before kids use the play equipment.

Wood Construction

Post-and-beam construction is a strong, time-honoured method of joining wood and is the standard for commercial wooden play equipment. Built with 4-by-4 or 6-by-6 timbers that span relatively large distances and form airy, boxy shapes, post-and-beam play structures are ideal for suspending

swings or supporting multilevel platforms. The straight lines and right angles created by such a framework make it easy to add guardrails to the platforms, to make ladders on the sides or to build a wall between uprights. And if half the lengths of the uprights are buried, a post-and-beam frame is structurally strong enough to resist a swing's lateral pressures.

The posts, beams and decking must be able to support the dead load (the weight of the structure itself) and the live load (kids, toys, snow, water and wind). Instead of trying to calculate the maximum load, use the building-code span tables, which list the sizes of lumber that keep the structure safely within recommended load allowances in residential construction (based on 40 pounds/square foot live load and 10 p.s.f. dead load). The aim is to use lumber which supports anticipated live and dead loads but which is not any bigger or more expensive than necessary. The size of lumber depends on the species of wood used, the gap it bridges and the distance between members. In general, the heavier the beam, the greater the distance it can span and the farther apart the posts can be set. For instance, a 4-by-6 cedar beam on edge spans up to 6 feet, a 4 by 8 spans 8 feet, and a 4 by 10 spans 10 feet. It may be cheaper to install a central post to break a 10-foot reach into two 5-foot spans that can be bridged with 4 by 6s than to pay for a 4-by-10 beam. If expanding or redesigning the structures in any of the following plans, consult building-code span tables to ensure that the structure is sound.

If necessary, minimize sway and keep the post-and-beam structure in square with diagonal cross braces. These triangles are the strongest structural unit, retaining their shape under stress because the three sides push against each other – unlike a square, which collapses if pressure is applied to one side. Avoid creating traps for a child's head, hands or feet by attaching each end of the brace at least 2 feet from the post-and-beam joint. Hold or tack-nail the brace at a 45-degree angle to the upright, mark it, then cut the brace to fit, and bolt it in place. It is not necessary to notch the beam and post for the brace. Solid bracing – plywood, diagonal boards – eliminates the hazards and can also enclose small nooks for dramatic play.

Posts and beams can be connected by

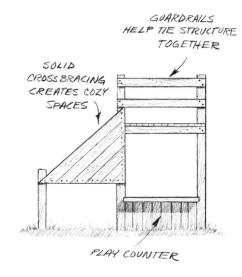

SOLID CROSS BRACING CREATES COZY SPACES

GUARDRAILS HELP TIE STRUCTURE TOGETHER

PLAY COUNTER

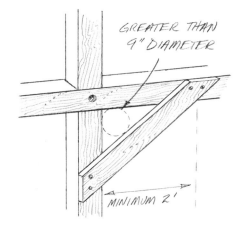

GREATER THAN 9" DIAMETER

MINIMUM 2'

toe-nailing or spiking, but bolting them together creates a stronger, more reliable joint. The size and number of bolts required depend on the load and the thickness of the joint. In general, a single ¼-inch bolt is adequate for a 2-inch-thick joint; wood that is 3 or 4 inches thick needs two ¼-inch bolts. Connect lumber that is 6 or more inches thick with at least three ⅜-inch bolts, which should be adequate for most backyard constructions. Drill the hole barely large enough for the bolt – it should have to be tapped through with a hammer. Do not drill holes too close to the outside edges of the wood, or it may split: position bolts no closer to the top of a beam or a post than four times the bolt's diameter and not within 1½ diameters of the side of the beam or post.

Wherever possible, bolt structural members together, notching the wood so that the joint fits tightly. Because physical play equipment is subject to many different stresses, avoid the metal post caps and joist hangers commonly used in house construction. Butt joints between beams cannot be secured by nailing into the end grain, which has little holding capacity. Instead, fasten this type of joint with angle irons bolted to both beams. Be sure they and other types of metal connectors are sturdy enough for the job, and use bolts, not nails, to fasten them to the wood.

Post-and-beam construction lends itself well to the use of cantilevers, those projecting beams that seem to extend unsupported into midair but are actually counterbalanced by weights on the opposite end. Cantilevers are especially practical for play equipment because a platform surface can be enlarged – adding a balcony to a play frame, for example – without increasing the number of uprights. They can also extend a potentially hazardous part of the equipment, such as monkey bars or a swing, away from the main structure so a child is less likely to bump into a supporting post if she falls. A good rule of thumb is to cantilever a beam beyond its supporting post up to one half its allowable span. Keep the beam short and well braced, though, if it is to support a swing or any other accessory liable to

Bracing helps stabilize post-and-beam structures, reducing sway and keeping them in square. Where possible, incorporate the bracing into the play-frame design as railings, playhouse walls or play counters, **top**. The space between the brace, the post and the beam should accommodate a circle greater than 9 inches in diameter, **bottom**, so that it cannot become a head trap for young children.

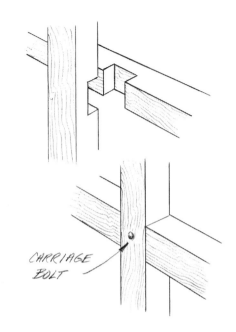

Posts and beams can be notched for a more secure fit, **left**, but all joints should be fastened with carriage bolts since their rounded heads will not snag kids' clothes or skin. Before assembling the play structure, sand the wood and round all exposed edges to soften the effect of the inevitable bumps and falls and to reduce the likelihood of splinters developing as the wood weathers. Slope the tops of posts so they shed rainwater, **right**.

CARRIAGE BOLT

put it under the combined stresses of kids' weight and movement.

Play-frame platforms are created by bridging beams with deck boards. Again, consider spans carefully: cedar 2 by 3s and 2 by 4s span a maximum of 42 inches, so reduce larger gaps between beams by adding intermediary joists. To build a safe, solid deck that is not springy, use 2 by 4s or 2 by 6s screwed or nailed into 2-by-8 beams on 32-inch centres, but leave at least a ⅛-inch space between deck boards to allow rainwater to drain off the platform quickly. Even a kiln-dried 2 by 6 may shrink ⅛ inch, making the ultimate gap ¼ inch. Be careful to avoid gaps greater than half an inch. If using nails, reduce the chance of splitting the board by flattening the tips slightly before driving them into the wood. Notch boards around posts if required, and trim irregular ends by snapping a chalk line along the edge of the finished deck and cutting it

straight with a saw. To protect the end grain of deck boards from rain and to prevent splintering, add edge nosing to the perimeter.

Whatever the fastening system, install hardware in a way that leaves a smooth surface with no points or sharp edges to snag kids' clothes or scratch their skin. Carriage bolts are preferred for post-and-beam connections because of their rounded heads; all other bolts, screws or nails should have a dome head or be countersunk or inset. If kids are likely to come into contact with a bolt, cut the threaded end until it projects beyond the wood no more than half the diameter of the bolt. Do not cut the ends of eyebolts on swings and cable rides – they are inaccessible to kids – but deform the thread with a cold chisel so the nuts cannot work loose. Be sure the sharp ends of nails and screws do not project through the wood, and countersink all bolt ends or cover them with smooth-finished cap nuts. Avoid drilling any more holes in structural members than is absolutely necessary, but prebore all the wood for nails, screws and bolts to minimize splitting.

Before assembling the parts, sand the wood smooth on all sides, and round the corners. The square edges of a 2 by 4 or 4 by 4 are not sharp to the touch, but they can deal a nasty blow if a child falls against them; furthermore, a square edge is more likely to develop splinters as the wood weathers. Round all exposed wood in the play structure with a jack plane or router to a minimum radius of ⅜ inch (some commercial play equipment is softened to a generous ¾-inch radius). Slope the tops of exposed posts to shed rainwater.

To connect the posts and beams, set the beam on the post and clamp or tack-nail it, then counterbore for the washers and nuts. Bore holes for the carriage

bolts, and cut them with a hacksaw if the threads will protrude when the lumber is bolted together. When the structure is finally fastened, secure the nut firmly to the bolt with thread-locking compound. For greater strength, notch the posts and beams, cutting the sides of the notch with a handsaw and splitting out the unwanted wood with a chisel.

To build low walls and sand gardens with 4 by 4s or 6 by 6s, stack the timbers so the joints are staggered, and fasten them with long spikes. Use 2 by 4s and standard house-framing techniques to frame in the sides of a play frame or to build a playhouse or storage cupboard.

Maintenance

This summer, after a year of fund-raising by parents and students and hefty donations from Wintario, the school board and the municipality, our local country school bought $10,000 worth of brand-new play equipment. This was the second time in less than a decade that the schoolyard was dug up to erect a play structure for the kids. Several years before, exchange students from Sri Lanka built an exciting creative playground using recycled tires and poles cut from

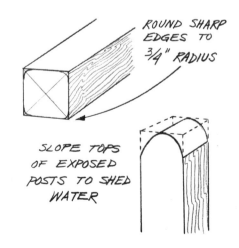

ROUND SHARP EDGES TO ¾" RADIUS

SLOPE TOPS OF EXPOSED POSTS TO SHED WATER

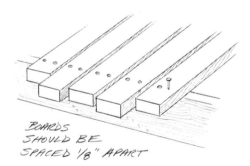

BOARDS
SHOULD BE
SPACED 1/8" APART

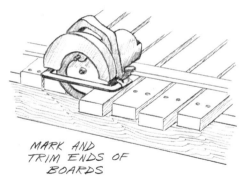

MARK AND
TRIM ENDS OF
BOARDS

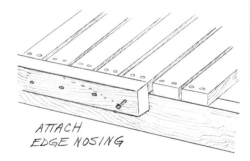

ATTACH
EDGE NOSING

Exposure to water causes wood to decay, but good construction practices can help preserve an outdoor play structure. Space decking so that rain drains quickly, **left**, mark and trim ends of boards, **centre**, and attach an edge nosing to cover the vulnerable end grain of the wood, **right**.

township woodlots. The kids loved the log cabin and tire climbers, but after years of steady use – and neglect – they were no longer safe and could not be repaired. The wood and rubber are now gone, and when buying replacement equipment, parents and school officials chose bright metal posts and chains instead of wood. Unfortunately, they failed to recognize that the short life span of the previous play structure was the fault not of the material but of the way it was constructed and the failure to maintain it properly. Like all constructions that are exposed to hard wear and weather, play equipment requires regular maintenance. Given a little loving attention, the wooden playhouses, blocks, swings and climbers detailed in this chapter will survive through more than one childhood.

Maintenance begins as soon as the equipment is erected. Before the kids scramble onto their new playthings, conduct a final inspection to make sure that recommended dimensions, clearances and safety precautions have been met. Feel the surfaces for sharp edges, splinters and protrusions, test the structure for stability, and look for faults that could cause injury or rapid deterioration. Make sure that all hooks

are clinched, all bolts tightened, peened or locked, all tubing enclosed and all moving parts properly aligned.

Once the play equipment passes muster and the kids are given free rein to enjoy the fruits of the family's labours, inspect it regularly and frequently – daily or weekly – for the first month or so. Design defects or problems show up quickly as the kids give the constructions a good workout. In fact, kids are the frontline maintenance inspectors: emphasize the importance of keeping the equipment in top shape, and encourage them to report loose bolts, splinters or broken parts immediately. It takes only a few minutes to tighten a nut or dab some extra moisture repellent on that bare spot, but if left uncorrected, those minor problems can cause major damage.

After this initial break-in period, a regular maintenance check every few months – at least twice a year – should be enough to spot the cracked ladder rungs, worn chain links and heaved footings that can cause accidents. Inspect all constructed components closely, checking wood for warps, checks, splits, splinters and worn finish. Check hardware for parts that are missing, bent, broken, loose or corroded.

Examine moving components for worn bearings or broken safety covers, and lubricate them if necessary. If using S-hooks to suspend swings, inspect them every couple of weeks. Make sure that the ground cover is loose and even and that it isn't kicked away from the hardwear areas under sliding poles, slide exits and swings. (See Maintenance Checklist on page 140.)

There is a Chinese proverb that says a person's house isn't finished until he dies; likewise, a playspace isn't finished until the kids leave home. Watching the kids at play, parents will discover new ways to expand and improve their handiwork, and the kids can be counted on to produce an unending stream of ideas and demands guaranteed to keep the playspace evolving. At our own house, several play structures have come and gone, but I can't recall one that was ever truly finished: they were either abandoned in mid-evolution as the kids grew into new interests or dismantled to create new and better constructions. And while that approach may run counter to the goal-oriented North American way of life, it is consistent with the true nature of play. May your backyard playspace always be in progress and never, ever be finished.

Swings

Suspension:

- The maximum drop height at 60 degrees from the vertical should be 6 feet.
- Pinch S-hooks closed.
- Choose handgrips that are ½ to 1 inch in diameter.
- Sheathe chain links, or buy them fine enough that kids can't poke their fingers through.
- On single-axis swings, install bolts so the eye is open in the direction of movement, and use a hitching ring to reduce wear on the S-hook; deform the bolt threads with a cold chisel so the nut cannot work loose.
- For stability, install the eyebolts slightly farther apart than the width of the seat.

Clearance:

- 30 inches or more between swings and between support frame and swing.
- At least 6 feet between the maximum extension of a multiaxis swing seat and any obstacles.

Design the swing support frame as an extension of the play frame or as a separate piece of equipment, **bottom left**. Fasten the cross beam to braced 6-by-6 uprights, or sandwich each end between two 4-by-4 posts. Increase the size of the beam from 4 by 6 or 6 by 6 to 4 by 8 or 6 by 8 in order to accommodate the longer span. Although public swings are sometimes 10 or 12 feet high, 8 feet is a good height for the backyard.

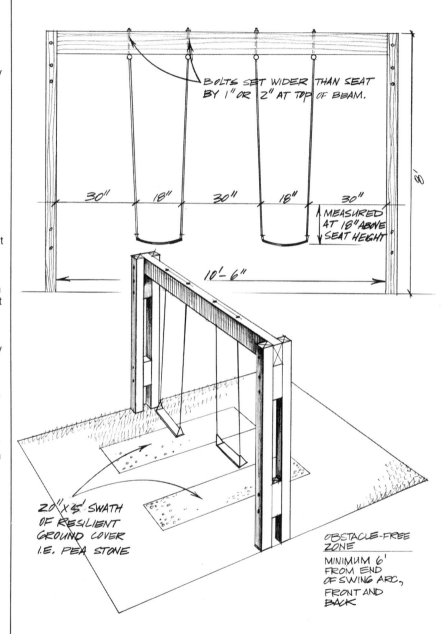

BOLTS SET WIDER THAN SEAT BY 1" OR 2" AT TOP OF BEAM.

30" 18" 30" 18" 30"

8'

MEASURED AT 18" ABOVE SEAT HEIGHT

10'- 6"

20"x5' SWATH OF RESILIENT GROUND COVER I.E. PEA STONE

OBSTACLE-FREE ZONE

MINIMUM 6' FROM END OF SWING ARC, FRONT AND BACK

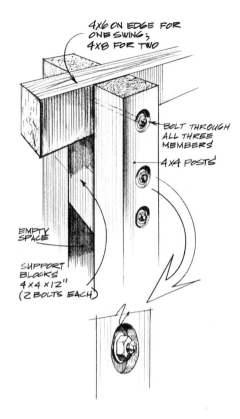

4X6 ON EDGE FOR ONE SWING; 4X8 FOR TWO

BOLT THROUGH ALL THREE MEMBERS

4X4 POSTS

EMPTY SPACE

SUPPORT BLOCKS 4X4X12" (2 BOLTS EACH)

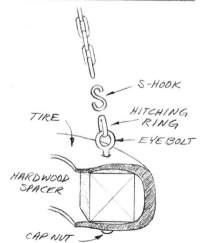

TIRE SEAT

S-HOOK

TIRE

HITCHING RING

EYEBOLT

HARDWOOD SPACER

CAP NUT

(Design information on page 22.)

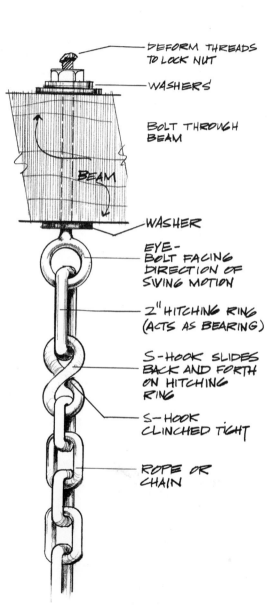

DEFORM THREADS TO LOCK NUT

WASHERS

BOLT THROUGH BEAM

BEAM

WASHER

EYE-BOLT FACING DIRECTION OF SWING MOTION

2" HITCHING RING (ACTS AS BEARING)

S-HOOK SLIDES BACK AND FORTH ON HITCHING RING

S-HOOK CLINCHED TIGHT

ROPE OR CHAIN

WOODEN SEAT

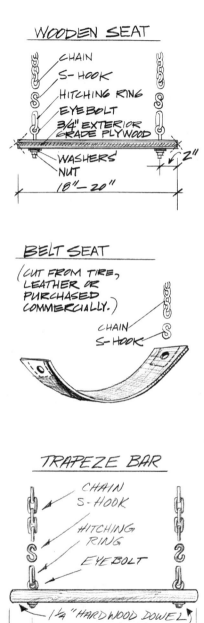

CHAIN

S-HOOK

HITCHING RING

EYEBOLT

3/4" EXTERIOR GRADE PLYWOOD

WASHERS

NUT

2"

18" — 20"

BELT SEAT

(CUT FROM TIRE, LEATHER OR PURCHASED COMMERCIALLY.)

CHAIN

S-HOOK

TRAPEZE BAR

CHAIN

S-HOOK

HITCHING RING

EYEBOLT

1¼" HARDWOOD DOWEL

CAP NUT

2"

24"

ADJUSTABLE ROPE SUSPENSION

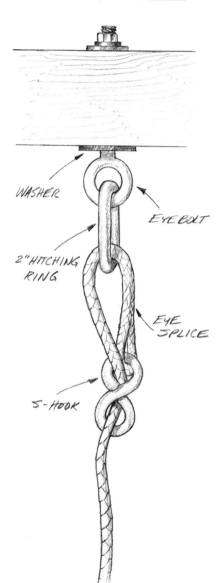

WASHER

2" HITCHING RING

EYEBOLT

EYE SPLICE

S-HOOK

Seats:
- Make seats of resilient material, textured to prevent slipping; soften sharp edges and corners.
- Make seats at least a foot wide and 5 inches deep.
- Install seats 14 to 18 inches high or so the child's feet touch the ground.
- Design toddler seats to support the child on all sides to waist level, with a strap between the legs and no movable or adjustable parts with which kids can tamper.
- Drill drain holes in tire seats; support tires at three points with "spreaders" to prevent collapse; use steel-belted tires with caution.

Suspended elements (trapeze bars, rings):
- Install 5 to 8 feet off the ground or within 6 inches of the maximum upward reach of the child.
- Rings must have an inside diameter of less than 4 inches or more than 9 inches to prevent head entrapment.

Suspend single-axis swings with a bearing hanger or a heavy-duty eyebolt, hitching ring and S-hook, **left**. If suspending the swing with rope, make an eye splice with a steel thimble to reduce wear, **right**. A multiaxis swing needs a specialized swivel; attach the purchased hardware to a new or recycled tire with eyebolts, **facing page**, **bottom right**. Buy or make swing seats, **centre**, connecting chains with S-hooks and ropes with secure knots on the underside of the seat, reinforced so the hole won't tear.

Cable Ride

Frames:

• Install the ride outside the traffic flow in the yard, parallel to a fence, building or property line.

• The site should be gently sloping (1:25); if not, create an incline with the frame.

• Design a support structure strong enough to withstand static and dynamic stresses without vibration or dislocation: either trees or 6-by-6 posts sunk 4 to 5 feet in the ground and stabilized with knee braces.

• Provide safe footing at the beginning and end of the run.

• Avoid single end posts; instead, bolt a cross beam at least 7 feet above grade between two uprights at least 6 feet apart.

• Install a brake at least 6 feet from the end of the ride.

Cable:

• Use ⅜-inch galvanized-steel cable attached to the frame with heavy-duty eyebolts; use rope only for one-day rides.

• Make the cable attachment inaccessible to kids.

• Provide a turnbuckle to adjust cable slack so the rider's speed is naturally reduced near the end.

• Suspend the cable high enough that no one inadvertently walks into it.

• Create a clear, obstacle-free zone under the entire length of the cable, with a resilient surface under the landing area.

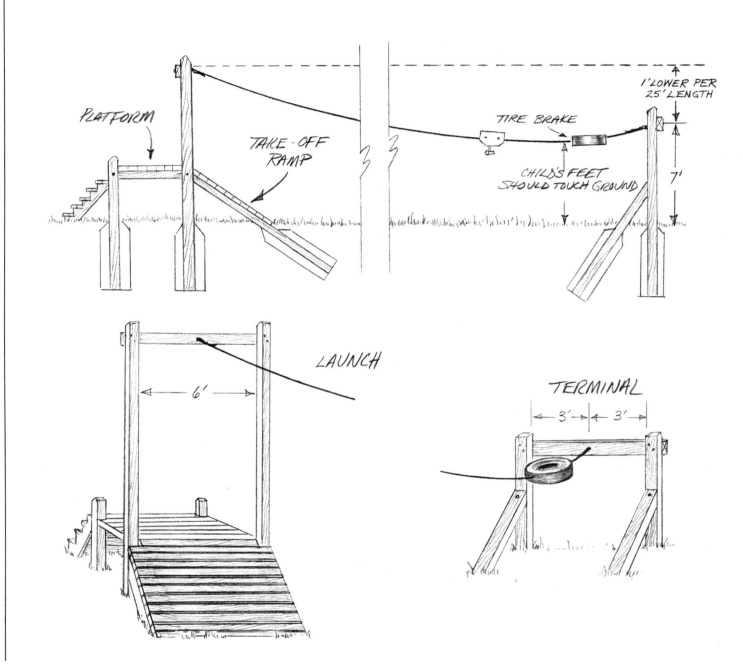

PLATFORM

TAKE-OFF RAMP

1' LOWER PER 25' LENGTH

TIRE BRAKE

CHILD'S FEET SHOULD TOUCH GROUND

7'

LAUNCH

6'

TERMINAL

3' 3'

(Design information on page 27.)

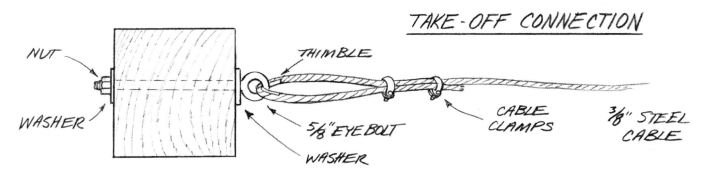

TAKE-OFF CONNECTION

NUT

WASHER

THIMBLE

5/8" EYEBOLT

WASHER

CABLE CLAMPS

3/8" STEEL CABLE

TIRE BRAKE

CLAMPS ON INSIDE & OUTSIDE OF TIRE

DIRECTION OF RIDE

MINIMUM 6'

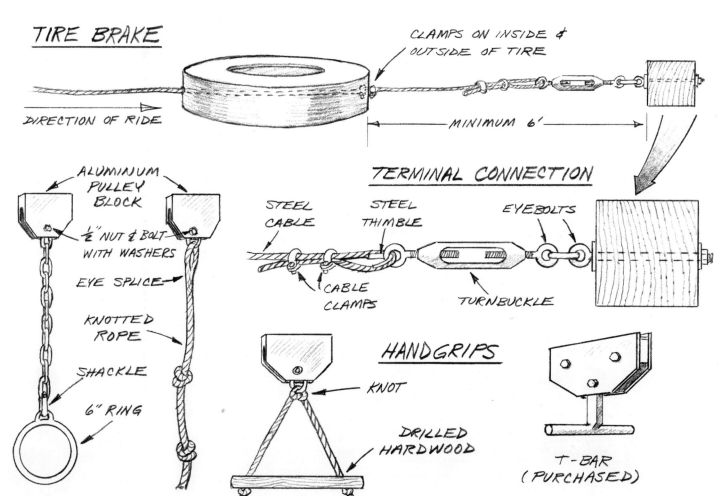

ALUMINUM PULLEY BLOCK

1/2" NUT & BOLT WITH WASHERS

EYE SPLICE

KNOTTED ROPE

SHACKLE

6" RING

TERMINAL CONNECTION

STEEL CABLE

STEEL THIMBLE

EYEBOLTS

CABLE CLAMPS

TURNBUCKLE

HANDGRIPS

KNOT

DRILLED HARDWOOD

T-BAR (PURCHASED)

Mechanism:
- Enclose wheels, pulleys or trolleys to prevent pinched fingers and snagged hair or clothing.
- There should be little risk that the mechanism will jam or jump off the cable.

Grips:
- Design so kids can let go without becoming entangled.
- Avoid large loops that could pose a strangulation hazard.
- Add a retrieval rope so kids can easily return the pulley to the starting point; make it long enough to be grasped without stretching or leaning.
- Handgrips should be higher than the tallest child but, at the highest point, no more than 6 inches above the child's maximum upward reach.

Existing trees are the best support for a cable ride because even well-entrenched poles may not withstand the rigours of kids flying through space. If there are no sturdy trees, sink posts very deeply and stabilize with knee braces, **facing page**. The take-off point can be a natural elevation or a constructed platform and the end, a cross beam. Cushion the end of the ride with an effective brake, **centre**. The steel cable attachment, **top**, is the same whether it goes through a tree trunk or a post, except that if the cable ride is to last through several children, the eyebolt should be a few inches longer than the diameter of the tree to accommodate future growth. Protect the tree wound with pruning compound before inserting the bolt.

Slides

(The following recommendations may not apply to all types of slides.)

• Slide height varies with the age of the children using it: 4 feet is appropriate for toddlers, 7 feet for elementary school children.

• For slides over 3 feet high, provide ladders or steps with handrails that continue onto the landing platform.

• The platform at the top must be horizontal and large enough to encourage kids to sit before sliding down; on freestanding models, it should be at least 20 inches long and the same width as the slide; provide guardrails to protect kids from falling while waiting to slide.

• Avoid joints in the slide bedway.

• The average incline of the slide bedway should be no more than 30 degrees; on wavy slides, any change in angle should have a radius of at least 39 inches.

• Provide side walls or handgrips at least 4 inches high, rounded and smoothly finished.

• The distance between the slide exit lip and the ground cover should be 3 to 5 inches for toddlers, 8 inches for preschoolers, 10 inches for young elementary school children and 14 inches up to adolescence; for kids under 3 years, bury the end of the slide in the ground cover.

• Provide a resilient ground cover at the base of the slide and 6 feet on either side of freestanding and combination slides.

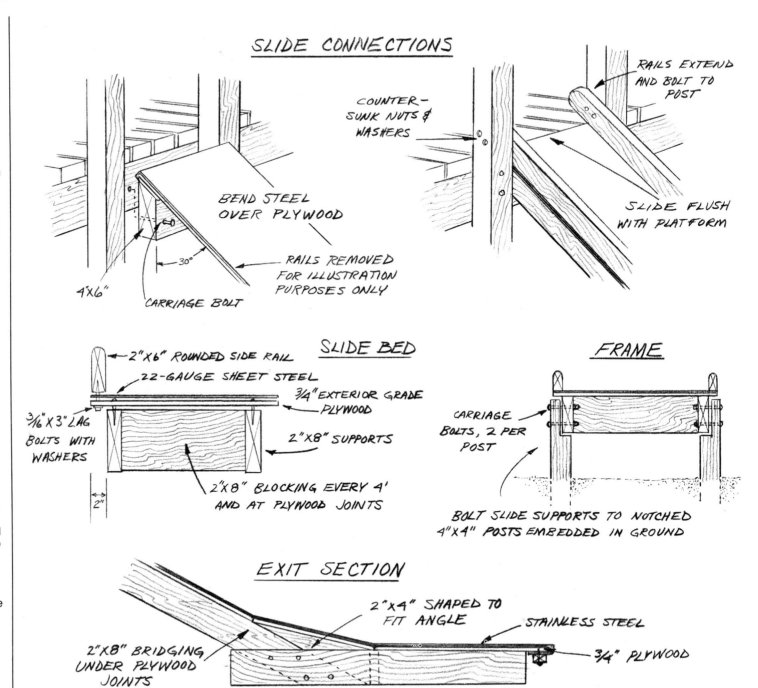

SLIDE CONNECTIONS

COUNTER-SUNK NUTS & WASHERS

RAILS EXTEND AND BOLT TO POST

BEND STEEL OVER PLYWOOD

30°

4"X6"

CARRIAGE BOLT

RAILS REMOVED FOR ILLUSTRATION PURPOSES ONLY

SLIDE FLUSH WITH PLATFORM

SLIDE BED

2"X6" ROUNDED SIDE RAIL

22-GAUGE SHEET STEEL

3/4" EXTERIOR GRADE PLYWOOD

3/16" X 3" LAG BOLTS WITH WASHERS

2"X8" SUPPORTS

2"X8" BLOCKING EVERY 4' AND AT PLYWOOD JOINTS

2"

FRAME

CARRIAGE BOLTS, 2 PER POST

BOLT SLIDE SUPPORTS TO NOTCHED 4"X4" POSTS EMBEDDED IN GROUND

EXIT SECTION

2"X4" SHAPED TO FIT ANGLE

STAINLESS STEEL

3/4" PLYWOOD

2"X8" BRIDGING UNDER PLYWOOD JOINTS

114

(Design information on page 29.)

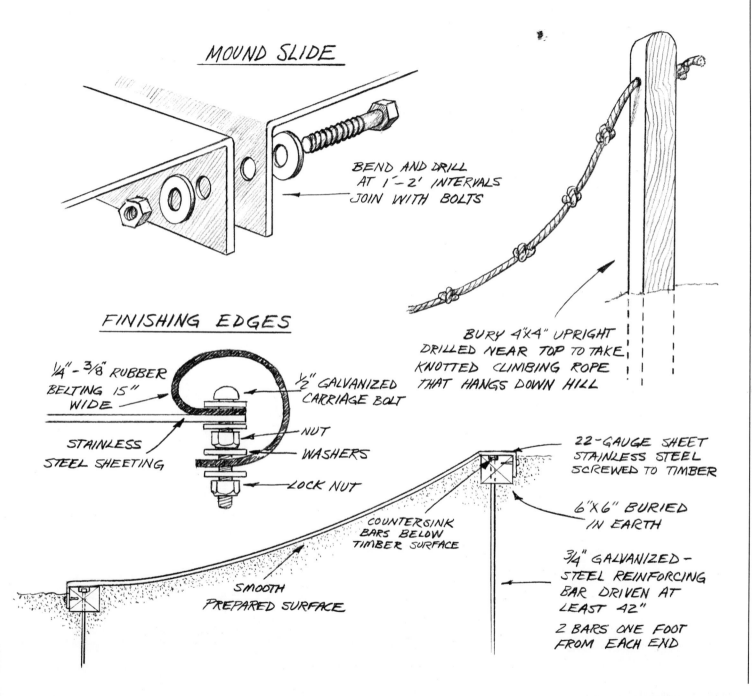

MOUND SLIDE

BEND AND DRILL
AT 1'- 2' INTERVALS
JOIN WITH BOLTS

BURY 4"X 4" UPRIGHT
DRILLED NEAR TOP TO TAKE
KNOTTED CLIMBING ROPE
THAT HANGS DOWN HILL

FINISHING EDGES

1/4"- 3/8" RUBBER
BELTING IS 15"
WIDE

1/2" GALVANIZED
CARRIAGE BOLT

STAINLESS
STEEL SHEETING

NUT

WASHERS

LOCK NUT

COUNTERSINK
BARS BELOW
TIMBER SURFACE

22-GAUGE SHEET
STAINLESS STEEL
SCREWED TO TIMBER

6"X 6" BURIED
IN EARTH

3/4" GALVANIZED-
STEEL REINFORCING
BAR DRIVEN AT
LEAST 42"

2 BARS ONE FOOT
FROM EACH END

SMOOTH
PREPARED SURFACE

A freestanding slide entails a lot of lumber and effort for a plaything with only one function; for the backyard, it is more practical to attach a slide to a play frame. The safety measures on page 114 are essential if the slide is raised above ground level, but kids have nowhere to fall if they tumble off a mound slide. Make the slide bedway of smoothly finished hardwood or plywood covered with stainless steel, galvanized sheet metal or Arborite, but before building one, compare its cost with that of a plastic model from a play-equipment manufacturer.

Just Climbers

- Match the dimensions and degree of difficulty of a climber to the child's size and abilities.
- Provide adequate hand- and footholds spaced at appropriate distances (see chart).
- The vertical rise of any climbing device should not exceed 10 feet; on high climbers, provide intermediate landings where a child can decide to continue upward or return to the ground.
- Cluster climbing elements (rocks, timbers) close enough together that feet, hands and limbs cannot be trapped; fill gaps with sand.
- For all stationary physical play equipment over 2 feet high, provide a resilient ground cover underneath that extends 6 feet on all sides.

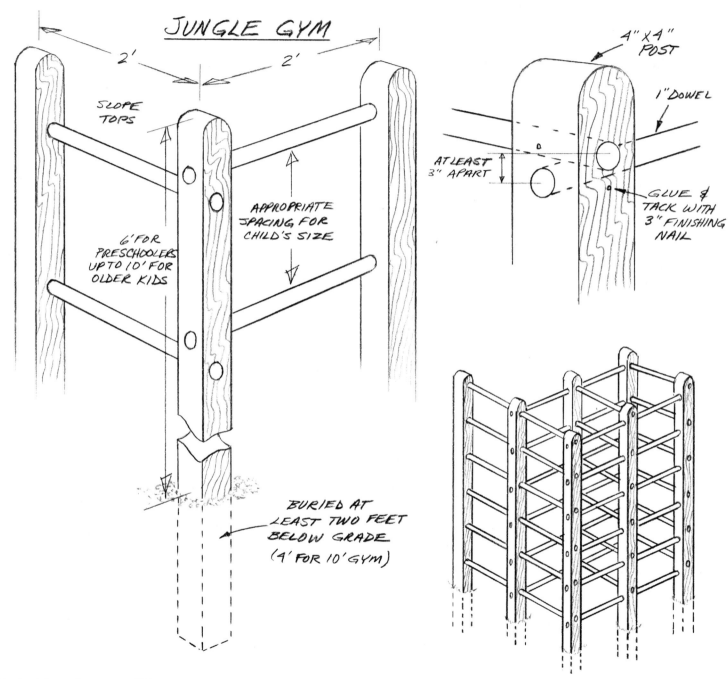

JUNGLE GYM

2' 2'

SLOPE TOPS

APPROPRIATE SPACING FOR CHILD'S SIZE

6' FOR PRESCHOOLERS UP TO 10' FOR OLDER KIDS

4" X 4" POST

1" DOWEL

AT LEAST 3" APART

GLUE & TACK WITH 3" FINISHING NAIL

BURIED AT LEAST TWO FEET BELOW GRADE (4' FOR 10' GYM)

(Design information on page 33.)

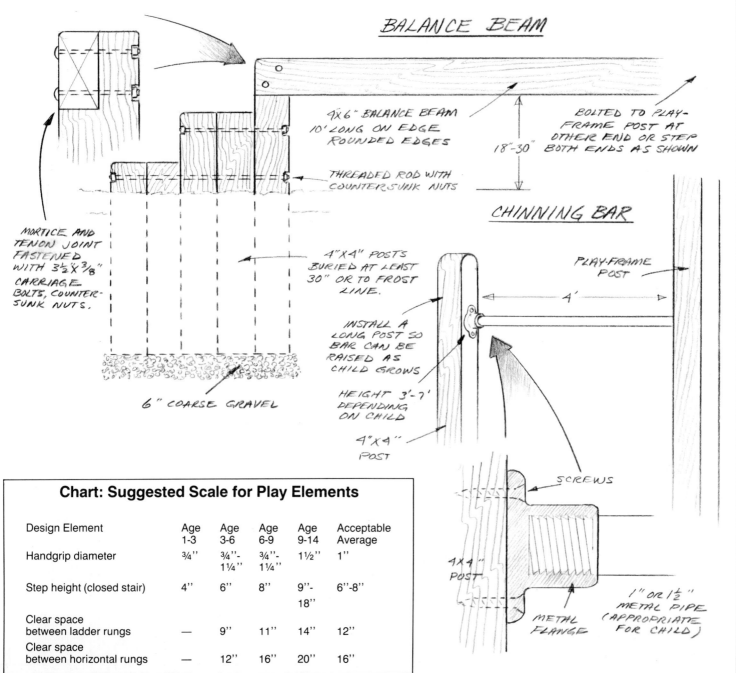

BALANCE BEAM

9×6" BALANCE BEAM
10' LONG ON EDGE
ROUNDED EDGES

BOLTED TO PLAY-
FRAME POST AT
OTHER END OR STEP
BOTH ENDS AS SHOWN

18"-30"

THREADED ROD WITH
COUNTER-SUNK NUTS

MORTICE AND
TENON JOINT
FASTENED
WITH 3½"×⅜"
CARRIAGE
BOLTS, COUNTER-
SUNK NUTS.

CHINNING BAR

4"×4" POSTS
BURIED AT LEAST
30" OR TO FROST
LINE.

PLAY-FRAME
POST

4'

INSTALL A
LONG POST SO
BAR CAN BE
RAISED AS
CHILD GROWS

HEIGHT 3'-7'
DEPENDING
ON CHILD

4"×4"
POST

6" COARSE GRAVEL

SCREWS

4×4"
POST

METAL
FLANGE

1" OR 1½"
METAL PIPE
(APPROPRIATE
FOR CHILD)

Chart: Suggested Scale for Play Elements

Design Element	Age 1-3	Age 3-6	Age 6-9	Age 9-14	Acceptable Average
Handgrip diameter	¾''	¾''-1¼''	¾''-1¼''	1½''	1''
Step height (closed stair)	4''	6''	8''	9''-18''	6''-8''
Clear space between ladder rungs	—	9''	11''	14''	12''
Clear space between horizontal rungs	—	12''	16''	20''	16''

These individual climbers are designed just for active physical play, unlike the play frames on the following page that are designed to be expanded with accessories. Based on plans originally published in 1950 by the Ottawa Citizen's Committee on Children, this simple jungle gym, **facing page**, is an excellent way to exercise young bodies. Composed of 2-foot-square modules, it can be expanded to any size: a 6-foot cube for preschoolers or a 10-foot cube for school-age kids. Combined with loose material such as cleated boards and blankets, it has limitless play value. Although not really a climber, the balance beam, **top**, nevertheless stimulates much the same type of activity as does the chinning bar, **bottom**.

(Design information on pages 32 and 35.)

The Play Frame

Platforms:

• Provide a resilient ground cover as for climbers.

• Maximum platform heights: 4 feet for toddlers, 5 feet for preschoolers, 8 feet for early-school-age kids and 10 feet for adolescents.

• If a child can climb on the roof, consider it a platform and follow the appropriate safety-design rules.

• On platforms over 6½ feet high, provide more than one way of getting up and down.

• Adjacent platforms without connecting stairs or ladders should differ in height by no more than 12 inches for kids 1 to 6 years old and 16 inches for kids 7 to 14.

• Design crawl spaces (hatches, tunnels) a minimum of 2 feet square.

• Provide access to very high platforms by play elements that can be negotiated only by older children, i.e., monkey bars, knotted rope.

Platforms are the core of a multipurpose play structure. They can be any size or height, and several can be attached at different levels to one set of uprights. Secure the posts in the ground with concrete or well-tamped earth, extending them high enough to accommodate guardrails on the top platform. Bolt 2-by-6 or 2-by-8 joists to the inside or outside of the posts as shown. Fasten additional joists between the posts, if it is necessary to reduce the span for the decking. For instance, for 2-by-4 or 2-by-6 cedar decking, joists should be no more than 32 inches apart.

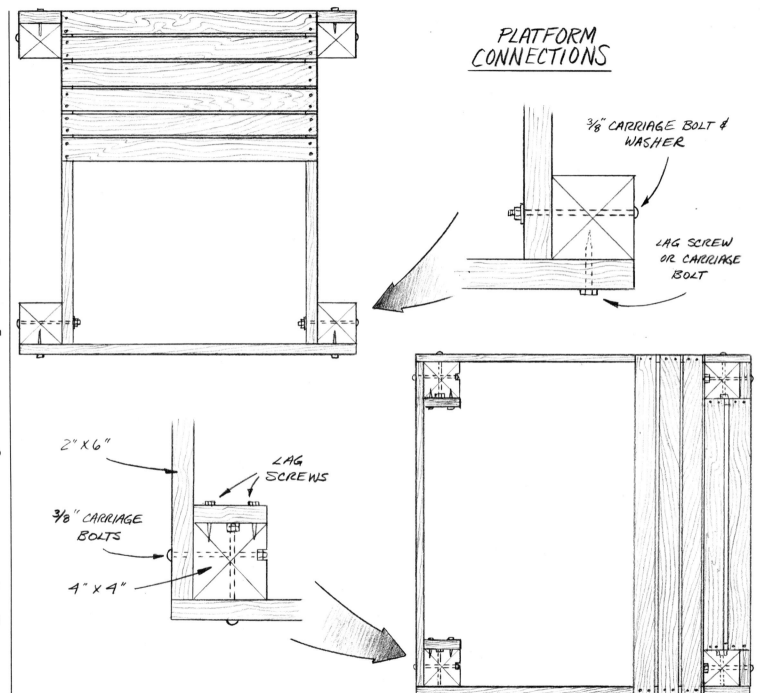

PLATFORM CONNECTIONS

⅜" CARRIAGE BOLT & WASHER

LAG SCREW OR CARRIAGE BOLT

2" X 6"

LAG SCREWS

⅜" CARRIAGE BOLTS

4" X 4"

(Design information on page 36.)

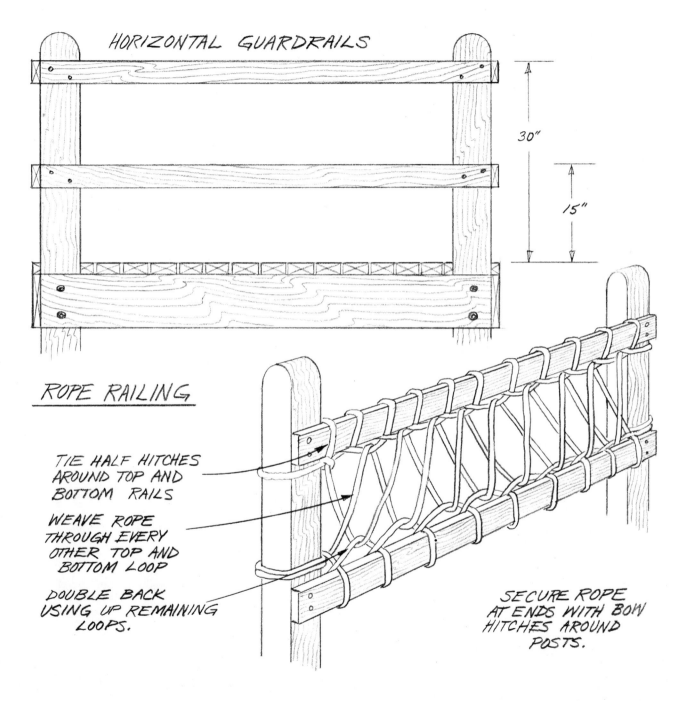

HORIZONTAL GUARDRAILS

30"

15"

ROPE RAILING

TIE HALF HITCHES
AROUND TOP AND
BOTTOM RAILS

WEAVE ROPE
THROUGH EVERY
OTHER TOP AND
BOTTOM LOOP

DOUBLE BACK
USING UP REMAINING
LOOPS.

SECURE ROPE
AT ENDS WITH BOW
HITCHES AROUND
POSTS.

Guardrails:
• On platforms over 2 feet off the ground, provide 28-to-30-inch-high guardrails around the perimeter, except at access points (stairs, ladders, et cetera).
• If guardrails have vertical pickets, space them less than 4 inches apart to prevent head entrapment.

All platforms over 2 feet high should have guardrails. Vertical guardrails have to be closely spaced to prevent head entrapment, giving the play frame a cage-like appearance, and they do not provide a handgrip for little kids. A two-tiered horizontal railing, **top**, is better, with the bottom rail 15 inches above the deck and the upper one 30 inches high for older children. On very high platforms, build solid railings with exterior-grade plywood or tarpaulins, or weave ropes between the railings for a barrier that is see-through but safe, **bottom**.

119

(Design information on page 36.)

Partially enclosing the space under a low platform makes a good hideaway; likewise, a roof over the top platform creates a crow's-nest playspace that is just as much fun as a tree house. Extend the posts a little higher than the guardrails and build a permanent roof, **top**, using cedar shakes or asphalt shingles, or let the kids add a temporary roof, **bottom**, whenever they want. Extend the centre posts 4 or 5 feet above the top deck and use post caps or metal plates to bolt on the cross beam. Punch grommets in the four corners of a sturdy weather-resistant fabric, and use ropes to lash it to the corner posts of the platform.

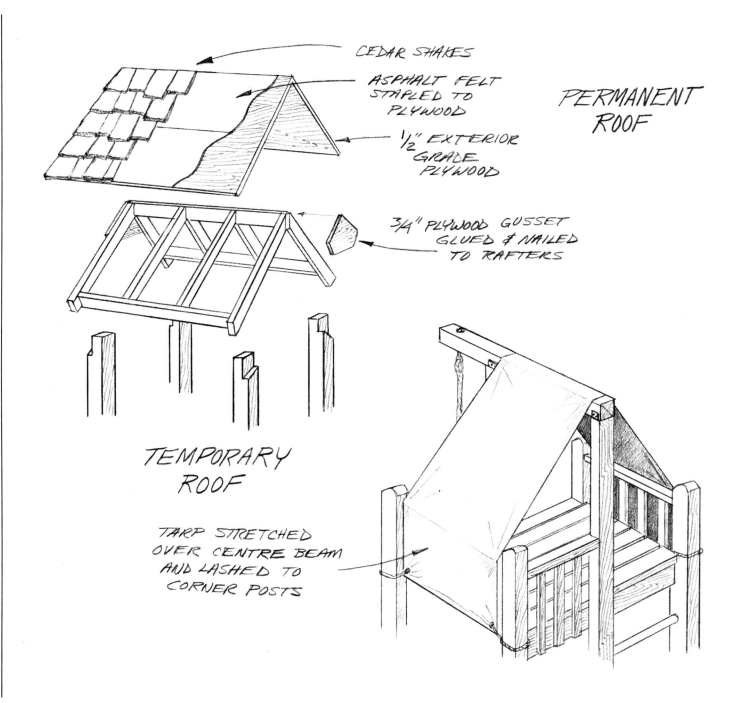

CEDAR SHAKES

ASPHALT FELT STAPLED TO PLYWOOD

1/2" EXTERIOR GRADE PLYWOOD

PERMANENT ROOF

3/4" PLYWOOD GUSSET GLUED & NAILED TO RAFTERS

TEMPORARY ROOF

TARP STRETCHED OVER CENTRE BEAM AND LASHED TO CORNER POSTS

120

(Design information on page 36.)

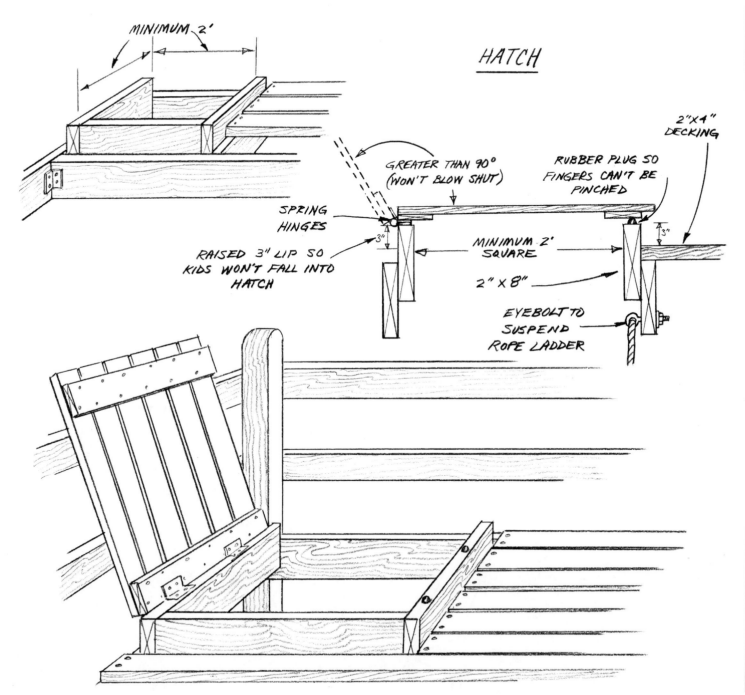

HATCH

MINIMUM 2'

GREATER THAN 90°
(WON'T BLOW SHUT)

RUBBER PLUG SO
FINGERS CAN'T BE
PINCHED

2"X4"
DECKING

SPRING
HINGES

3"

RAISED 3" LIP SO
KIDS WON'T FALL INTO
HATCH

MINIMUM 2'
SQUARE

3"

2" X 8"

EYEBOLT TO
SUSPEND
ROPE LADDER

The following pages show plans for play-frame accessories—the slides, ramps, ladders and nets that provide optional ways of getting to and from the platforms, but a hatch such as the one shown here gives kids access from inside the play frame. It can also be used to restrict a high platform to kids who are able to manipulate the latch or master a difficult climber such as a knotted rope. The raised lip prevents kids from slipping into the gap in the decking, and the rubber plugs prevent pinched fingers when opening and closing the hatch.

Access

- Adults must have access to all platforms so they can reach children in case of emergency.
- Ramps, steps and treads should have nonslip surfaces, i.e., cleats or wood that is not finely sanded.
- Inset rungs and steps into support rails so their structural security does not depend solely on nails or screws.
- Space steps and rungs evenly at distances appropriate for the child.
- Ramp inclines should not exceed 30 degrees.
- Ladders are best for inclines of 55 to 90 degrees; rungs should be 12 to 20 inches wide and uniformly spaced at least 9 inches apart to avoid creating a head trap.
- Rungs should be ¾ to 1½ inches in diameter and should not turn when grasped.
- For stairs with a fall height of more than 2 feet, provide continuous handrails.
- Provide two levels of handrails to accommodate kids of varying sizes: an upper rail 28 to 30 inches high and a lower rail 15 inches high.
- Round the top edge of rails to a ¾-to-1½-inch diameter to provide good grip.
- Support handrails so the child's hand can move smoothly along the surface.

RAMP

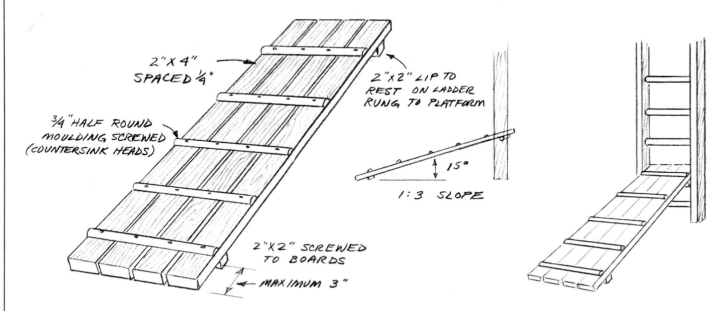

2"X4" SPACED ¼"

¾" HALF ROUND MOULDING SCREWED (COUNTERSINK HEADS)

2"X2" LIP TO REST ON LADDER RUNG TO PLATFORM

15°

1:3 SLOPE

2"X2" SCREWED TO BOARDS

MAXIMUM 3"

SLOPED LADDER

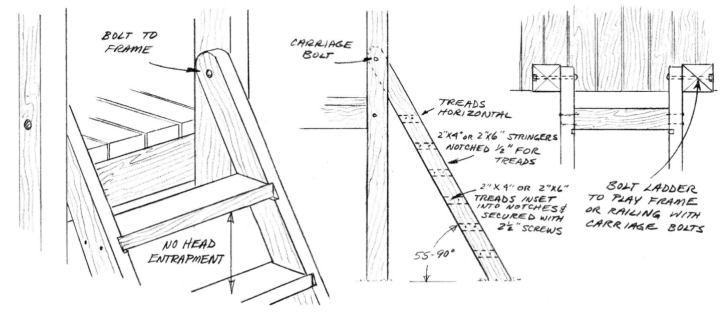

BOLT TO FRAME

CARRIAGE BOLT

TREADS HORIZONTAL

2"X4" OR 2"X6" STRINGERS NOTCHED ½" FOR TREADS

2"X4" OR 2"X6" TREADS INSET INTO NOTCHES & SECURED WITH 2½" SCREWS

BOLT LADDER TO PLAY FRAME OR RAILING WITH CARRIAGE BOLTS

NO HEAD ENTRAPMENT

55-90°

(Design information on page 35.)

VERTICAL LADDERS

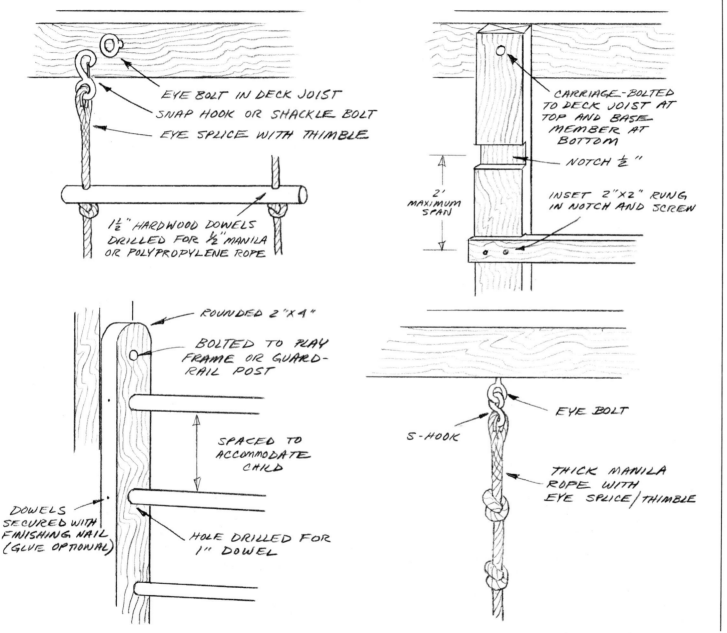

EYE BOLT IN DECK JOIST

SNAP HOOK OR SHACKLE BOLT

EYE SPLICE WITH THIMBLE

1½" HARDWOOD DOWELS DRILLED FOR ½" MANILA OR POLYPROPYLENE ROPE

CARRIAGE-BOLTED TO DECK JOIST AT TOP AND BASE MEMBER AT BOTTOM

NOTCH ½"

INSET 2"X2" RUNG IN NOTCH AND SCREW

2' MAXIMUM SPAN

ROUNDED 2"X4"

BOLTED TO PLAY FRAME OR GUARD-RAIL POST

SPACED TO ACCOMMODATE CHILD

HOLE DRILLED FOR 1" DOWEL

DOWELS SECURED WITH FINISHING NAIL (GLUE OPTIONAL)

EYE BOLT

S-HOOK

THICK MANILA ROPE WITH EYE SPLICE/THIMBLE

The way a child gets to and from a platform is both muscle-building and fun, with movable ramps and stairs providing as much exercise for very young children as sloped and vertical ladders do for older kids. The designs on these pages, together with the monkey bars, sliding pole and cargo net that follow, should be used to build into the play frame as much variety of activity, shape and texture as possible.

123

(Design information on page 33.)

Horizontal Climbers

Monkey Bars:

• Rungs should be 1 to 1½ inches in diameter and fixed securely so they don't turn when grasped.

• Centre rungs 12 to 20 inches apart, depending on the size of the child.

• Space the ladder rails 24 to 48 inches apart; choose dowelling strong enough to bridge the span.

• Position monkey bars so kids are discouraged from climbing on top of them and possibly falling through.

• Design overhead bars so kids can start and finish safely.

• Install horizontal ladders 5 to 8 feet off the ground or within 6 inches of the maximum upward reach of the child.

• Position monkey bars over a resilient ground cover.

• For increased challenge, incline monkey bars (maximum 1:3 slope).

Extend monkey bars from the play frame, or install them as a separate piece of physical play equipment. Construct monkey bars like a vertical ladder, except that the rails must be strong enough to span the supporting posts.

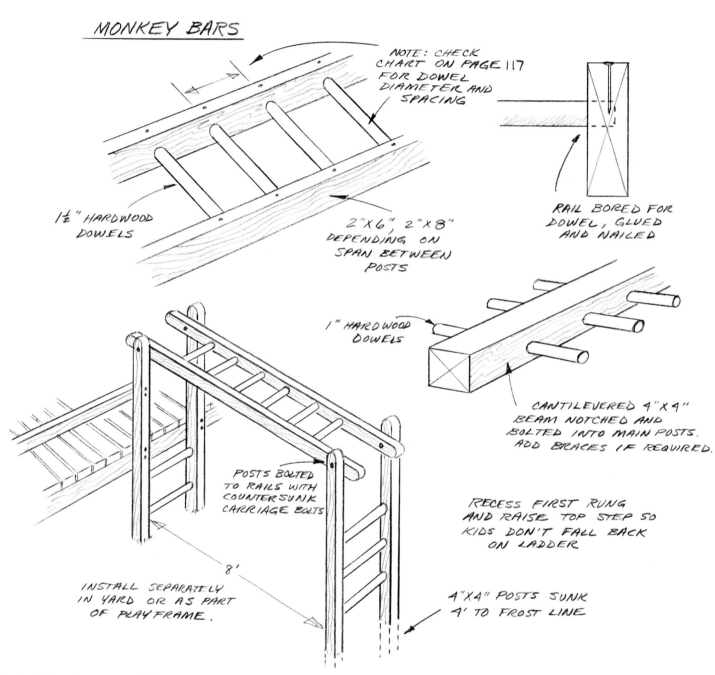

MONKEY BARS

NOTE: CHECK CHART ON PAGE 117 FOR DOWEL DIAMETER AND SPACING

1½" HARDWOOD DOWELS

2"x6", 2"x8" DEPENDING ON SPAN BETWEEN POSTS

RAIL BORED FOR DOWEL, GLUED AND NAILED

1" HARDWOOD DOWELS

CANTILEVERED 4"x4" BEAM NOTCHED AND BOLTED INTO MAIN POSTS. ADD BRACES IF REQUIRED.

POSTS BOLTED TO RAILS WITH COUNTERSUNK CARRIAGE BOLTS

RECESS FIRST RUNG AND RAISE TOP STEP SO KIDS DON'T FALL BACK ON LADDER

INSTALL SEPARATELY IN YARD OR AS PART OF PLAY FRAME.

8'

4"x4" POSTS SUNK 4' TO FROST LINE

(Design information on page 35.)

TIRE CONNECTIONS

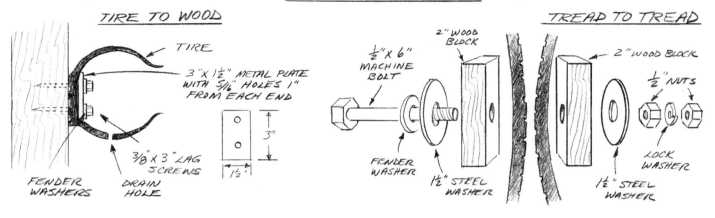

TIRE TO WOOD

TIRE

3" X 1½" METAL PLATE WITH 5/16" HOLES 1" FROM EACH END

3"

1½"

FENDER WASHERS

DRAIN HOLE

3/8" X 3" LAG SCREWS

TREAD TO TREAD

½" X 6" MACHINE BOLT

2" WOOD BLOCK

2" WOOD BLOCK

½" NUTS

FENDER WASHER

1½" STEEL WASHER

LOCK WASHER

1½" STEEL WASHER

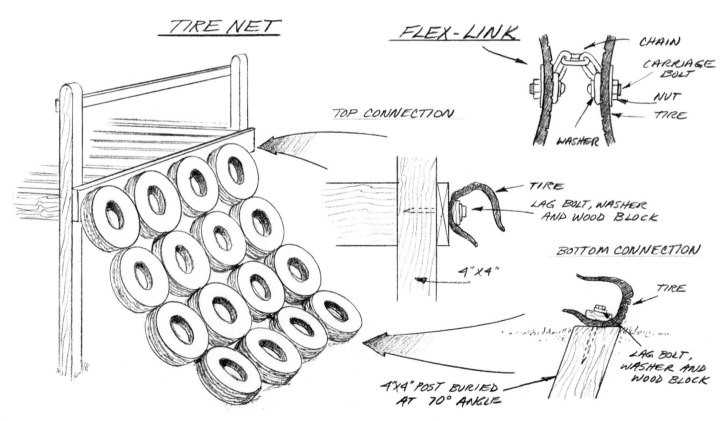

TIRE NET

TOP CONNECTION

FLEX-LINK

CHAIN

CARRIAGE BOLT

NUT

TIRE

WASHER

TIRE

LAG BOLT, WASHER AND WOOD BLOCK

4"X4"

BOTTOM CONNECTION

TIRE

LAG BOLT, WASHER AND WOOD BLOCK

4"X4" POST BURIED AT 70° ANGLE

Tire Connectors:
Good flexible climbers, tires can be attached to the play frame in a variety of ways. Using a metal plate (top left) to prevent tearing, bolt a row of tires vertically, one above the other, to one of the play-frame posts for a climber that really moves. For more stability, bolt the stack of tires to posts on either side, or erect three posts in the ground and bolt tires horizontally inside the circle about 18 inches apart. To build a cargo net (bottom left) or bridge out of recycled tires, fasten the tires together using a single carriage bolt, washers and a wooden "spreader" (top right), or use a flex-link connection (centre right). Bolt the top row of tires to a 2-by-6 plate that is bolted to the play-frame posts. Secure the bottom tires to 4-by-4 posts set at an angle below the ground cover (bottom right).

(Design information on page 101.)

Sliding Poles

• Install sliding poles 18 to 20 inches from any platform, deck or structural member.
• If the pole passes two platforms, provide a barrier in front of the lower one so children can mount only from the top.

Extremely popular with school-age kids, sliding poles are often incorporated into their dramatic play as fire-fighters' poles or as quick exits from an alien space ship. They are easy to make using a length of galvanized plumbing pipe, an elbow joint and a shorter length of pipe screwed into a flange mounted on the play-frame post. Sliding poles made with hardwood dowels should be sanded very smooth and attached with a U-bolt to a cantilevered beam. Whatever the material, bury the base of the pole deeply, tamping the earth firmly around it.

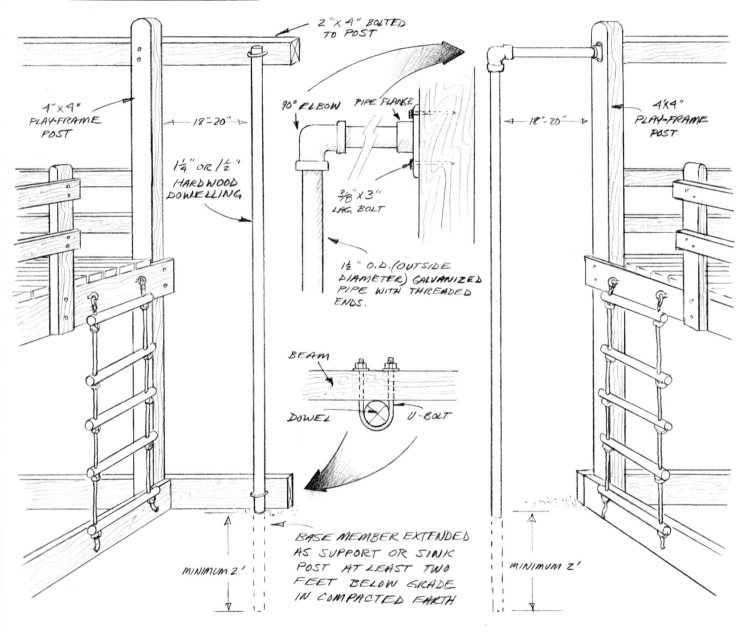

SLIDING POLES

2" X 4" BOLTED TO POST

4" X 4" PLAY-FRAME POST

18"-20"

1¼" OR 1½" HARDWOOD DOWELLING

90° ELBOW

PIPE FLANGE

3/8" X 3" LAG BOLT

1½" O.D. (OUTSIDE DIAMETER) GALVANIZED PIPE WITH THREADED ENDS.

4"X4" PLAY-FRAME POST

18"-20"

BEAM

DOWEL   U-BOLT

MINIMUM 2'

BASE MEMBER EXTENDED AS SUPPORT OR SINK POST AT LEAST TWO FEET BELOW GRADE IN COMPACTED EARTH

MINIMUM 2'

(Design information on page 35.)

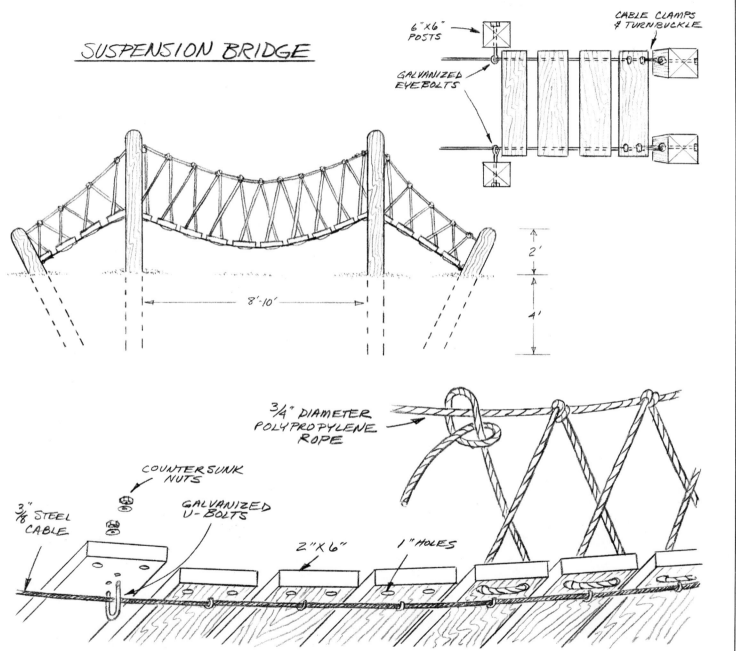

SUSPENSION BRIDGE

6"x6" POSTS

CABLE CLAMPS & TURNBUCKLE

GALVANIZED EYEBOLTS

2'

4'

8'-10'

3/4" DIAMETER POLYPROPYLENE ROPE

COUNTERSUNK NUTS

GALVANIZED U-BOLTS

3/8" STEEL CABLE

2"x6"

1" HOLES

Bridges

Bridges can span two adjacent platforms or connect a play frame with the crest of a hill or a nearby tree house. The cedar slats of this clatter bridge are suspended with sturdy steel cable. Attach it to the play-frame posts or build it as an independent unit to span a play stream or ravine. The knotted-rope railing shown below is also appropriate for low platforms, but a wood railing is safer for heights.

(Design information on page 35.)

Playhouses

• Sand all surfaces and round all sharp edges; have no protruding hardware, especially from the roof.
• Do not combine active play areas with the playhouse: stairs, ladder or ramp access to a raised playhouse should be used primarily for ascent and descent, not for rowdy play.
• Keep the design generic, avoiding too much detail that limits imaginative potential.
• Bigger is not better; design room for only two or three kids at a time, i.e., 3-by-6-foot floor space for preschoolers, 6 by 6 for school-age kids.
• Limit furnishings, but scale details (window-ledge counters, bench) to the child.
• Raise the floor off the ground to avoid dampness.
• Raise the door sill off the ground at least 4 inches to encourage winter use.

For yards that lack good tree-house trees, an elevated playhouse is a good alternative. Construct a raised platform and extend the corner posts to support the roof. Close in the walls with wood siding, securing door and window openings with battens. Joists can be cantilevered up to half their recommended span to create a balcony off one side, though braces may be necessary, especially if a rope-and-dowel ladder dangles from the edge.

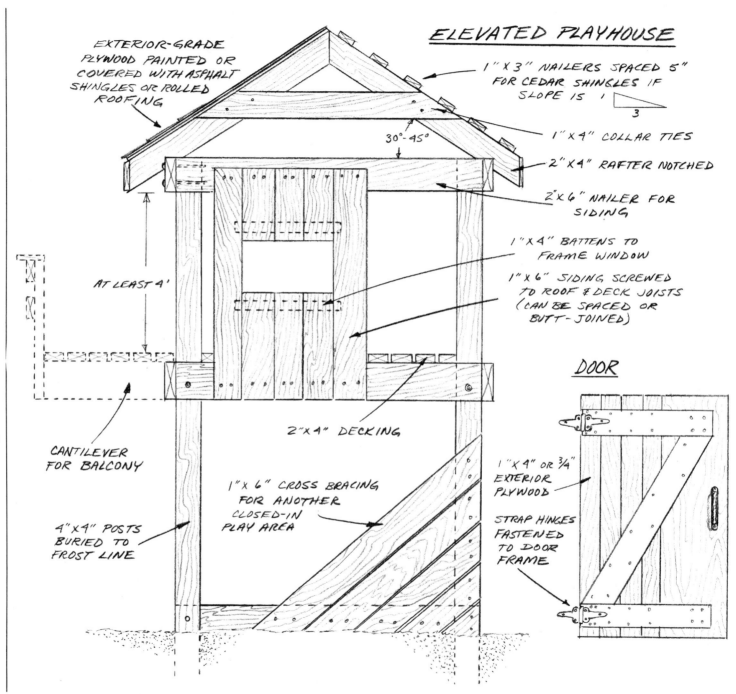

ELEVATED PLAYHOUSE

EXTERIOR-GRADE PLYWOOD PAINTED OR COVERED WITH ASPHALT SHINGLES OR ROLLED ROOFING

1" X 3" NAILERS SPACED 5" FOR CEDAR SHINGLES IF SLOPE IS 1/3

30°-45°

1" X 4" COLLAR TIES

2" X 4" RAFTER NOTCHED

2" X 6" NAILER FOR SIDING

1" X 4" BATTENS TO FRAME WINDOW

1" X 6" SIDING SCREWED TO ROOF & DECK JOISTS (CAN BE SPACED OR BUTT-JOINED)

AT LEAST 4'

2" X 4" DECKING

DOOR

CANTILEVER FOR BALCONY

1" X 6" CROSS BRACING FOR ANOTHER CLOSED-IN PLAY AREA

1" X 4" OR 3/4" EXTERIOR PLYWOOD

4" X 4" POSTS BURIED TO FROST LINE

STRAP HINGES FASTENED TO DOOR FRAME

(Design information on page 37.)

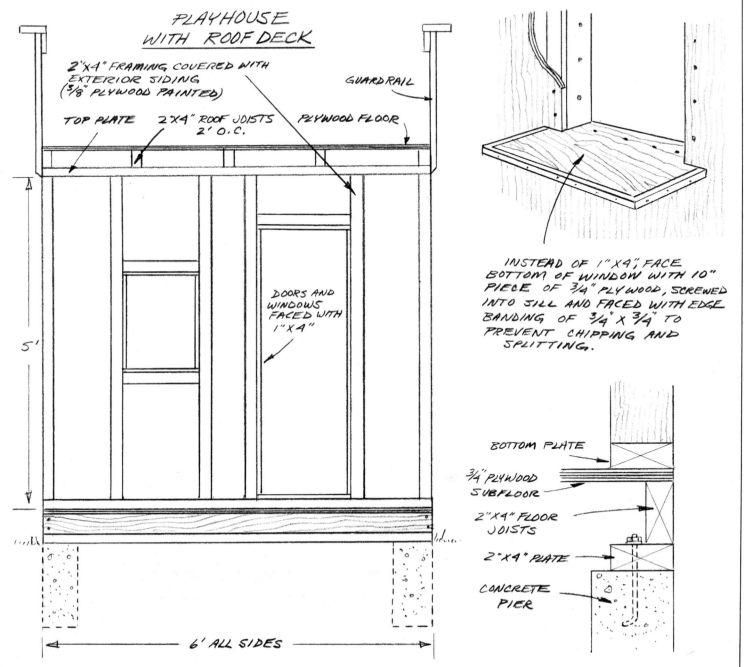

PLAYHOUSE WITH ROOF DECK

2"x4" FRAMING COVERED WITH EXTERIOR SIDING (3/8" PLYWOOD PAINTED)

TOP PLATE

2"x4" ROOF JOISTS 2' O.C.

GUARDRAIL

PLYWOOD FLOOR

DOORS AND WINDOWS FACED WITH 1"x4"

5'

6' ALL SIDES

Playhouses do not have to be high or large to be fun. Built on low concrete piers, **bottom right**, this design is framed with 2 by 4s on 16-inch centres using conventional house-construction techniques. The roof deck, **left**, gives the playhouse twice the play area at only marginally increased cost. To reach the deck, add stairs or a ladder to the outside or a hatch and knotted-rope climber inside. To give the house even greater play potential, extend one of the window sills to create a play counter, **top right**, that will become a ticket wicket, a grocery-store shelf or a fast-food take-out.

INSTEAD OF 1"x4", FACE BOTTOM OF WINDOW WITH 10" PIECE OF 3/4" PLYWOOD, SCREWED INTO SILL AND FACED WITH EDGE BANDING OF 3/4" x 3/4" TO PREVENT CHIPPING AND SPLITTING.

BOTTOM PLATE

3/4" PLYWOOD SUBFLOOR

2"x4" FLOOR JOISTS

2"x4" PLATE

CONCRETE PIER

Loose Material

• Sand sides and round the edges of constructed wooden components.
• Sand and repaint recycled materials (except in adventure play area).
• Paint all loose material the same colour, preferably a dark green or blue.
• Provide storage accessible to children.
• Adhere strictly to dimensions of modular loose material.
• For older children, provide raw materials for construction—tires, boards, et cetera.

Loose material is a must, especially for preschoolers. Compared with a play frame, these blocks, boards and sawhorses cost very little, yet they repay the investment many times over. The hollow blocks, originally designed by U.S.-based educator Caroline Pratt, will be used year-round and can simply be stacked against the fence or garage wall when the kids are finished playing. The Swedish blocks, from a design published by the Canada Mortgage and Housing Corporation's Children's Environment Advisory Service, should be sanded and sealed with a high-quality marine spar varnish. These blocks, together with a couple of small sawhorses, will occupy kids for hours, as they build forts, ramps and their own versions of mini-play frames.

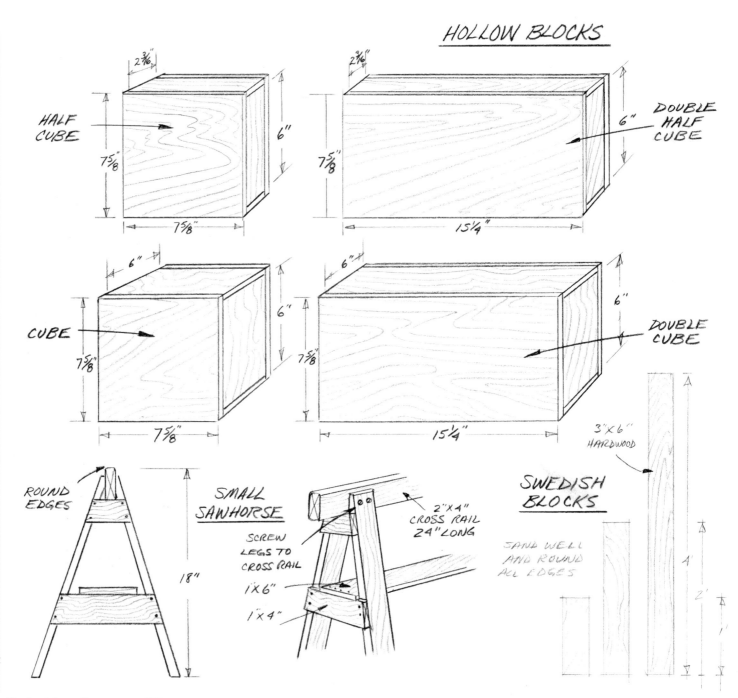

HOLLOW BLOCKS

HALF CUBE — 2³/₁₆" — 6" — 7⁵/₈" — 7⁵/₈"

DOUBLE HALF CUBE — 2³/₁₆" — 6" — 7⁵/₈" — 15¼"

CUBE — 6" — 6" — 7⁵/₈" — 7⁵/₈"

DOUBLE CUBE — 6" — 6" — 7⁵/₈" — 15¼"

ROUND EDGES — 18" — SMALL SAWHORSE

SCREW LEGS TO CROSS RAIL — 1"x6" — 1"x4" — 2"x4" CROSS RAIL 24" LONG

SWEDISH BLOCKS — 3"x6" HARDWOOD — SAND WELL AND ROUND ALL EDGES

(Design information on page 39.)

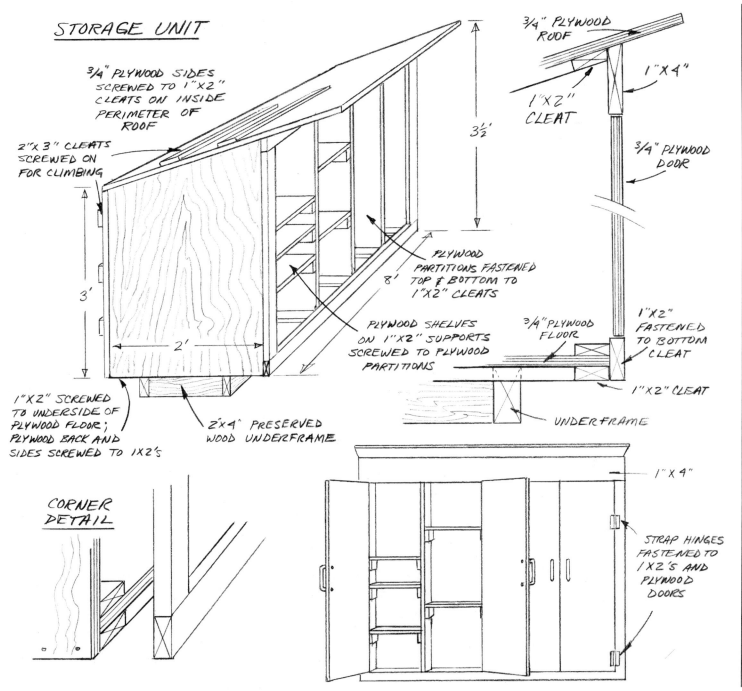

STORAGE UNIT

3/4" PLYWOOD SIDES SCREWED TO 1"x2" CLEATS ON INSIDE PERIMETER OF ROOF

2"x 3" CLEATS SCREWED ON FOR CLIMBING

3'

2'

1"x2" SCREWED TO UNDERSIDE OF PLYWOOD FLOOR; PLYWOOD BACK AND SIDES SCREWED TO 1X2's

2"x4" PRESERVED WOOD UNDERFRAME

3/4" PLYWOOD ROOF

1"X4"

1"x2" CLEAT

3/4" PLYWOOD DOOR

3½'

8'

PLYWOOD PARTITIONS FASTENED TOP & BOTTOM TO 1"X2" CLEATS

PLYWOOD SHELVES ON 1"X2" SUPPORTS SCREWED TO PLYWOOD PARTITIONS

3/4" PLYWOOD FLOOR

1"X2" FASTENED TO BOTTOM CLEAT

1"X2" CLEAT

UNDERFRAME

CORNER DETAIL

1"X4"

STRAP HINGES FASTENED TO 1X2's AND PLYWOOD DOORS

Storage

- Don't combine play with storage other than to make the outside of the storage cupboard climbable.
- Scale cupboards to kids, with low, shallow shelves (maximum 36 inches deep).
- Divide the interior of the storage cupboard to encourage organization and neatness.
- Design shelves to fit specific play items, i.e., hollow blocks.
- Avoid heavy top-hinged lids that can fall shut on kids' fingers.
- Be sure cupboards can be opened from the inside so kids won't be trapped if they crawl inside.
- Set cupboard doors high enough off the ground that they will open in winter, encouraging year-round outdoor play.
- Make outdoor storage weather-tight and solid (particularly if it is climbable).

Constructed almost entirely with plywood and 1 by 2s, this storage cupboard is sturdy and weather-resistant, but it represents only one of many possibilities. The bottoms of the walls are screwed to 1 by 2s fastened around the perimeter of the underside of the floor, and the tops of the walls are screwed to 1-by-2 cleats fastened around the perimeter of the inside of the roof. Similarly, the partitions are screwed to 1 by 2s on the floor and the inside of the roof. The front of the cupboard has a 1-by-4 facing board at the top and 1 by 2s on the bottom and sides where the door hinges are attached.

(Design information on page 41.)

Sand Garden

- Design a sand play area distinct from the sand ground cover under active play equipment.
- Use washed masonry sand, with particles no larger than 1.5 mm.
- Use sand that is free of organic matter.
- Fill the sandbox to a depth of 8 to 20 inches.
- Fill only to within 4 inches of the top of its container.
- For good drainage, spread the sand over 4 inches of gravel and a foot of granular fill; in clay soils, install a 4-inch perforated drainage pipe (protected with filter paper) that drains to a dry bed or ditch.
- Provide a sand table and storage for sand toys.
- Provide access to water, if possible.
- Round all exposed wood edges.
- Shade the sand garden from intense summer sun.
- Protect the sand from dogs and cats.

Sandboxes can be any size or shape, but they should be well drained and deep. In heavy soils, excavate a pit and lay drainage tile in gravel under the sand, separating the two layers with bricks, **top**. For in-ground sandboxes, build retaining walls of timber or brick, **bottom left**. Aboveground designs constructed with 2 by 10s, **bottom right**, make a good temporary sandbox, but they are more obtrusive; be sure to dig up the sod and check the drainage before pouring the sand.

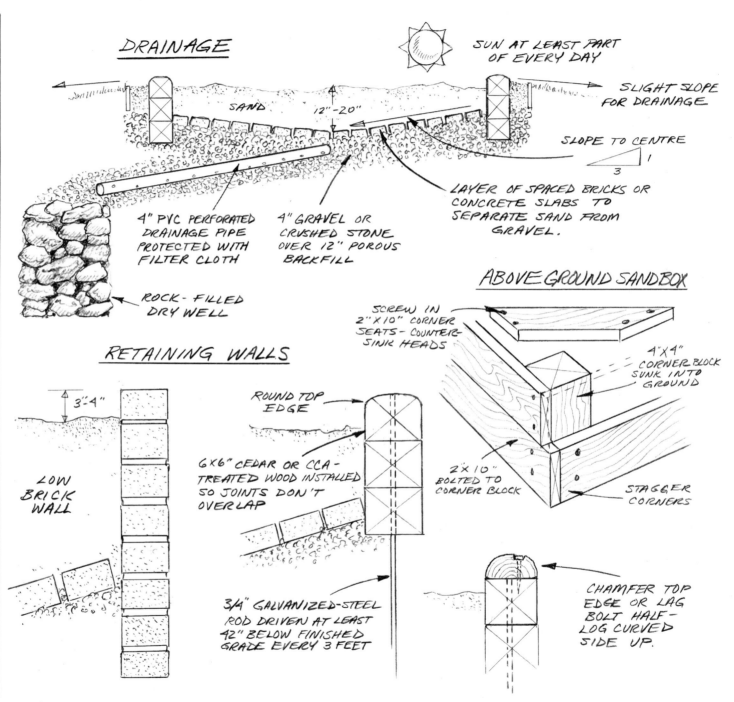

DRAINAGE

SUN AT LEAST PART OF EVERY DAY

SAND   12"-20"

SLIGHT SLOPE FOR DRAINAGE

SLOPE TO CENTRE

3   1

LAYER OF SPACED BRICKS OR CONCRETE SLABS TO SEPARATE SAND FROM GRAVEL.

4" PVC PERFORATED DRAINAGE PIPE PROTECTED WITH FILTER CLOTH

4" GRAVEL OR CRUSHED STONE OVER 12" POROUS BACKFILL

ROCK-FILLED DRY WELL

ABOVE GROUND SANDBOX

SCREW IN 2"X10" CORNER SEATS - COUNTER-SINK HEADS

4"X4" CORNER BLOCK SUNK INTO GROUND

2"X10" BOLTED TO CORNER BLOCK

STAGGER CORNERS

RETAINING WALLS

ROUND TOP EDGE

3"-4"

LOW BRICK WALL

6X6" CEDAR OR CCA-TREATED WOOD INSTALLED SO JOINTS DON'T OVERLAP

3/4" GALVANIZED-STEEL ROD DRIVEN AT LEAST 42" BELOW FINISHED GRADE EVERY 3 FEET

CHAMFER TOP EDGE OR LAG BOLT HALF-LOG CURVED SIDE UP.

(Design information on page 50.)

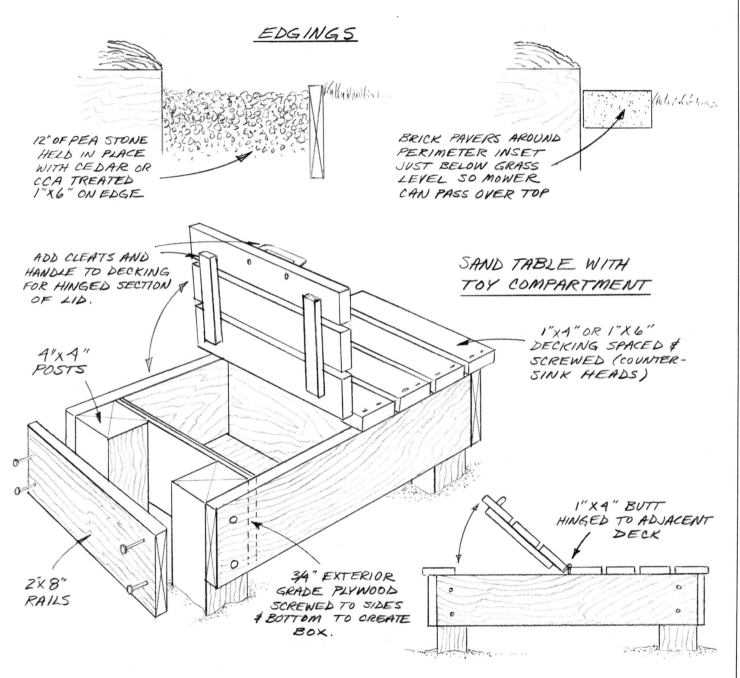

EDGINGS

12" OF PEA STONE HELD IN PLACE WITH CEDAR OR CCA TREATED 1"X6" ON EDGE

BRICK PAVERS AROUND PERIMETER INSET JUST BELOW GRASS LEVEL SO MOWER CAN PASS OVER TOP

SAND TABLE WITH TOY COMPARTMENT

ADD CLEATS AND HANDLE TO DECKING FOR HINGED SECTION OF LID.

1"X4" OR 1"X6" DECKING SPACED & SCREWED (COUNTER-SINK HEADS)

4"X4" POSTS

2"X8" RAILS

3/4" EXTERIOR GRADE PLYWOOD SCREWED TO SIDES & BOTTOM TO CREATE BOX.

1"X4" BUTT HINGED TO ADJACENT DECK

The major drawback to this important piece of play equipment is that the sand rarely stays in the box. To minimize spillage, discourage kids from using the edges as tables and seats by rounding the tops or by bolting a half-log to the timbers, then provide a ''cake table'' on which kids can shape and display their creations. For convenience, include storage space for sand toys in the table. To reduce the amount of sand tracked across the yard and into the house, install paving stones or gravel around the edge of the sand garden.

Water Play

• Create a streambed by laying reinforced concrete or asphalt over a granular base.
• Maximum depth of 6 inches.
• Provide a nonslip surface on the bottom of the play stream and the surface around pumps and taps.
• Slope the streambed to a drain connected to a dry well.
• Locate the drain and water source at opposite ends of the play stream to create a current.
• Provide a sand filter for the drain and a screw-in plug permanently chained to the streambed.
• Dish the surface around hand pumps and taps slightly; if the soil is not porous, install drainage tile.

Paths

• Build a smooth surface to prevent tripping and tricycle spills.
• Grade for drainage.
• Design at least 2 feet wide; create play oases by widening sections.
• Design a continuous loop for wheeled toys.
• Visually integrate paths with landscape.

A backyard path is not a means to an end but an avenue of exploration, a way of delineating and linking activity areas, an extra measure of fun for the kids. Make paths of brick, gravel or sand, wood, asphalt or just a series of stepping-stones.

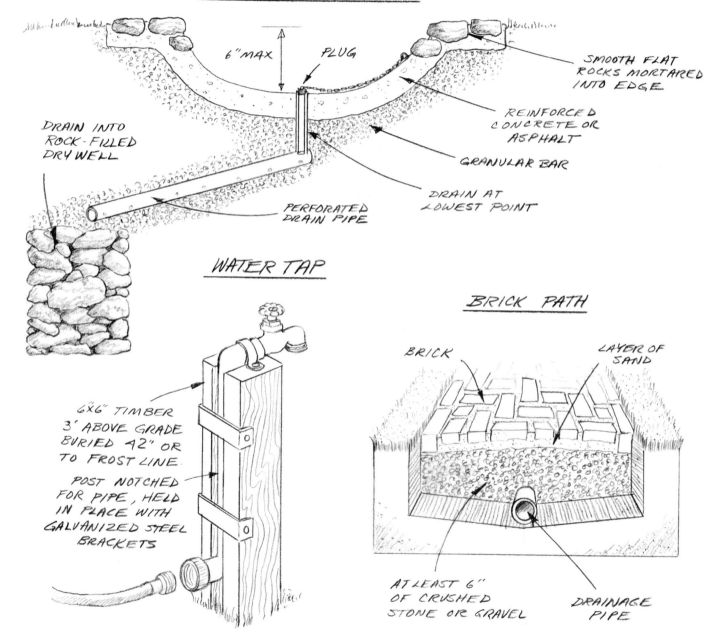

PLAY STREAM DRAINAGE

6" MAX

PLUG

SMOOTH FLAT ROCKS MORTARED INTO EDGE

REINFORCED CONCRETE OR ASPHALT

GRANULAR BAR

DRAIN AT LOWEST POINT

DRAIN INTO ROCK-FILLED DRY WELL

PERFORATED DRAIN PIPE

WATER TAP

6"x6" TIMBER 3' ABOVE GRADE BURIED 42" OR TO FROST LINE.

POST NOTCHED FOR PIPE, HELD IN PLACE WITH GALVANIZED STEEL BRACKETS

BRICK PATH

BRICK

LAYER OF SAND

AT LEAST 6" OF CRUSHED STONE OR GRAVEL

DRAINAGE PIPE

(Design information on page 53.)

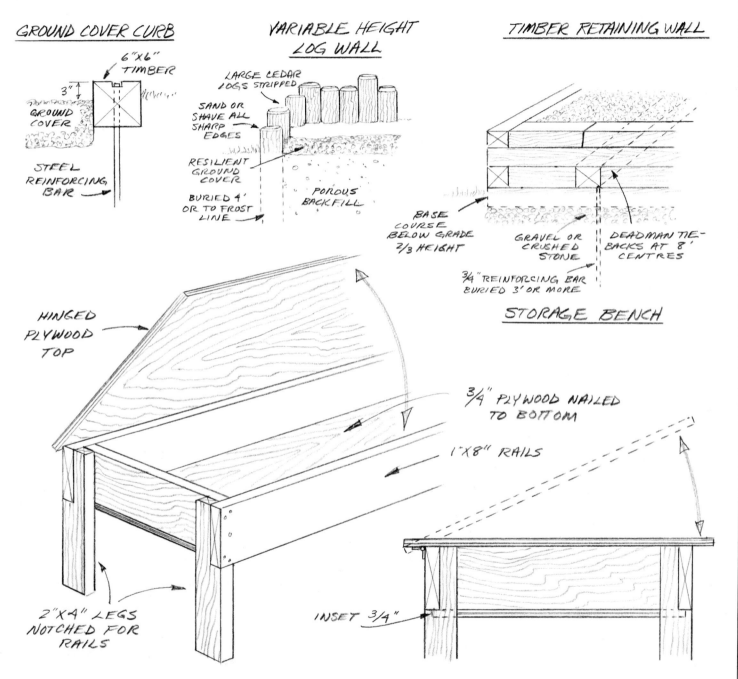

GROUND COVER CURB

6"x6" TIMBER

3"

GROUND COVER

STEEL REINFORCING BAR

VARIABLE HEIGHT LOG WALL

LARGE CEDAR LOGS STRIPPED

SAND OR SHAVE ALL SHARP EDGES

RESILIENT GROUND COVER

BURIED 4' OR TO FROST LINE

POROUS BACKFILL

TIMBER RETAINING WALL

BASE COURSE BELOW GRADE 2/3 HEIGHT

GRAVEL OR CRUSHED STONE

DEADMAN TIE-BACKS AT 8' CENTRES

3/4" REINFORCING BAR BURIED 3' OR MORE

STORAGE BENCH

HINGED PLYWOOD TOP

3/4" PLYWOOD NAILED TO BOTTOM

1"x8" RAILS

2"x4" LEGS NOTCHED FOR RAILS

INSET 3/4"

Borders

• Build very low borders (6 inches) to contain the ground cover.
• Build low borders (2 to 3 feet) to contain children without blocking them from view, to separate activity areas or to create elevation changes.
• Build high borders (5 to 6 feet) to shield adventure areas from sight, to protect kids from danger zones or to control microclimate.
• Design borders with play value: colourful bird-attracting shrubs for hedges, borders that double as benches, climbable fences (except where intended to block access) as supports for loose material.

Depending on its height, a constructed border serves a variety of functions, from very low curbs to high fences that are practical barriers to unsightly messes or unsafe areas such as ravines or busy streets. Incorporate borders into kids' constructive play, bridging the rails with sawhorses and cleated boards.

Seating

• Widths and lengths may vary, but an adult bench should be 14 to 17 inches high.
• Include storage in bench seats close to sand garden or play stream.
• Use weather-resistant lumber and hardware.
• Make movable benches light enough that kids can pull them into the sunshine or use them for creative play.

(Design information on pages 55, 56 and 57.)

Appendices

Natural Components

Component	Page	Age	Design Variables
Berms	44	all	−1:3 slope for sledding, rolling, mound slide −1:4 or gentler for wheeled vehicles −half-berm for small spaces, bridges −height and position for wind/sun control −height and position as barrier to danger zones
Plants	47	all	−species to attract birds −berry-, cone-bearing species for loose material −species for year-round colour and texture for sensual stimulation
		3-8	−drooping branches for cozy retreat −children's gardens −spiny, dense species as barrier to danger zones −species and position for wind/sun control
Sand	50	3-6	−central sand table −storage for toys −buffer zone with pavers
Water	52	6-10 3-6	−excavated pond −temporary rock stream −permanent concrete play stream −play tap/pump near sand garden
Animals	54	6-13 all	−pets −wildlife
Borders	55	3-8 all all	−cozy retreats −climbing surfaces −design fences to be included in construction −design and position for wind/sun control −design and position to define activity areas of the yard −double as benches
Paths	56	3-6 all	−trike paths: circular, good surface −exploration, reflection −visually integrate the landscape
Seating	57	all 3-6	−low benches for kids' reading, drawing, et cetera −picnic table: part of loose material −adult supervision

Constructed components

Component	Page	Age	Modifications for Different Age Groups
Swings	22		
traditional		all	-raise seats as kids grow
horizontal tire		3-8	-big enough for 2 or 3 kids
Tarzan-type		8-15	-single knotted ropes, tires in series
			-suspend over rugged terrain
trapeze-bar rings		8-15	-raise as kids grow
hammock		adult	-cozy and large for adolescents
toddler		8-18 mos.	-secure infants around waist
			-strap between legs
Cable ride	27	all	-increase length, slope, height for challenge
Slides	29		
freestanding		all	-interest wanes unless height and complexity increase
combination		3-6	-low (4 feet), wide
		6+	-higher (7 feet), wavy as they grow older
mound		all	-safe, all-season
			-best for bumps
Climbers	32		
climbing mountain		3-8	-higher, more complex for older kids
balance beam		3-6	-fixed beam; doubles as a bench, fencing
		6-14	-increase slope; moving beam, log roller
			-use as link between equipment
tire crawler		3-6	
tire tree, net		5-14	-increase height, complexity with age
jungle gym		3-6	-6-foot cube; cleated boards for movable ramps
		6-14	-increase height and complexity
Play Frames	33	3-14	-vary accessories for maximum play value and graduated challenge
ladders		3-14	-space ladder rungs to match arm and leg reaches
			-raise rungs to restrict young kids from height
			-vary material and incline

Component	Page	Age	Modifications for Different Age Groups
knotted rope		6-14	-access to restricted zones
sliding pole		6-14	-increase height with age
ramps		3-6	-movable, low slope
		6-14	-increase slope, difficulty
monkey bars		6-14	-space bars, match diameter to kids
			-raise as child grows
			-link platforms
chinning bars		6-14	-raise as child grows
bridges		3-14	-increase height, complexity with age
			-link platforms
cargo net		5-14	-increase height with age
platforms		3-14	-increase height or complexity of access with age
			-fixed, small to mark levels of climbing difficulty
			-increase size for dramatic play
			-movable
Playhouses	37	3-6	-small (3 by 6 feet), not completely enclosed; generic; big box
		6-14	-cozy (6 by 6 feet); private; enclosed; self-built
Loose Material	39	3-6	-monochromatic, generic, enough to build structures; ladders, sawhorses, blocks, cleated boards
		7-14	-gradual shift to real-life raw materials; adventure play area
Storage	41		-loose material
			-swing accessories
			-sand, water, snow toys
			-wheeled vehicles
			-make outside climbable

Backyard Plants

Common Name	Botanical Name	Comments
Shrubs for Spring		
Cornelian Cherry	*Cornus mas*	Yellow flowers, large red edible fruit
Forsythia	*Forsythia ovata*	Hardiest and earliest to bloom
Judas-tree	*Cercis canadensis*	Pink flower clusters in early spring
Lilac	*Syringa amurensis*	Over 200 varieties; white, lilac, crimson
Prinsepia	*Prinsepia sinensis*	One of first shrubs to leaf; small bright yellow flowers, edible cherry-like fruit
Viburnum	*Viburnum carlesi*	Pink and white flowers, blue-black fruit
Witch-hazel	*Hamamelis*	Fragrant yellow flowers in spring, yellow and orange leaves in fall
Shrubs for Fall		
Acanthaponax	*Acanthaponax*	Pollution-tolerant, dense
Cotoneaster	*Cotoneaster* spp	Good hedges, red fruit, yellow leaves in fall
Hobblebush	*Viburnum alnifolium*	reddish-purple leaves in fall, white flowers, blue-black berries
Honeysuckle	*Lonicera* spp	white, pink or red flowers, red fruit, leaves green into winter
Matrimony vine	*Lycium chinense*	Leaves green until late fall, purple flowers in early summer, orange-red berries

Common Name	Botanical Name	Comments
Potentilla	*Potentilla*	Profuse yellow flowers all summer until late fall, very hardy
Smoke tree	*Cotinus coggyria*	Large panicles, feathery flowers, foliage colours in fall
Wayfaring tree	*Viburnum lantana*	Light green leaves, deep red in fall
Shrubs for Winter		
Barberry	*Berberis dictophylla*	Scarlet leaves and berries persist into late fall; stems reddish-brown; good barrier
Forsythia	*Forsythia viridissima*	Stems bright green
Japanese Kerria	*Kerria japonica*	Light green stems, yellow June flowers, leaves yellow in fall
Rugosa rose	*Rosa rugosa*	Spiny, good barrier; holds leaves and fruit into winter; very hardy
Shrubs that Attract Birds		
Bayberry	*Myrica caroliniensis*	
Chokeberry	*Aronia*	Red and black berries
Dogwood	*Cornus* spp	White, red, blue fruit; leaves red in fall
False-bittersweet	*Celastrus scandens*	Yellow flowers, waxy red fruit
High-bush Cranberry	*Viburnum opulus*	Red fruit; very hardy
Mountain Ash	*Sorbus americana*	Red fruit clusters; leaves red in fall

Hazardous Plants *Reprinted with permission of the Co-operators Insurance Service.*

Plant	Toxic Parts	Possible Effects
Garden Plants		
Crocus	All parts, especially bulb	Vomiting, severe diarrhea; bone-marrow suppression.
Daffodil Narcissus Hyacinth	All parts, especially bulb. May be mistaken for onion	Abdominal pain, vomiting, diarrhea, shivering.
Foxglove	All parts	One of the sources of the cardiac medication digitalis. May cause abdominal pain, vomiting, diarrhea; irregular slow pulse; rarely, delirium, convulsions, death. Children have been known to pick the drooping tubular flowers and suck the toxic nectar from the base.
Lily-of-the-Valley	All parts, especially the roots	Another source of digitalis-like effects. Stomach upset and irregular heartbeat may occur.
Ornamental Plants		
English Ivy	Berries, leaves	Oral irritation, nausea, vomiting, diarrhea, abdominal pain.
English Holly	Berries	Vomiting, diarrhea, drowsiness.
Common Privet	Berries, leaves	Nausea, vomiting, severe diarrhea; may cause kidney damage.
Daphne	Fruit	Burning of mouth and throat; abdominal pain, vomiting, diarrhea, kidney damage; rarely, convulsions, coma, death.
Rhododendron Azalea	All parts	Poisonings are rare but potentially dangerous. May cause salivation, vomiting, low blood pressure, convulsions.

Plant	Toxic Parts	Possible Effects
Yew	Leaves (needles), bark, seeds, but not pulp of fruit	Abdominal pain, vomiting. In severe cases, muscular weakness; cardiac and respiratory depression.
Rosary Pea	Chewed seeds	Burning pain in mouth; delay in onset of abdominal pain, vomiting, severe diarrhea; kidney failure; death.
Castor Bean	Chewed seeds	Delay in onset of burning in mouth and throat; vomiting, diarrhea, blurred vision; convulsions; renal failure; death.
Trees and Shrubs		
Apple	Seeds	Many types of fruit seeds contain a minute amount of cyanide. May cause death if very large numbers of seeds chewed.
Black Locust	Bark, leaves, seeds	Burning pain in mouth; abdominal pain, vomiting, severe diarrhea.
Wild Black Cherry Choke Cherry	Leaves, pits, bark	Cyanide is present in large, tender leaves of shoots and sprouts. May cause nausea, vomiting, low blood pressure; coma; death.
Elderberry	Stems, unripe or raw berries	Nausea, vomiting, slow heartbeat, low blood pressure; coma; death. The berries are harmless if cooked.
Horse Chestnut	All parts	Abdominal pain, vomiting, weakness, if large amounts ingested.
Oak	Raw acorns, young sprouts	Abdominal pain, vomiting, diarrhea, if large amounts of raw acorns eaten.

Maintenance Checklist *(as suggested by the Canadian Institute of Child Health)*

Element/Component	Look for . . .
Structure	Bending, warping, cracking, loosening, frost heaving, distortion, splintered or decayed wood, corroded or damaged metal, exposed footings
Hardware	Loosened, missing, bent, broken, open hooks or rings, protruding nails or hardware, missing protective caps
Surface finish	Rust, corrosion, cracks, splinters, worn water-repellent finish
Edges	Sharp points or edges, protrusions
Pinch or crush points	Broken covers exposing mechanisms or junctures of moving components
Moving parts	Worn bearings, jammed equipment, lack of lubrication, excessive or noisy motion, missing protective pieces, loose spring castings
Guards, handrails	Missing, bent, broken, wobbly components
Access	Missing or broken rungs, steps or treads; loose or missing planks; splinters in handholds; blocked exits
Seats	Missing, damaged, loosened, sharp edges or corners, insecure fittings or attachments
Foundations	Erosion, rot, looseness in ground, exposed surfaces
Ground cover	Compaction, erosion, displacement to ineffective levels, protected area not extensive enough, unsanitary conditions, litter, poor drainage
Sand garden	Rancidity; stains on clothing or skin; debris; need for replenishing, raking or disinfecting
Water play area	Leaks, clogged drains, improper drainage, debris, growths, nonfunctioning components
Ropes, cables	Worn spots, fraying, deteriorating fibres, joints, splices, insecure attachments
Plastics, rubber	Splitting, cracking, breaking, discoloration, abrasion, wear, clogged drainage holes in tires
Paths	Worn patches, holes, cracks, uneven surface

Safety Checklist

Kids at play are subject to six general types of accidents. Avoid these by considering the following when buying or designing and building play equipment.

1. Falls from heights

-design no standing surfaces over 10 feet high
-install guardrails around platforms more than 2 feet off the ground
-make high levels accessible by play elements that only older children can handle
-design intermediate platforms on high climbers
-discourage climbing on high horizontal supports
-install resilient ground covers under equipment
-be sure free-fall zones are clear
-design playspace to eliminate collisions
-locate equipment so kids can approach, use and depart safely

2. Injuries from sharp or rough edges or projections

-use round-headed hardware, countersink screw heads and bolt ends, or finish with cap nuts
-round the edges of all woodwork
-roll or cap exposed edges of sheet metal or plastic
-plug or cap exposed open ends of tubing
-design structures with adequate head clearance

3. Injuries from moving parts

-design to avoid shear, pinch or crush points
-if unavoidable, make junctures of moving components inaccessible

4. Suspended hazards

-don't suspend cable wires, ropes or cords where kids might run into them

5. Head entrapment

-avoid openings large enough for a child's head to pass through (4-9 inches in diameter)

6. Abrasion

-sand all wood surfaces: where roughness is desirable for a better grip, be sure there is no danger of abrasion or splinters
-seating and sliding surfaces should have no joints or rough textures capable of cutting skin or snagging clothes
-design structures and choose material to minimize risk of skin burns
-cap or roll edges of materials to a radius of not less than ¼ inch

Sources

Books

On Public Playgrounds:

Aaron, David and Bonnie P. Winawer. **Child's Play**. New York: Harper and Row Publishers, 1965. A critical assessment of traditional play equipment and one of the first books to promote creative playspaces.

Chu, Paul and Alec Topps. **A Guide to Creative Playground Development**. Toronto: Ontario Ministry of Culture and Recreation, 1982. Copies available for $2.50 from the Ontario Government Bookstore, 880 Bay Street, Toronto, Ontario M7A 1N8.

Frost, Joe L. and Berry L. Klein. **Children's Play and Playgrounds**. Boston: Allyn and Bacon, Inc., 1979. One of the most comprehensive books on public playgrounds, including historical and psychological background and some good design and construction information as well as a thorough section on designing play equipment for handicapped children.

Hewes, Jeremy. **Build Your Own Playground**. Boston: Houghton Mifflin Company, 1974. Subtitled "A Sourcebook of Play Sculptures, Designs and Concepts From the Work of Jay Beckwith," this book offers a good overview of the design and construction issues in community-built playgrounds.

Hogan, Paul. **Playgrounds for Free**. Cambridge, Massachusetts: The MIT Press, 1974. Advocating community involvement and the use of recycled materials, the book is highly readable, if somewhat dated.

On Home Playgrounds:

Friedberg, M. Paul. **Handcrafted Playground**. New York: Vintage Books, 1975. A sketchbook of play-equipment ideas, short on theory and instructions but full of stimulating concepts within the capabilities of most homeowners.

Stiles, David. **The Treehouse Book**. New York: Avon Books, 1979. An excellent step-by-step guide for kids on the art and craft of tree-house construction.

On Play:

Caplan, Frank and Theresa. **The Power of Play**. Garden City, New York: Doubleday, 1973. An academic but readable overview of the importance of play; for adults as well as kids.

McCullagh, James C., ed. **Ways to Play: Recreation Alternatives**. Emmaus, Pennsylvania: Rodale Press Inc., 1978. This book constitutes an inspiring guide to play and recreation that the whole family will be sure to use and enjoy.

Sutton-Smith, Brian and Shirley. **How to Play With Your Child (and when not to)**. New York: Hawthorn Books, Inc., 1974. An informative guide from one of the leading researchers in children's play.

On Landscape Design:

Bennett, Jennifer, ed. **The Harrowsmith Landscaping Handbook**. Camden East, Ontario: Camden House Publishing Ltd., 1985.

Bird, David M. and Sandra Letendre. **City Critters**. Montreal, Quebec: Eden Press, 1986.

Dobson, Clive. **Feeding Wild Birds in Winter**. Scarborough, Ontario: Firefly Books, 1981.

Luttman, Rick and Gail. **Chickens in Your Backyard**. Emmaus, Pennsylvania: Rodale Press, 1976.

Luttman, Rick and Gail. **Ducks and Geese in Your Backyard**. Emmaus, Pennsylvania: Rodale Press, 1978.

Matson, Tim. **Earth Ponds**. Woodstock, Vermont: Countryman Press, 1982.

Tekulsky, Mathew. **The Butterfly Garden**. Boston, Massachusetts: The Harvard Common Press, 1985.

Sunset Books produces an excellent series of how-to books, including **Garden Pools, Fountains and Waterfalls, How to Build Walks, Walls and Patio Floors** and **Fences and Gates**.

Information

Canada Mortgage and Housing Corporation
682 Montreal Road
Ottawa, Ontario
K1A 0P7
CMHC sells a variety of publications on children's play, including "Creative Playground Information Kit 1," "Adventure Playground Information Kit 2," "Play Opportunities for School-Age Children" and "Play Spaces for Preschoolers." Write to CMHC Publications at the above address, or contact the local CMHC office.

Canadian Council on Children and Youth
323 Chapel Street
Ottawa, Ontario K1N 7Z2
Publishes "Play Space Guidelines," a resource document for planning community playgrounds.

Canadian Institute of Child Health
17 York Street, Suite 105
Ottawa, Ontario
K1N 5S7
Publishes "Moving and Growing," I and II, illustrated booklets on children's physical development, and a bibliography of children's playspaces and equipment.

Plans

Popular Mechanics, June 1982, pp. 130-135. Plans for a roofed play frame and slide, monkey bars, ladder and swing.

Popular Mechanics, June 1983, pp. 98-103. Plans for a physical play structure including a balance beam, monkey bars, sliding pole and single rope climber (no platforms).

Better Homes and Gardens Shopping Service
Box 374
Des Moines, Iowa 50336
Project Plan #50465
Blueprints costing $5.95 (U.S.) for a play frame, including three platforms, a tire swing, ramp, two traditional swings, chinning bars and ladders.

Kidstuff
Box 154
Kipton, Ohio 44049
Plans for a playtower with swings and teeter-totter sell for $15.

Play-Equipment Manufacturers

Playworks! and Children's Playgrounds Inc. manufacture a line of wooden play equipment specifically for the backyard, and PlayTech and Henderson distribute Backyard BigToys. Although the other companies design and build exclusively for public playgrounds, most will sell components and hardware to individuals on request.

Blue Imp Playground Equipment of Canada
Box 567
Medicine Hat, Alberta T1A 7G5
1-800-661-1462

Children's Playgrounds Inc.
Box 370
Unionville, Ontario L3R 2Z7
(416) 475-7648

Childspace Manufacturing Ltd.
Box 2459
Olds, Alberta T0M 1P0
(403) 475-7648

Finnskoga Play Systems Inc.
289 Gordon Avenue
Winnipeg, Manitoba R2L 0L7
(204) 667-8296

GameTime of Canada
57 Simcoe Street South
Oshawa, Ontario L1H 4G4
1-800-263-3774

Henderson Recreational Equipment Ltd.
Box 10
Norwich, Ontario N0J 1P0
1-800-265-5462

Hilan Creative Playstructures Ltd.
Box 1300
Almonte, Ontario K0A 1A0
1-800-267-7984

Kompan Playscapes Inc.
Box 4430
Ottawa, Ontario K1S 5B4
(613) 737-1195

Paris Playground Equipment Inc.
Box 125
Paris, Ontario N3L 3E7
1-800-265-9953

PlayTec Distributors Inc.
11940 Mitchell Road
Richmond, British Columbia
V6V 1T4
1-800-663-5973

Playworks! Recreational Equipment Ltd.
Box 74
Canning, Nova Scotia
B0P 1H0
(902) 582-7811

Index

(Bold-face numbers indicate plans.)

Credits